"Bill Heavey is James Thurber in camouflage overalls, with an unrelenting geyser of slapstick comedy and serrated wit. If he doesn't make you laugh, consult a coroner."
—Jonathan Miles, author of *Dear American Airlines*

"I've read Bill Heavey's [*Field & Stream*] page since the earliest days of my career. He's one of my all-time favorite writers. He's funny, fearless, and always up for anything. If he could fish as well as he writes, I'd be in trouble. Fortunately, he can't."
—Kevin VanDam, winningest professional bass angler of all time

"If you think of Bill Heavey as 'just' a humorist, you'll be selling him short, but it's his intelligent, unforced humor that hits you first and stays with you the longest."
—John Gierach, author of *At the Grave of the Unknown Fisherman* and *All Fishermen Are Liars*

"A reader doesn't have to hunt or fish to appreciate Heavey's gift for storytelling . . . The best essays, here, in fact, are heartbreakingly tender . . . This is a hard book to classify, and that's its biggest strength."
—*Christian Science Monitor*, "10 excellent books you might have missed in 2014"

"If Bill Heavey felt like it, he could write a book about something as boring as shuffleboard and it'd turn out to be good."
—Steven Rinella, author of *The Scavenger's Guide to Haute Cuisine, Meat Eater*, and *American Buffalo*

"The art of the story, a casualty of the era of Internet fixation, is a thing of beauty in Bill Heavey's voice." —*San Francisco Chronicle*

You're Not Lost if You Can Still See the Truck

Also by Bill Heavey

If You Didn't Bring Jerky, What Did I Just Eat?:
Misadventures in Hunting, Fishing, and the Wilds of Suburbia

It's Only Slow Food Until You Try to Eat It:
Misadventures of a Suburban Hunter-Gatherer

You're Not Lost if You Can Still See the Truck

The Further Adventures of America's Everyman Outdoorsman

Bill Heavey

Grove Press
New York

This book is published by arrangement with *Field & Stream* magazine, in which many of the book's pieces originally appeared.

"Shopping Is Fun, but Not for Men" (September 1994), "The Girls of Summer" (1996), "It's a Bass World After All" (August 1998), "Alone with a Pretty Woman in a Small Room with a Big Mirror" (April 1988), and "Truce and Consequences" first appeared in the *Washington Post*. "Suddenly, She Was Gone" (February 2001) first appeared in *Washingtonian*.

Published simultaneously in Canada
Printed in the United States of America

ISBN 978-0-8021-2432-6
eISBN 978-0-8021-9186-1

Grove Press
an imprint of Grove Atlantic
154 West 14th Street
New York, NY 10011

Distributed by Publishers Group West

groveatlantic.com

15 16 17 18   10 9 8 7 6 5 4 3 2 1

For Mom

The human race has only one really effective weapon and that is laughter.

—Mark Twain

Contents

Contents

Part II: It's Always November Somewhere, 2000–2004

Part III: Not Entirely Untrue Stories, 2005–2009

Contents

Part IV: I Wouldn't Try That if I Were Me, 2010–2014

Contents

Introduction

Have you ever experienced one of those days when every cast seemed to land right in front of a willing fish or your arrows flew toward the target like guided missiles or you crushed fifteen clay pigeons in a row at a skeet range?

Neither have I. In fact, whenever some bright-eyed geek is recounting such a moment—people who have experienced "flow" are always dying to tell you about it—I immediately ask if they've experienced the opposite phenomenon, which one groundbreaking behavioral psychologist (me, although I don't share that part) has called "flu." No? Quite understandable, I tell them. It's a recent discovery.

Flu, I explain, is the vague but unmistakable sense that, while you're sort of immersed in the moment, you're pretty much doing everything wrong. Further, although you're aware that you're screwing up, you feel powerless to do much about it. If you've ever spent six hours in a tree-stand without seeing a deer, started your descent, and then startled a big buck that has been bedded for hours right beneath you, that's "flu." Maybe you've sat in a boat with a bunch of lures at your feet, tied one to your line and then tossed it out, the better to reel it up to the proper height for casting. Except that you didn't toss out the lure you tied on—but rather the one next to it, which has just sunk and is gone forever. That's flu.

I'm telling you all this so that you, dear book buyer, can make an informed decision about the outdated media format currently in your hands.

1

If you've ever experienced flow or are in any way interested in learning more about it, this is *not* the book for you.

If, on the other hand, you've ever experienced flu, or—like me—felt as if most of your life has taken place under its influence, you are in the right place. Here you will find aid, comfort, and validation.

Why do you need this? It's because the public has been hoodwinked into believing that being good at what you like to do is of great consequence. It's not. Enthusiasm is a lot more important than skill. On numerous occasions, for example, I have traveled thousands of miles to catch certain types of fish, failed utterly, and had a hell of a good time doing so. A competent person who did likewise—even the competent get skunked occasionally—would have been miserable.

I'm able to fail and have a good time simultaneously because I am—by nature and by preference—an amateur rather than a professional. The sources of those two words are instructive. The root of "amateur" is the Latin *amātor*, or "lover." The root of "professional" is the medieval Latin *professiō*, "the taking of vows upon entering a religious order."

If the question is whether I'd prefer being a lover to becoming a monk, I can tell you the answer right now.*†

---

* (Scary asterisk warning) Several women and children appear in this book. One is my first wife, Jane. Another is Michelle—to whom I hope to be married by the time this appears—who appears as my girlfriend. Our kids also appear: my daughter, Emma, and Michelle's two boys, Jack and Cole. Jane's daughter Molly—my stepdaughter—is here as well. None of these children were seriously harmed in the making of this book.

† (*Don't-say-I-didn't-warn-you* warning) Although this book is mostly about hunting and fishing, it contains a few other pieces: stories about my dad, my fear of dancing, why I hate to shop for clothes, and one about losing my baby daughter, Lily. In all cases, I have operated under the assumption that there is nothing particularly special about me, and that if it happened to me it has probably happened to other people. If you recognize your own experience in any of these stories, rest assured that it is strictly on purpose.

I

TAKING THE BAIT, 1988–1999

PARTNERS

"Think they might be moving," says a voice on the phone. It's Greg. We last spoke four months ago, but he talks as if the conversation has been interrupted by someone burping instead of winter. Every spring when the sun reaches a certain angle and the water's edging up toward 60 degrees, Greg and I seem to find each other. It's been like this for six years now.

"I'm working a job nearby," he continues, not waiting for me to say hello. "Primer's got to dry for at least five hours. I got the boat on the car, and if I pick you up in fifteen—"

"'Preciate all this advance notice, bud," I interrupt sarcastically.

"Why?" he asks, his voice full of innocent surprise. "You busy looking through *GQ* to see how many pleats your pants are gonna have this summer? Want me to call you back in July?"

I'm already smiling. These are ritual insults, our way of saying we missed each other over the season of antifreeze, catalog fishing, and despair. Greg is an artist and self-employed floor refinisher who drives what's left of a midseventies station wagon the size of Brazil. In his part of town, the guy at the corner store passes your donuts through a Plexiglas wall with 9 mm spiderwebs on it. I, on the other hand, labor with the tips of my fingers in an office with windows that can only be opened by throwing heavy furniture through them, and live in an area where espresso shops have suddenly begun to grow like shower mold. In a universe without fish, we would probably not be friends. As it is, there are times when we're almost telepathic.

"Think they're still deep?" I ask casually.

"I'm thinking shallow. Find someplace the sun will have warmed some rocks near—"

"Like that riprap below the ferry where it—"

"Nope. Motor-accessible. That'll be a mob scene." He thinks for a moment. "'Member where that carp hit on a red shad Slug-Go last—"

"Too open," I tell him. "No structure. What about that skinny water up—"

"Okay," he agrees. "Yeah."

"Make it twenty minutes," I tell him. "I got three rods to string up. And, uh, Greg?"

"What?" he asks impatiently.

"Park up the street. I don't want any of my friends seeing me get into your car." I hang up before he can get a word in.

The fact is, of course, we enjoy each other. Greg routinely and publicly tells me I'm spineless yuppie scum who has sold his soul for mammon. (He especially likes to do this in the dives we stop in for coffee on the way home.) I return the favor, explaining that he digs the starving artist act because it lets him simultaneously dress like a slob and feel superior to people like me who have full-time jobs.

But that's just the surface noise. Here are the important things I know about Greg: He will be ten minutes late; he will park right out front; and his car will smell like it always does—a mixture of resins and solvents, unwashed dog (a 140-pound bloodhound with minimal saliva control), and Berkley PowerBaits (the car doubles as a tackle box). Out on the water, he is one of the best guys with a spinning rod I've ever seen. Because he's wiry to start with and because waltzing a 250-pound floor sander has given him wrists like twin boa constrictors, he can throw a 1/16-ounce rig thirty yards back into overhanging trees and never have the lure rise five feet off the water, the fishing equivalent of hitting a one-iron three hundred yards. He's an aggressive caster, and he loses more lures than I do. But when he's hot, he can throw from his off side around a tree and drop a plug into an opening the size of a shoe box as if that lure wasn't even considering landing anywhere else.

Like all fishermen, we both have our odd proclivities. I, for example, am fond beyond all reason of the four-inch white grub. I'm comfortable with it, I believe in it, and I generally make the fish prove they don't want it before I take it off one of my three active rods. Greg, on the other hand, is just plain bent. He will throw any crankbait in the book, as long as it's a Countdown Sinking or Original Floating model Rapala in silver or gold. These, Greg maintains with the demented reasonableness of people who only shop on Mars because everything is always on sale there, are the only hard-bodied lures that look like real fish. And yet he routinely throws plastics in shades they won't sell to minors except in New York City. One favorite crawfish pattern— hazardous-waste-orange claws on an about-to-be-sick-fuchsia body— could only have been thought up by someone deep inside the penal system of one of those Scandinavian countries where everybody goes crazy six months a year due to light deprivation.

All of this is especially galling because Greg catches more fish than I do. Actually, I can handle that part. (I'm five years younger and better-looking.) The real problem in the relationship is that he can fish whenever he wants and I can't. This has necessitated my developing a number of chronic-but-unspecified medical problems that flare up on short notice April through November and seem to be related to barometric pressure and water temperature. (I think people at work know I'm faking, but as any criminal prosecutor will tell you, knowing and proving are two different animals.)

Greg and I once tried getting together socially, that is to say with our girlfriends. But I think we did it more because we felt we were supposed to than because we actually wanted to. The results were predictable: a dinner of lasagna and long silences that neither of us has ever mentioned again.

Last year, however, I heard a local gallery was having a show of his work. He didn't invite me; I just decided to show up. One of the paintings was a memorial triptych for a friend who died when a drunk's car jumped a curb and drove through his windshield. It was painted on a piece of ancient wood he'd gotten off the front of a boarded-up store in his neighborhood and combined some strange images: a detailed calendar of the waxing and waning of the moon over several months; painstakingly rendered bits of the cotton plant shown as seedling, bud, flower, and withered stalk; a fireman's yellow boot and, off in a corner, a larger image of the full moon in whose shadows you finally saw the face of the dead man smiling faintly at you, his name, SIMON, scratched below. It's a haunting piece, unflinching, charged with the knowledge of how quickly what we take for granted passes into nothingness. It's too bleak for people who want something that matches the green sofa in the den and doesn't take up too much wall space. It's like one of those books people admire but don't read. And Greg knows this, of course. But it's like the way he is about Rapalas—he's just not the compromising sort.

The critic in a major newspaper the next day lauded the show, praising its "elegiac power" and calling my fishing buddy "a master of metaphor." I didn't say anything about all this to Greg. He'd seen me that night and nodded, but I'd left him, dressed in clothes only slightly more stylish than what he fishes in, surrounded by men in black silk shirts buttoned up to their necks and women who had gone to great pains to make themselves look as if they'd been freeze-dried, brought back to life, and then painted by undertakers.

But the next time we went fishing, Greg uncharacteristically threw a large silver Rapala high into a sycamore, where it spun around a limb four times, sealing its fate. "Damn," he said. "Just threw five bucks up a tree." We looked at it for a moment, waiting as if it might fall. It didn't.

"Look at it this way," I finally said. "At least you're a master of metaphor."

He looked at me to see if I was consoling him on the loss of a lure, acknowledging his art, or simply pulling his chain. I think he realized it was all three about the same time I did. He smiled, then bit the line, laid his rod across the thwarts, and began to paddle.

"Running outta daylight," he announced. "We got time for one more stop on the way back. The big eddy by the island or the bar off the point?"

"Your pick," I told him.

He pondered. "The sandbar," he finally murmured almost to himself as I picked up my paddle and fell to under the failing light. "I'm betting they're moving into the shallows to feed."

FALLBACK FLATS

It's the place you can get to in under an hour, the place that gets pounded like a dead tree at a woodpecker convention, the place big fish avoid, the place where the waters are stocked with compromise. It's the place you go when time is short and the act of fishing is more important than the catching. In short, it's your fallback.

My personal version is a scenic portion of a good-sized river fifteen minutes from my front door. I could draw you its features in my sleep: the two-foot ledge running diagonal to the current; chunky little islands in the middle where some resident Canadas have opened their own fertilizer farm; a line of celery grass off a sandbar that tapers into the current the way the last hairs of your eyebrow peter out into the skin on your temple. While I'd hardly ever been skunked here, neither had I ever unhooked a smallmouth over thirteen inches in the ten years I'd been visiting. Until last Friday, that is.

It was one of those days they couldn't put enough numbers on your paycheck to make it worthwhile, when you feel like you might pour sugar in your boss's gas tank unless you get away to a place where the only thing tugging at you will be a fish. I couldn't slide out early enough to make it to Lunker City, a two-hour drive. So I did what big people do: I waited until 4:59 and hit the gas for Fallback Flats. The way I look at it, thirteen inches of fish is a hell of a lot more than zero inches, which is what you catch if you stay home.

Traffic was worse than usual and I knew I'd be lucky to get an hour on the water. Redemption came just as the sun was becoming tangled in the trees and three night herons flapped silently overhead (why is it getting to be that you see more kinds of wild birds near cities than in the country?). I was massaging the rocky bottom just upstream of the ledge with a four-inch Scoundrel "live"-colored worm (call me crazy, but I was actually fishing a worm-colored worm) Texas-rigged on an $1/8$-ounce slip sinker, when there came the most tentative of taps, the twitch of a sleeping baby's finger. I raised my rod tip and held my breath, not quite sure I'd felt what I thought I'd felt. When I felt a second bump, I set that hook like it was connected to the backside of an IRS auditor. The ball of adrenaline on the other end began stripping six-pound on a diving break for points north and east and I just held on. My spinning reel was making a sound like someone pulling masking tape off a roll, my arms were shaking, and I knew instantly this was not a catfish because although the fish stayed down, the line was cutting all through the water in a kind of fevered handwriting that could only spell "smallmouth."

I couldn't remember if this was the rod I hadn't changed line on for three months or the fresh one, and I didn't have time to check. But I made a bunch of promises about product loyalty to whoever's line this was, because I wanted this fish. He jumped once, fifteen yards out and as big as I'd imagined, then put on a final surge close to the boat when he saw what I looked like. But I kept pressure on him, and then it was over. He was dark and heavy, and as soon as I lifted him the hook fell from his mouth and thocked the deck of the canoe as if he'd been holding on to it out of pure courtesy.

"Oh, buddy, look at you," I said, as if greeting an infant. I held him down gently with one hand and measured with the other. When stretched full out, my hand measures exactly nine inches from thumb to little finger. The bass was all of that and an inch more and just over three pounds on my right-hand heft-o-meter. He stared back with his wild orange eye and snapped his body, refusing to be friends. How many thousand empty casts had I made at this place to arrive at the one connecting me to this creature? I had the sensation of watching an odometer turn over, of it all beginning again.

I lowered him back into the water, my thumb still in his mouth, and swished him back and forth a couple of times while he lay stunned. I don't think anybody had ever treated him in this manner before. He wasn't used to it. Suddenly, with a vicious swipe of his head, he was gone. I held my hand up. There was a little line of blood coming from where he'd nicked my thumb. I sucked it and smiled. The sun had gone for the night, leaving a soft molten glow on the underside of the farthest clouds.

I was back the next morning before the crowds, armed with fresh line and high hopes that the river hadn't undergone a mood swing during the night. It hadn't. I hammered them. I got 'em on the Scoundrel, on a three-inch white grub, on a six-inch red shad Slug-Go with insert weights. They weren't in the eddies or more obvious still water, but holding in the tiniest pockets in relatively strong current about four feet deep. None were as big as the one from the night before, but by fallback standards they were trophies. I didn't keep strict count, but I bet there were five fish in the 14–16-inch range, including one brawler who got loose in the boat and fought his way forward until he wrapped himself up in my sweatshirt. I fished for several hours, concentrating so hard it was like being in a trance.

When I finally took a break, everything around me seemed more vivid: the throbbing of a drowned limb caught in the current, the river's endless self-applause as it completed a little ladder of riffles, the ancient scalloped rocks that look like shoulder blades. You can fish for years, not thinking about anything but where your next cast will be, and then look up and see everything around you as if it had just been created. That's how it felt that day.

I wasn't able to get back to that place for a week, and then I found about what I expected, which wasn't much. But it was okay. I'd had my moment of glory, the mystery had been restored. About a month later a friend called up and said he'd like to get out on the water.

"I don't have much time," he said almost apologetically, "but we could hit that place nearby on the river if you're up for it."

"You think we're gonna catch anything there?" I asked, not having decided whether I wanted to tell what had really happened.

"Well, prob'ly not," he admitted. "I just want to get out. But we gotta get lucky there someday."

"Come on over," I told him. "We'll give it a shot."

SHOPPING IS FUN,
BUT NOT FOR MEN

I have just made the biggest mistake of my life. I have agreed to go shopping with my current girlfriend. "C'mon," she urged. "We'll start small. A shirt and a pair of pants. You dress like you haven't bought any clothes in twenty years." Actually, it's only been ten years. It was at Sunny's Surplus, the one in Georgetown. I bought nine identical pairs of black socks. I understand that is also where Ralph Nader shops.

We leave behind the world of sunlight and fresh air as we descend into the fifth circle of Mazza Gallerie in my Honda. Lose your ticket stub and you stay here until Jesus comes back. "Where are we going?" I ask as calmly as possible. "Filene's," says my companion. "You'll like it. It's cheap." We take the elevator up with a young women's professional gum-chewing team. All have on the kind of canvas coats men wear on dairy farms. "Tourists?" I whisper. "No. Those are barn jackets. They're in."

On the way to Filene's we pass stores that are anything but cheap. Places that sell only Belgian chocolate molded into shapes like a tennis racket or a woman's leg or a Mercedes hood ornament. Places that sell platinum fountain pens shaped like overstuffed sausages and endorsed by men who have walked on the moon. A store that sells only bonsai trees. There is a sign in the window: WILL HOLD YOUR TREE WHILE YOU SHOP. Why bother? They could just pin it to your lapel.

It's warm and airless in Filene's, which appears to operate without sales staff, just people who put merchandise back on hangers after it has been flung on the ground and trampled. Men, I am reminded as

13

my brain begins to shut down, are basically hunters. We like to focus on a single thing to the exclusion of all else, stalk or run it to ground, and then kill it with spear or credit card. Then we go watch television. Women are gatherers. They have wide-angle vision and can actually look at hundreds of things simultaneously, imagining how they would taste or feel, what they could be combined with, and how often they would need to be dry-cleaned. What's more, women can do this for virtually unlimited amounts of time. My friend, I'm vaguely aware, is as charged as the Energizer Bunny, while I've got all the zip of a man on a chloroform binge.

I'm aware of something else, too. Filene's is not really a store at all. It's a hospice for new clothes with incurable diseases: orange polyester designer sweatshirts with enough scales for the Miss Carp U.S.A. Pageant, dresses made of viscose and rubber-coated cyclone fencing, suits that virtually guarantee freedom from sexual harassment in the office. We take the escalators up to Menswear, where I first notice the presence of black globes suspended from the ceiling at regular intervals. I instinctively know what these are: death stars, stuffed with microphones and heat-sensing scanners, that are connected to an office building full of minimum-wage security guards who are cramming for night school instead of watching the monitors. My companion tugs me toward wire racks of shirts and sweaters marked CLEARANCE. Here are the untouchables among fashion's outcasts: plaid flannel shirts the colors of milk shakes and motor oil, rayon garments designed to be worn to professional mustard fights, a white silk number with a postage stamp where the pocket used to be and cuneiform writing all over the front. The stamp is canceled, and if you look hard it reads, CASABLANCA, MOROCCO, 3:31 P.M. 9 NOV 1993. Perhaps this is where the designer wanted to be when he was creating this. Tough call. You can't wear it, mail it, or use it for scratch paper. I pat its sleeve as if everything's going to be all right. But I know it's not. I drift away.

I've been fighting hard, but this is not a healthy environment. Maybe some kind of low-level kryptonite seepage from those death stars is depleting my life force. Maybe you're not even supposed to buy these clothes, just come to try and cheer them up. But it's too late. These clothes know. I'm measuring the distance to the door when my friend pulls me over to Pants, where, among the somber ranks of grays and browns, one of Ralph Lauren's costlier mistakes is repeated dozens of times in waist sizes 30 to 46. They're Polo Enduring Quality Dungarees in a multicolored plaid visible from Saturn. This could be a designer's inside joke, a comment on the seventies, or an impassioned plea for the freedom to be wrong, terribly wrong. All I know is these pants are bouncing off the walls, and if they could talk, they'd be begging for lithium. My companion says, "Wait here," breathes deeply, and plunges back into the racks. I look around. There are other men here, and some of them are holding up rather well, under the circumstances. Maybe they just walked in. Hell, for all I know, they're enjoying themselves. But for every functional soldier there are three guys like me, guys who look like they've just been hit in the face with a frying pan.

My friend returns and looks at me like a nurse doing triage. "You're not doing too well, are you?" she says tenderly. I shake my head. "C'mon. We'll try Woodies. It's calmer there, and they have chocolate." Good. With some chocolate, I might rally for another half an hour.

The light is even brighter at Woodies, but there are doors leading to the outside world at each end and more ambient oxygen. Plus it has chocolate. I buy a 1.75-ounce treasure chest of Godiva—four pieces, four bucks—and eat them. The chocolate works on the pain centers of the brain, temporarily stunning them. I rally.

In the men's department, Ralph Lauren, Liz Claiborne, Tommy Hilfiger, and Alexander Julian have all staked out little zones where they vie with one another to test your intelligence. Alexander opens with a bold gambit: Why wouldn't you pay $65 for a blue sweatshirt with the Briticism COLOURS written on it in bumpy thread? Liz counters with a sophisticated gray cotton tee devoid of ornamentation for $35. I think she's bluffing. Tommy's in your face with the following deal: You give me $92, I'll give you a made-in-Taiwan rugby shirt with my name printed over your heart, and, on the back, a heraldic griffin clutching a fistful of arrows. Above the griffin floats a kind of brick crown, on either side stand sheaves of wheat à la Budweiser, and below ripples a ribbon that reads EST. MCMLXXXV, as if this marked the Norman Conquest instead of the year Billy Joel and Christie Brinkley decided to make it legal. But for sheer chutzpah, Ralph, as always, stands alone. His $127.50 cotton-acrylic sweatshirt features an old-timey teddy bear in a snowsuit on skis. This is genius. It's like jazz. If you have to ask why adult males will be wearing old-timey teddy bears on their sweats, you'd never get it anyway. The other clever thing that sets Ralph apart is that attached to everything are these little plastic antitheft devices containing two tiny cylinders, one black, one red. A warning states that any tampering will result in the cylinders breaking, presumably combining to form an invisible gas that would make you change your name back to something unmarketable.

My friend, sensing my disorientation, shows me to a display of shirts and promptly stuffs an olive-colored one into my chest. "Go put this on. There's the dressing room." In the dressing room I step in front of a three-way mirror before trying the shirt on and notice that I need a haircut and my head has changed shape since the last time I saw the whole package. My skull has gotten longer, or maybe it's just that my hairline is retreating. It's fascinating. I never really knew I had a profile. I spend several minutes getting reacquainted with my body, wondering if this is really how I look to other people. "Sir?" a young salesman calls out unsteadily, waking me from my trance. "Your, ah, lady friend asked me to see if everything's okay."

"Oh, yeah, fine, fine," I assure him, putting on the shirt, careful not to look at myself with it on. "That's a great color on you," my friend gushes. "But your undershirt's showing. You button it up to the neck."

"No."

"But that's how they're worn. It'll look great. Just try it."

"No way. Where I grew up only dweebs buttoned their shirts up to the neck without a tie. It's like stamping MORON across your forehead."

"Just try it," she pleads.

"You don't understand. I can't. My friends would beat me up. And I'd have to help them."

16

"Okay, okay. What about these?" She motions to a stack of Perry Ellis Portfolio silk shirts, marked down to thirty-five dollars. "These you wouldn't necessarily have to button all the way up."

"Silk?" I ask, managing to make the word sound like *cholera*.

"Silk," she says sternly. "Look, I didn't make you come here. You wanted to. And you must have wanted to try to do something about your wardrobe or you wouldn't have brought me."

It's true. She's got me. "Which one do you like?" I ask. She thinks, fingering the shirts, finally selecting two: one with brown and blue bars and a funny red squiggle, the other subtler, a pattern of blue and green watercolor brushstrokes with flecks of pale yellow.

"That one," I say, picking up the second, careful of the pins.

"Aren't you going to try it on?"

"Don't need to. That's the shirt. One giant leap for mankind. Let's get outta here."

Two weeks later, I wear the shirt to a close friend's birthday party. Nobody makes fun of me. Several women friends pat me on the shoulder. "Nice shirt. I wish I could get Jim into something like that," says one I've known for years.

I square my shoulders and smile into the pleasant thrum of the party. "Yeah, well," I say, figuring I might as well go for it. "Some guys lead, some guys follow." I look back at her, and the top half of her body has disappeared. She has turned away from me and is laughing silently but so hard she has bent in half. White wine is coming out of her nose.

MONSTER IN A BOX

I keep opening the hatch to the livewell to make sure this is really happening to me. Inside is a largemouth twice as big as any I've ever caught before: eight, maybe nine pounds. Actually, I can't really see it too well down there in the dark, but every once in a while it throws a shoulder against the bulkhead like a sumo wrestler locked in a motel closet.

Even Jerry Martin, a guide from Bass Pro Shops who is taking me out for the day on Stockton Lake, doesn't want to commit to a guess on weight. "I just haven't seen enough fish that big, to tell you the truth. If we'd got her before she spawned out, you might have the lake record there," he says.

The lake record is 9 pounds, 11 ounces. In forty years of fishing—including some when he was on the water 250 days a year as a guide and tournament fisherman—Jerry has caught just two fish over nine pounds. And now I—a pale out-of-towner with airplane peanuts still in my pocket—have got a monster in the box.

In late summer on Stockton, Jerry says, the bass spend the early-morning hours chasing schools of shad in the flats. If it's overcast, the fish may chase them on and off all day. But on a bluebird day like this one, the bass retreat to pole timber, where they hold so tight you've got to bop 'em on the nose to get a strike. Jerry's been doing this with more success than I have, releasing three sublegal fish while I lose two of his worms to stickups.

Jerry maneuvers the boat to a big lone tree on the edge of the channel and casts his worm to one side while I take the other. Suddenly he grunts, sets his hook hard, then mutters, "Wrapped me."

Just as his line goes slack, somebody gives my bait a big, dull thump. The next thing I know I'm fighting a fish that moves like a bass, only stronger, the oscillations on the other end slower and more deliberate. It makes three diving runs; my line slashes through the water like the Z that stands for *Zorro*, and somehow stays clear of the timber. It's all over in half a minute or two minutes or an hour. I don't remember. Then Jerry hoists her up and I'm looking at a bass that could swallow a cantaloupe.

When I stop dancing long enough to listen, Jerry asks what I want to do with her. "We can always use a big fish in the aquarium back at the shop," he says. "If you don't want to have her mounted, I mean."

This is a no-brainer: pay $150 so the fish you killed can stare you down from the wall for the rest of your life, or donate it to the people who were nice enough to take you fishing. I tell him I'd be honored to have my fish in their aquarium.

It's a good life, he tells me. A fish like this is probably nearing the end of her life in the wild. In a temperature-controlled tank, swimming lazily down to a scuba diver twice a day for a nutritionally complete fish cake before adoring crowds, she might live another ten years.

Jerry phones from his truck, and when we get back to Bass Pro Shops, there's already a photographer waiting. They put a baseball cap on my head; I climb back on the trailered boat, pull my fish up out of the livewell, and smile. By this time I'm starting to have second thoughts about the whole thing. Fish don't look right in parking lots.

Then one of the aquarium guys comes and takes her away in a cooler filled with water to transfer her to a holding tank while she acclimates to her new home. I watch them push the cooler away in a shopping cart. Suddenly I have a fleeting impression of what it might feel like to commit my mother to a rest home against her will.

Two days later I went back to the showroom near the athletic shoe section. My fish was in a shallow pool—an intermediate step on her way to the big aquarium. The pool was artfully landscaped with rocks and logs. There were turtles on the rocks and bass and catfish in the pond. All were resting quietly under the fluorescent lights, oblivious to the people and the carpet of pennies and nickels beneath them.

I couldn't find her at first. Then I spied her off by herself, nose turned into the farthest corner, refusing to cooperate. I stood at the edge of the pond. With their leathery necks extended from their perch on the rocks, the turtles looked like trustees. The dark shapes of the fish looked like sleek, docile inmates.

I suddenly realized what I'd done. I wanted to scoop her up and run, but it was too late. "I'm sorry," I whispered.

THE GIRLS OF SUMMER

It takes us a little over three hours to drive from Arlington to Ocean City, just enough time for two giddy girls in the backseat to perform the Macarena . . . about six thousand times. No sooner have our suitcases hit the floor in the 120-year-old Atlantic Hotel, near the town's south end, that Molly—my girlfriend Jane's daughter—and her best friend, Carsie, are sprinting down the long second-floor hallway to the porch overlooking the boardwalk. Ten feet below are two perpetual counter-currents of humanity strolling the boards in flip-flops and tank tops. The timeless smells of this oldest of Ocean City institutions waft up: popcorn and salt air, suntan lotion and steamed crabs, fudge and antici-pation. There are racks of colorfully spangled T-shirts, glowing signs for "Dolle's Original Salt Water Taffy," "Kohr Bros. Frozen Custard Since 1919," and "Q-ZAR, Earth's Favorite Laser Game." As Jane and I arrive, the girls turn toward us, eyes shining. Molly struggles momentarily for the words to fit her feelings. "I mean, who wouldn't love this place!" she crows. "Let's go!" Add two more names to the list of the seduced.

We walk directly from the hotel lobby onto the boardwalk, turn right, and find ourselves swept along onto the Pier, the Times Square of O.C. (It's the only pier along the ten-mile beach; it's been here forever; it doesn't even stoop to advertise in the Sunny Day Guide, the coupon-rich visitors' guide.) We enter and pass the Whac-A-Mole and the Shoot-Um-Up, a huge Ferris wheel and a small roller coaster, dart games and squirt gun games, and horizontal ladders on swivels that flip you upside down as soon as you are halfway across and the attendant lifts her steadying finger from the cable.

21

"C'mon folks, you didn't come here to start a savings account," calls the young sharpie who'll guess your weight, age, and birth month (within two). "Can't win it unless you're in it," says a raspy-voiced guy at the Bowler Roller. For those especially slow on the uptake, there is a sign at the Softball Toss beneath the red plush bulldogs and yellow Tweety Birds: "Have fun . . . spend money." We shell out $22.95 for a book of one hundred tickets and are soon in line to buy more fun.

At ages ten and eleven, Molly and Carsie are enjoying what may be their last summer before adolescent self-consciousness sets in, flying along just beneath the radar of boys with fledgling goatees and the visors of their caps all shaped to a special roundness. They break into a hyper version of the Macarena while we stand in line for the 1001 NACHT, a flying carpet ride that came from Stuttgart, Germany, and rides around on an enormous steel arm. Waiting to get on the Hurricane, their skinny arms spell out the letters to the Village People's "YMCA" over their heads.

There are strange moments of human poignancy going on all around here. I watch as a crew-cut little boy sandwiched between two bulky men emerges from the darkness of the Ghost Ride. The metal bar holding them in their seat rises, signaling termination. "Ah," the boy says with infinite regret. "A pity." A huge fellow in Harley-Davidson nylon shorts and a menacing Fu Manchu mustache waves tenderly to his little girl on the Ferris wheel. He holds a rough hand up next to his eyes and waves just the tips of his fingers at the light of his life as she ascends into the night.

The Bottle-Up game is simplicity itself. You hold a stick with a string attached to the tip. At the end of the stick is a ring. Slip the ring over the neck of a prone beer bottle and stand it up. The aging hippie attendant does it effortlessly in four seconds. "Did it on my second try, how I got the job," he says. "It's easy. You wanna try?" It's two bucks a shot or three for five bucks. I give him two and watch as the bottle pivots wildly like a compass at the North Pole and falls off its Formica pedestal as soon as I begin to lift. "You can't give up that easy," he says, seeing my crushed expression. "Tell you what. Give ya two tries for four bucks." I'm so confused by now that this sounds like a special deal. This time it's over in six seconds. "This game is stupid," I explain to Jane. The girls, ecstatic at this show of adult frustration and ineptitude, break into the Macarena.

The next day, sitting on the beach, I watch two people being pulled around the sky in parachutes attached to speedboats. "Isn't that just the silliest thing you ever saw," a woman three towels over says to her husband, who is wearing a tennis hat and shielding a can of beer from the beach patrol. Instantly I decide I must go parasailing or die.

Three blocks behind the hotel, on the bay side, I find a booth for Island Watersports. The attendant tells me, "We have a four-hundred-foot, an eight-hundred-foot and Ocean City's highest ride, twelve hundred feet. The question is, how high do you want to go?" To fully appreciate this moment, you need to understand that the attendant is a young babe and that I am a pale forty-one-year-old bald man who won a Kewpie doll last night when the age-guesser pegged me for forty-seven. "Gonna, uh, gonna go all the way up," I stammer, handing her a credit card from which she deducts fifty-five dollars (with a ten-dollar coupon from the Sunny Day Guide) for a ten-minute ride.

Half an hour later, I'm standing on the rear platform of a speedboat slamming through the waves while a tanned young guy shaped like an inverted pyramid fastens a mountain climber's harness around my hips as if I'm his incontinent grandfather. He clips the harness to the guylines of the parachute and tells me to sit down on my butt. The boat speeds up and goes away, and I am rising up in the air like Icarus in rubber sandals.

It's effortless, dream-flight. The roar of the boat fades to a distant mosquito buzz, the wind rocks me gently in my harness, and I am looking down at the white backs of gulls below me. I wave placidly to some people who are looking up at me from a sailboat and they wave back. I arch my back into the harness to tilt my chute to catch more air. I want to go higher. I want this to last forever. This must be how it is when your soul rises up, freed at last from its mortal suitcase.

From here Ocean City and its mighty high-rises look puny, the whole shebang built on a narrow spit of sand that one good wave would wash back into the sea. The wakes of boats look like long white feathers ever growing and fading in the water. The line reels me in, and I land standing up from exactly where I left.

That night, back at the pier again, Jane wants to try the Bottle-Up. She can't do it, either. "How 'bout you, sir," the guy says, lazily righting her fallen bottle with the stick. I tell him he already got me last night. "Oh, yeah, I remember," he says, his face brightening with recognition. "You the guy almost won it."

A CHIP OFF THE OLD ROOT

All I know is the tug in my blood that announced itself suddenly in my late thirties must have come from someplace. I can't lay it at the feet of my father. In the seven generations since we left Ireland, there has been not a single hunter recorded among the Heaveys. On the other hand, there had to be a few guys back in the deep end of the gene pool who had a talent for bringing home meat or I wouldn't be here, right? Maybe I'm just atavistic, a chip off the old root.

The way the urge hit reminded me of that ad on television where the guy answers his doorbell to find the pizza delivery man there with a smile on his face, pizza box open with the fragrant steam rising up out of the box. He didn't order the pizza, but now that he's got a whiff of pepperoni and mozzarella, there's no way that pie is leaving his porch. Same thing happened to me. On a whim, I went along with some guys going duck hunting one morning, and as soon as the first bird flew overhead I knew it wasn't binoculars I wanted to be holding. Some neural switch had been thrown, some connection made. And now I'm sitting with a stiff back against a tree, a Polar Heat seat under my butt, and a rifle in my lap. It's opening day of deer season, and I'm hoping to get lucky.

Some guys hunt smart, some guys hunt stubborn. Being a late entry in the game and self-schooled to boot, my learning curve has been on the flat side. Sure, I'd like to be one of those guys who grew up steeped in the finer points of hunting lore, waiting in ambush for a buck with a rocking chair on its head, which I'd been stealthily patterning for months. I wish I could look at a patch of woods and break it down into deer subdivisions: restaurant, bedroom, escape route, and commuter line, knowing that just after shooting light, old Mr. Many Tines would come waltzing through the acorns. Heck, I wish I could get into a tree stand fifteen feet off the ground without killing myself. But I can't. (I'm not stupid. I've seen them in my local gun shop. If you wanted to design a baitless mousetrap for humans, this is pretty much where you'd start.) So I'm going at this thing freestyle, hunkered down behind a tangle of vines twenty-five yards from where two deer trails intersect along a little stream. My boots smell like a fox with serious bladder control problems. I've got six little tufts of cotton doused with doe-in-estrus urine arranged in a circle around me. And I'm waiting for something with horns on its head to walk by.

What I lack in smarts I hope to make up for in persistence, what a friend calls the middle-linebacker mentality. The deer have me way outclassed in woods savvy. I'm as green as the cheese in the back of your refrigerator. But they have to be right all the time, and I only have to be right once. I arrived by flashlight, freshly showered with scent-killing soap and wearing a camouflage face mask that would get you handcuffed within thirty seconds if you put it on in an airport. I'm prepared to leave by flashlight, too. I have a set of cheapo binoculars that make my eyes feel like they've been doing twenty-five-pound curls, aspirin to counter that pain, an ample supply of cookies, a quart bottle of water, and an empty quart bottle with a tight cap to pee in. You can lose the battle all day long and still win the war with one shot.

Distant fire sounds all around me. Sometimes it comes in volleys of three, which I imagine to be a miss, a wide miss, and a final gunpowder curse from a greedy hunter. I suppose I should thank those guys. Maybe one is sending a buck my way right now. The squirrels that crash through the dry leaves seem oblivious to me, approaching within ten feet and giving me reason to be cheerful. A flicker hops backward down the trunk of a pine tree thirty feet in front of me, cocking its head to one side as if deciding whether to believe the wood when it swears there are no bugs beneath its bark. Around ten thirty a red fox comes trotting boldly up the trail, with a gait that is neither dog nor cat. Sixty feet away it pauses, thinking for a moment. I hold my breath, trying to melt into the scenery. It lowers its nose and resumes its weightless amble through the dry leaves and is gone. Hey, bubba, things are looking up.

Only they're not. For the next four hours, the woods close for business. Nothing stirs. Maybe the garlic in last night's spaghetti has begun to seep from my pores. Maybe the deer have cordoned off a circle with a radius of a hundred yards, using me as the center. Maybe they're talking amongst themselves, saying, "You know, I love the smell of commercially bottled fox urine. It always reminds me of fall." I scrunch my toes in my boots to ward off numbness, arch my lower back to fine-tune the ache. Hey, it could be worse. I could be playing golf.

At three o'clock, contact. The faintest shuffle of leaves. I slide my eyes to three does along the top of the far ridge, 125 yards away, and adrenaline floods my body. They are dainty and tentative: heads down and sniffing, stopping and starting incessantly, tails lowered but twitching. I move the glasses up to my eyes in slow-mo. My hands are shaking, but I can make out the does' dark muzzles and a white patch across each throat. Seeing deer is still magic to me, like a cave painting becoming animated, a contact with the spirit world. My blood remembers things my head has never even had the chance to forget. The deer quarter away and dissolve into the trees.

The sighting is enough to keep me on full alert for the next two hours, sure that at any moment something is going to happen. By five the day is already turning to dust, the light soaking back into the ground. The wind rises for a few minutes and dies away. The woods are absolutely still. At last I lean away from the tree and fall back slowly until I'm flat on my back and looking straight up. From a hollow in a tree fifty feet above my head, the night shift is reporting for work. Two raccoons poke their noses out for a sniff, then lumber out and spend the next five minutes rubbing their heads with their hands, scratching themselves, then grooming each other. They walk out and back along several of the larger limbs to stretch their muscles. As the last of the light leaves, I can just make out two shapes inching down the trunk headfirst. I wait till they're down and gone before I switch on my flashlight, shuck the cartridges from my gun, and begin the walk out. I'm stiff, bone-tired, and strangely happy. I'm making friends with my ancestors.

CAN I TELL YOU SOMETHING?

"Can I tell you something?" the famous outdoor writer asked suddenly. We'd been in his Jeep for about a hundred miles on our way to a tidal river on Maryland's Eastern Shore to fish for largemouth bass. I'd called him up because I was a smaller fish in the same pond and hoped to learn a trick or two at the feet of a master. I'd been surprised when he immediately invited me along on a fishing trip. He checked the rearview before continuing.

"I don't like fishing and hunting that much anymore." I looked at him closely. This was not some retiring aesthete, but a tough old bull with an ego to match, a guy who'd outhustled a lot of competition to get his job, then cut a wide swath doing what the rest of us dream about. He'd been all over the world fishing for brook trout and marlin, crappie and tarpon, bass and bonefish. Closer to home, he had his pick of blinds in duck and goose season, and access to private clubs where he could hunt trophy bucks each fall. And now he was telling me his heart wasn't in it.

"What I mean is that I don't like killing animals anymore. I still love being out there in the woods or on the water. That part never gets old. But the shooting . . . I haven't told anybody this but I had a big buck in my sights at forty yards last November and I just let it walk."

"What about fishing?" I asked, buying some time to think all this over. "I'm sure you release just about everything you catch."

"I do. I hardly ever use anything except a fly rod and barbless hooks. But that's not the point. I've started feeling like I don't even want to bother the fish unless I'm going to eat them. I just want to let them go

29

about their lives. Does that make any sense to you?" He looked as if he'd already told me more than he'd intended.

Sure it made sense, I told him. Part of the problem was political. As hunters and anglers, we must constantly justify our sport to people who think we're witless barbarians. It's hard to explain to someone whose mind is already made up that you hunt because of how it connects you to the natural world. Someone who has never taken up a gun, bow, or rod will never understand how that act suddenly transforms you from an observer to a participant in life. We who possess that knowledge count ourselves a lucky but beleaguered minority. So it seems almost treasonous to deviate from the code, even when that's what a man's feelings are telling him to do. I know of more than one hunter who, after decades of filled tags, went down to his workshop one day and, without telling anybody, replaced the barrel on his rifle stock with a telephoto lens. Now he shoots pictures instead of bullets. He is neither better nor worse than his friends. He does what's right for him.

We talked about how a young man wants passionately to make his mark upon the world, to see how he measures up. Over time, a certain kind of man will develop more than a good roll cast and an instinct for where a big buck might lie up on a windy day. He'll also be wondering how he stalks. He'll kill cleanly or pass up the shot. He'll land and release a fish before exhaustion threatens its recovery.

But for some men, there comes a time when even that isn't enough.

The outdoor writer and I went out on a small tidal river near the Chesapeake Bay under perfect conditions, fished hard for nearly seven hours, and got skunked. It was a beautiful place. There was almost nobody else around and we were casting well. As dusk turned to dark, we reeled in and headed home.

"I'm not gonna tell you I'm happy we didn't catch anything," my companion noted, "in spite of what I said before."

I liked this guy. I liked his honesty, how he matched his words to his feelings, even if they contradicted something he'd said earlier. On the drive back we talked about writing and swapped stories. Neither of us mentioned what we'd talked about on the way down.

My own predator instinct is very much intact. The only hope for a big buck in my sights at forty yards is that I'm shaking too much to shoot straight. My girlfriend Jane says I have two driving speeds: regular and on-the-way-to-fishing. I love this urgency, this thing that pulls at my blood like the moon pulls at the oceans. But I can imagine a day when I look at a wild trout with my hook in its mouth and suddenly feel that I've caught enough trout. I can picture a buck locking eyes with me in what it somehow knows is its last moment, and discovering that my finger doesn't want to pull the trigger. I'm not looking forward to that day. But to be a hunter is to have the courage and humility to honor your instincts, even if they tell you the time to hunt has passed.

A BOWHUNTING OBSESSION

I found the only other guy at the party who wasn't wearing a tie. Pretty soon we were talking bass and trout, ducks and doves. It wasn't long before he was telling me about bowhunting for whitetails. "Any dolt with a scope and a rail to rest his rifle on can shoot a deer at three hundred yards," he insisted, swirling the bourbon in his glass. "Shooting one that's so close you can see his whiskers . . . now that's a different deal."

A little orange flare arced up in a dark cave in my brain. You could do this, it signaled.

"You don't need a bow named after nuclear weapons, military aircraft, or Clint Eastwood characters," my newfound friend continued, slowly reeling me in. "If it has the word *turbo* in it, pass. Any compound out there has the power to turn a monster whitetail into chipped venison."

Thus began my descent into bowhunting obsession.

The next week, after asking around, I settled on a PSE Nova, an entry-level one-cam. I went out and promptly began burying arrows in the back lawn. It was humbling to watch a thirty-inch shaft disappear so fast you couldn't be sure you'd really owned that particular arrow in the first place. Then I discovered that I'd stored my bow upside down before tightening the sight pins. I fiddled with them, worked my way back to twenty yards, and began smacking the target consistently.

"Hooked" would be an understatement. I was filleted, battered, and deep-fried. It was like having a rifle with a silencer on it. My bag target actually shuddered under the impact of every shot. I loved the feeling of stored energy in the bow's limbs as the let-off kicked in, the Zen of relaxed strength, the way you maintain form and look the arrow home after it has sprung from the bow. Soon I'd worn a path from the back deck to the target. In my dreams, every branch in the forest turned into antlers.

To shoot at thirty yards, I had to improvise. Cranking open the little casement window in my office, standing with my right heel touching the back wall and shooting over my computer just about did it. I noticed that the neighbors stopped inviting us to cookouts. Now it was mid-August. I figured one hundred arrows a day would make me lethal by the start of deer season in October.

What I was turning into became clear the morning I scared the bejesus out of the UPS man. By this time I had taken to replicating field conditions as closely as I could for my morning fifty. A rickety stool atop the picnic table on the back deck got me near-tree-stand height. I wore my fleece camo parka in 85-degree heat, a full-face Scent-Lok hood, with binoculars and a grunt tube slung around my neck. I was an unlikely centaur: deer slayer above the waist; the white hairy legs, gym shorts, and bedroom slippers of the suburban male below.

UPS drivers witness a wider daily range of aberrant human behavior than your average psych ward nurse. Weird doesn't particularly faze them. But the eyes of the guy in the brown uniform and clipboard told me that he had never seen anything like the Ninja of North Arlington.

"Okay if I just, uh, leave this one on the front porch?" he asked in the overly friendly voice you use on lost children and muggers. He was holding a tiny box of broadheads and keeping the fence between us in case he had to duck and cover.

At times like this, explanations just make you look crazier. "Sure," I told him. I made a gesture of conciliation with my right hand, which still had a string release on it.

Opening day found me sixteen feet up a tree on a ridge overlooking a stream crossing. I was wearing rubber boots, camo everything, a charcoal-activated suit, scent killer, and fall masking scent. As light filled the woods, I rattled hard for thirty seconds and watched as a doe and still-dappled fawn came running to see who was new to the neighborhood. She sniffed and stomped. Something was off; she just couldn't tell what. My heart was trying to jackhammer its way out of my chest.

Two weeks later a spike buck came in to the same sound and was actually sniffing at the doe-in-estrus scent on the boot pads I'd left on a screw-in step. What I didn't have was a shot. I waited, my heart again trying to make a prison break. The deer drifted away, taking the woodiest possible route. At twenty yards he turned his shoulder, and I let one go. The arrow clattered harmlessly against the limbs I hadn't seen, and he trotted off to another appointment. I was disconsolate for days.

Then my hot spot turned cold. Despair made me reckless. I rattled, grunted, and bleated to excess. I lit deer-luring incense sticks and watched them turn to ash. I sprinkled Deer CoCain on the ground. I wondered briefly about real cocaine. I bought several rounds of doe-in-estrus pee for every buck in the house. No gimmick was too stupid for me to buy. If someone had marketed an Ole Buckster Fart Tube, I'd have ordered two. Some nights back home I'd set up candles by my target and fling arrows out of my office while the rest of the world slept.

The strain was beginning to show in the blue hollows under my eyes. My wife held my hands in her lap one night. "You're sick," Jane said tenderly.

"I know," I replied.

I moved my stand to a trail intersection deeper in the woods. I bought a second stand and put it up along a small bench on a gentle hillside. Forget those articles about how a fixed stand can be set up quietly in twenty minutes and hunted the same day. My personal best was ninety minutes. And it sounded like a Bon Jovi concert.

Thirty of the forty days of bow season were now gone. I bit the bullet and moved my stands again. I chained one twenty yards in from a fence line at a crossing where I'd found tiny tufts of hair on the top wire. The other I relocated off to one side of a saddle between my original ridge and its brother.

The dawns and dusks were getting colder. Four days before the end of the season, I spied at a great distance a doe scampering through the leaves. A larger shape, with its head lowered, was tailing her. There was a moment when something that looked like antler caught the slanting afternoon light, but I couldn't be sure.

On the last day of the season, I got to my saddle stand at 2 P.M., climbed up, clipped in, and slowly pulled my bow up. My heart wasn't in it, but I knew I'd kick myself for the rest of the year if I didn't finish it out.

I grunted and rattled. About three thirty, the deer began to appear. A doe came cautiously into view, so well camouflaged that if I took my eyes off her for a moment, I wouldn't be able to find her again until she moved. Two more does came straight up the saddle, trailed by a four-pointer with his head down. My heart dropped the clutch and floored it. They were forty yards out. I rose slowly to my feet, and my stand squeaked. The deer snorted, stomped, and jumped three long lengths away, then stood. I concentrated on taking fast shallow breaths and didn't look directly at them.

The first doe began feeding again. Then another buck, this one sporting five points, appeared and began trailing her downwind. They did figure eights through the trees for forty-five minutes. As dusk fell, she led him toward my tree. I drew and held. A minute later he turned broadside. I put my pin on his shoulder and released.

The two deer jumped once, then trotted off into the dark woods. I heard hooves clatter on stone. I waited fifteen minutes, climbed down with a flashlight in my mouth, and found my bloody arrow nine steps from the base of the tree. Thirty yards away, where I'd heard the clatter, lay the five-point buck. It took me an hour to drag him forty yards.

The guy at the slaughterhouse guessed his weight at 180. "That's a big buck," he said.

It occurred to me that I'd shot six thousand arrows to hear that one sentence. It was worth it.

THE WAITING

During the last weeks of the pre-rut, bucks get together in bachelor herds to click antlers and size each other up before the madness of mating season sets in. Bowhunters have a similar instinct, but to a different end. In this neck of the woods, they meet at Hoffman's, a low-slung brick building next to the Buckland Farm Market out on Route 29. On the last Saturday before the season opens, it would be difficult to prove that a bow is the silent way to hunt. Auto body shops are quieter. Both saws are in use, milling carbon and aluminum shafts to order. Dave Hoffman hasn't had a moment in the past three hours to get over to the VCR by the worn sofa in the corner, so it's blaring *Monster Bucks, Volume IV* for the third time today. And through the door to the twenty-yard range comes the *guh-fwack!* of archers who can't resist one last chronograph or paper check. It's not that their speed or alignment has changed in the three days since their last check; they just don't know what else to do. As Tom Petty sang, the waiting is the hardest part.

Dave is talking to a guy in overalls and muddy boots who has brought in his two little boys and an ancient, pre-camo Bear Kodiak compound that creaks mightily on its way to full draw. He buried his last arrow in a tree and needs more, only he doesn't know the length or size. "I killed a squirrel and a groundhog with it," he says. "After I get me a deer, I'll buy a good bow. Got to get my money's worth out of her first." He slaps his checkbook against his leg and laughs uproariously. It's a farmer's joke.

Dave's prices are competitive with the catalogs, especially when you consider the cost of shipping and the agony of waiting for the truck to show up. And the store's policies are pretty straightforward. Dave services what he sells. And there's a gentleman's agreement that you can shoot all afternoon at his targets in the back as long as you buy something. A set of field points qualifies. A hand-lettered sign lists his services: Three shots with the chronograph: $1. Fletching: $1.50 per arrow. Our stories: Free. Listen to your stories: $25.

Nine months a year, Hoffman's is quieter than a plaid-carpet warehouse. In August, things start to pick up a little. By September, bemusement seems to steal into the glass eyes of the deer, bear, and boar mounted on the wall, as guys who've been on the fence all summer about a new bow suddenly teeter into gotta-have-it land. By the first of October, vehicles are ringing the entrance two deep as hunters decide they need more broadheads, new servings, maybe a fifth tree stand. Mostly, of course, they just want to rub shoulders with fellow hunters.

Two guys are standing with their arms crossed and big hard-shell bow cases at their feet, waiting for a word with Dave. They plant their feet and remain motionless, as if rehearsing for the woods. One finally looks at the other. "Pumped?" he asks.

The other guy's body goes slack as he exhales a breath that's been building up all summer. "Shoot, man. So itchy I can hardly sleep. Shot all the video deer I can stand. I want to get up in a tree."

The discussion ranges from expanding broadheads (not as durable as fixed blades, but they fly just like field points and cut an awful big hole in a deer), releases (ball bearings eat up your serving faster than calipers or a bar, but you can't beat them for smooth), and Scent-Lok camo ("Buddy of mine nailed an eight-pointer last year that came in downwind of his stand to a rattle bag and just stood there, bellerin'").

There's also the problem of what to do about the lack of mast this year. The first guy is targeting a stand of persimmon trees. The other's working a pokeberry patch where he's seen some purple droppings. "Tell you what," the first guy says. "Let's shoot three while we're

37

waiting." They nod at the guys behind them in line to reserve their places, open their cases on the floor, and adjourn to the range to settle their nerves.

Dave Hoffman took up a bow twenty-five years ago, when he was a section foreman in a coal mine in West Virginia. "There were so many guys with seniority that you couldn't get any vacation during rifle season," he says. He started off on a secondhand Jennings compound. First time out, he shot twice over a doe at about twenty-five yards. "When I paced it off, it turned out she was twelve yards away," he remembers. "That's how stoked on adrenaline I was. But, man, was I hooked." It took him four years to get his first deer, with that same Jennings. He no longer shoots it, but can't bring himself to sell it.

For Dave, the quintessential story of what keeps bowhunters battling the odds isn't about success. It's about deer-induced meltdown, the epiphany of failure that all true hunters know firsthand. "I was watching a buddy up in a tree stand nearby when a big buck wandered in. You should have seen this old boy shake. He drew an arrow back all of two inches, held for ten seconds, then let it clatter down out of the tree, sending the buck running. Later, I asked him how far away the deer was when he shot. 'I don't know,' he said. I asked him if he came to full draw. 'I don't know.' I asked if the deer was walking or had stopped. 'I don't know.' It was like talking to somebody who'd just been hit by a truck."

Dave smiles broadly. "See, that's what I love about bowhunting."

Dave greets the next customer and starts ringing up Bright Eyes fluorescent thumbtacks, a half dozen arrows, and a camouflage rattling bag. As they wait for the electronic go-ahead from the credit card company, the guy confesses that the waiting is making him crazy. "Me, too," Dave says happily. "Just like everybody else."

IT'S A BASS WORLD AFTER ALL

There is no place the nation's 20 million bass anglers would rather be than out fishing. Except in winter, of course, when we sink into our Barcaloungers like hibernating mud turtles to watch TV bass-fishing shows until the ice melts. Or when it's a blazing 96 degrees out there with air quality in the lethal-only-if-inhaled range, when I personally prefer to retire to a cool room to read my latest issue of *Bassmaster*. Come to think of it, there's an awful lot of the time when the great outdoors would be better if it were indoors. Which may be why there's Bass Pro Shops Outdoor World in Springfield, Missouri.

The single biggest tourist attraction in the Show-Me State is not the Ozark Mountains, the Gateway Arch in St. Louis, or one of the theaters in Branson where Wayne Newton and Tony Orlando croon their ancient hits to packed houses. It's this megastore, a retail theme park of Disneyan proportions dedicated to the pursuit of America's favorite game fish, *Micropterus salmoides*, the largemouth bass. Four million people a year push through these doors. When my wife, Jane, drops me off while she goes to visit friends in this, her hometown, she asks when she should pick me up.

"As late as you can," I answer.

"Okay," she says. "Seven. Right here. And don't buy anything you can't fit on the plane."

It was the bass that gave Johnny Morris, Outdoor World's creator, his leg up in the world. And he has never forgotten it. Morris started out in a corner of his father's liquor store on this very spot in Springfield, selling lures and bait to men who had stopped in for beer and ice on their way to bass-fish one of the nearby lakes. In 1974 he sent out his first Bass Pro Shops catalog. This year he'll be sending out 40 million, listing 30,000 items and fighting archrival Cabela's for the No. 2 catalog ranking. (L.L.Bean is No. 1 in the country). Morris has already opened other Bass Pro Shops megastores in Georgia and Illinois, and a specialty saltwater flyfishing store in Florida. Four more Outdoor Worlds—in Nashville, Fort Lauderdale, Houston, and Grapevine, Texas—are scheduled to open by 2000. Not far from here is another successful Morris project, Big Cedar Lodge, a resort with a Jack Nicklaus–designed golf course and a ten-thousand-acre nature park stocked with elk and bison. But he's still primarily in the bass business.

Outdoor World is an ever-expanding work in progress—200,000 square feet at the moment, with plans to increase to 300,000 this year. Naturally, it houses the world's largest fishing department: a forest of high-modulus graphite fishing rods flanking aisles displaying more than seven thousand lures, 3-D electronic fish finders, and one-piece aluminum reels with LCD line counters.

But while fishing is Outdoor World's foundation, there have been some whopping big add-ons. The store has, to name a few, sections devoted to archery, black-powder firearms, flyfishing, knives, and sporting optics. You can buy golf clubs, ladies' wildlife jewelry, or a deer rifle you may sight in at the indoor range right behind the gun counter. You can buy a canoe or a $30,000 bass boat that will do zero to 60 mph so fast you think you're in a rocket sled. You can buy chaps that will stand up to a rattlesnake's fangs or a four-hundred-dollar Nautica leather jacket or Orvis luggage.

At Hemingway's Restaurant, you can see the skiff that legendary guide Bonefish Willie used to take the great writer fishing in Florida, watch the pink and blue fish parade back and forth in the thirty-thousand-gallon saltwater tank behind the bar, and sip a Monsoon, a fruity concoction containing six shots of booze served in a glass the size of a goldfish bowl. There's a wildlife museum, a free knife-sharpening service, and the Tall Tales Barber Shop, where they'll not only cut your hair but use a tuft of it to make you up a special Hair Trigger fishing lure.

Outdoor World casts a wide net. Good ol' boys in pickups mix with older bus tourists wearing nylon jackets that proclaim them to be Tulsa Keenagers. Minivans outnumber trucks in the parking lot 3:1. Like other intensely American phenomena, Outdoor World has an appeal that extends beyond national boundaries. Bass clubs from as far away as Japan and Zimbabwe have made the hajj here. Heck, George W. Bush has been here so many times the help doesn't even get excited anymore.

The real, the artificial, and the artificially real coexist happily here. A hundred-pound alligator snapping turtle born sometime in the 1800s lies motionless in a tank near Marine Accessories. It holds its breath forever, seldom moves, and consequently doesn't quite look real. But something inside you knows that it is, knows it could take your hand off at the wrist and not even feel bad about it. The four-story waterfall with headwaters near the in-store McDonald's tumbles past trophy elk and mountain goats and the live snake exhibit near Triple Play Sports Collectibles ($1,300 for a signed Michael Jordan jersey), then spills into a reflecting pool where dark catfish motor endlessly beneath the paddling feet of teal and wood ducks. A little farther on, the reflecting pool turns into a 64,000-gallon aquarium housing all manner of freshwater fish. The star here is Gertie, a nineteen-pound largemouth bass believed to be the biggest in captivity. Every day except Christmas, a scuba diver descends into the tank for the fish-feeding show, while visitors watch from the Uncle Buck Auditorium through Plexiglas. After the show, the faithful nuzzle up to the glass to pay homage to Gertie. She's a few pounds shy of the holy grail of bass fishing, the 22-pound, 4-ounce monster that was caught by George Washington Perry in Georgia back in 1932. Guys have come close to the magic number in recent years, mostly in a few lakes around—of all places—Los Angeles. There is general agreement that the record breaker is even now finning its way around out there, swallowing ducklings, water snakes, and smaller fish whole. She (girl bass get bigger than boy bass) may even be showing up now as a blip on some angler's sonar.

The fish that breaks the record that has stood for more than half a century will be worth a million bucks to its owner in product endorsements alone. It will be a bittersweet victory in some ways. Bass anglers take a perverse pride in knowing that all our high-tech boats, tackle, and electronics don't impress the fish. We like it that the world record was taken by a guy who built his own skiff with seventy-five cents' worth of scrap lumber, using a $1.33 rod and a wooden Creek Chub Wiggle Fish with glass eyes. Still, you have to admit that Gertie is one boss hawg, a Rubenesque beauty of a bass. Any fisherman worth his salt would gladly pawn his wife's engagement ring for a shot at a fish like that.

Outdoor World is founded on the golden rule of retail: The longer you entice people to stay in the store, the more likely they'll open their wallets. But after three hours, I find the opposite is happening. I'm paralyzed by the abundance. Numbly strolling through the crankbait aisles, I come upon an old standby bass lure, the Rat-L-Trap. When I started fishing, it came in two sizes and three colors, I think. Now it comes in six sizes and forty-seven colors, from Bleedin' Shiner to Firetiger. If you bought one in each size and color, your boat would sink, all the lures would catch on your clothing, and then they'd drag you down to Lunker Land.

I slide over to soft plastics, another huge market segment. There are Super Squirts, Squirmin' Squirts, Sparkle Squirts, Lightning Squirts, and (my personal favorite) Squirmin' Jerks. There are tackle boxes small enough to slip into a shirt pocket and others big enough to use as a life raft. There is braided fishing line and mono fishing line, stuff that glows fluorescent yellow in the water and stuff that turns invisible. I can't keep up with all of it. Maybe I'm the Squirmin' Jerk.

Over in Hunting, it's the same, but more so. Every garment comes in fleece, cotton, and cotton-polyester blend and in twelve shades of camouflage. Do the deer and turkeys and ducks appreciate the subtle differences between Apparition and Mossy Oak, Realtree X-tra Brown and Blaze Camo? I'm drawn by the sound of falling water into the Gore-Tex section, where a mannequin stands in a shower stall beneath a perpetual jet of water wearing that company's waterproof laminate in his parka, boots, and pants. You want to throw him a towel and give him some hot soup. I listen to two guys debating the purchase of a video called *The Magic of Squirrel Hunting*. A guy blows into a bull elk grunt tube that is big enough to unclog a toilet. It sounds sort of like it's trying to warn all the other toilets in the area. At the gun counter, I pick up a rifle stock with a twelve-power scope on it, damn near as big as the Hubble, and aim it down the aisle. I see a gob of flesh and realize it's the earlobe of a woman standing eighty feet away. She sees me, too. Sees me pointing a rifle stock her way. I put the gun down, smile sheepishly, give her a little wave. She is not amused.

At seven, I'm out front to meet Jane. In six hours at Outdoor World, all that I have purchased is a dark green Redhead chamois hunting shirt. It's a discontinued color, marked down from $24.95 to $9.99. The outer lobes of my brain are on the blink, leaving only the reptilian core functioning. But I'm still a sucker for a deal. When I get in the car, she looks at my face, sees it's drained of color.

"Too long in Disney World?" she asks.

I nod. I feel as if I'm five years old.

A MORNING IN THE BLIND

The sun is little more than a reddening inflammation in the east, the clouds low and scudding over the Chesapeake when Charlie Laird spots the ducks, spots them so far out they look like motes floating across my eyes, which are tearing up from cold.

"Don't move," he tells the three other men in the blind. Not moving is the easy part. There are mummies wrapped in fewer layers than I am. The interesting part is whether I can raise a 12-gauge to eye level.

"Canvasbacks," Charlie confirms happily when they're still three hundred yards out. "Remember, one apiece," he says.

The last thing he wants is some itchy out-of-towner—me—going home with a bad taste in his mouth and a hole in his wallet. Scott, the local warden, is one of our party, enjoying a rare couple of days of hunting ducks instead of poachers at the tail end of the season. Charlie and Scott have been friends for years. And they both know Scott would have his pen out to write up the violator, no matter who it is, before the second duck hit the water. ("It's a real small world down here," Scott says of the Eastern Shore. "You lose your reputation once, you're over.")

The cans, numbering about twenty, come by high and purposeful, like they've got someplace else to be. But there's something about the lay of the dekes that gets to them. They fly past, bank right, do a figure eight that brings them back for another look, and head down the shank of the hook to the calm water in front of the blind. You can see the chestnut red of the drakes' heads and necks, hear the hissing of their wings as they descend. Charlie waits until the birds at the bottom tier of the flock have their landing gear down. Then he calls, "Take 'em." Scott immediately knocks down a drake. Bob and I each need two shots to tumble a bird, a drake for him, a hen for me. It's all over in seconds. "Hold up!" shouts Charlie. The danger of overshooting past, his voice returns to normal. "Nice shootin', guys." While he gets the boat to pick up the ducks, the rest of us just grin at each other. It's not fifteen minutes into legal light and we've already limited out on the fastest-flying, best-eating duck there is.

"They don't come to the 'coys any prettier'n that," says Bob, who manages an insurance agency up the road.

"Boy knows his stuff," agrees Scott.

Charlie's knowledge of the marsh is bred in the bone. The Lairds have been living here for five generations, no great stretch of time by local standards. Some folks trace their line back to the English colonists who waded ashore nearby at St. Mary's City in 1634. For generations men molded their lives to the rhythm of the seasons along the Indian-named rivers—Nanticoke, Wicomico, and Big Annemessex. They netted the running fish in spring, farmed the loamy soil, tonged oysters, and set crab pots in the summer, hunted ducks, geese, and deer in the fall, trapped muskrats and coons in the winter. You didn't get fat at this life, but it worked its way into you the way salt rubbed into a ham works its way to the bone. After a while, you weren't fit for life anyplace else. And you didn't care to be.

The old way is disappearing faster than a falling spring tide. The estuary the Algonquins called Chesepiooc, Great Shellfish Bay, now produces a tiny fraction of the protein it did two generations back. Small farming makes the state lottery look like a prudent use of your money. Many families have done the arithmetic and moved to take indoor work in Baltimore, Norfolk, or farther. Then there are guys like Charlie, too in love with the marsh or just too proud to be the one to break the chain.

"I learned these marshes the same way my daddy and his daddy did. Got my first pair of hand-me-down hip boots at seven, started trapping at eight. Got my older brother's .410 and a .22 the same year.

Always had a boat, always had a dog, spent all summer getting ready to duck hunt. My dad would have to chase me down and throw me in the shower every so often just to get the mud off. How you gonna leave a place like that?"

Charlie works a full-time job as a guard at the prison nearby, raises nearly a million chickens a year with his brother and sister, rises at four each morning to check traps for coons and muskrats. On top of that he takes about one hundred clients a year waterfowling or bow-hunting for deer on 1,300 acres of land he leases. He doesn't log a lot of sack time, wouldn't know *Seinfeld* from a signpost, doesn't get to take his fiancée and her three boys out to eat as much as he'd like. But he counts himself a lucky man. He loves his work, and it shows up in repeat customers. In seven years, he'll have his twenty in as a guard and with the pension as backup, figures he'll be able to guide full-time. "If I can show folks how beautiful this place is, put them on to the birds, and make 'em feel they got their money's worth, I'm happy," he says.

The next day brings sleet but no wind. But the serious business of hunting ducks gives you license to build forts with the fervor of a six-year-old, and Bob and I throw ourselves into the task. We heap armfuls of cordgrass until the walls are so high you have to stand up to shoot out of it. Then we sit inside and feel the intimacy of the blind sneak up on us, stripping away the layers of modern life that conspire to keep one man separate from another. It's a magic that never gets old.

Prompted by no one, Bob starts telling how he and his wife of twelve years are headed for a divorce. They still talk on the phone each day, even go to church together, but he has moved out of the house. The counseling didn't seem to take. They're trying to make it easy on the kids. He talks as if the whole thing were a moving train and he just happens to be a passenger on it. I don't say anything, because all I can think of are the pat words that carry no meaning. Hey, it happens. Rough on everybody concerned. Way of the world.

But Charlie is made of sterner stuff, doesn't look up or down to anybody, doesn't set much store by "tact" when it's truth a guy needs to hear. He looks Bob straight in the eye. "Listen," he says abruptly. "I ain't known you but two days and I can read you like a book. You're a nice guy, anybody can see that. And just from hearing you talk, I know you got a good woman. But you're stubborn and selfish and you got your priorities backwards. And you're both hurting and drifting into a divorce neither of you wants." He scans the sky for birds and turns his attention back to Bob. "I'm not sayin' this outta meanness, and I'm not looking for a policy discount."

Bob manages a little laugh. "I know you're not," he says softly. But Bob's eyes are widening and a little glassy.

"How old are you, thirty-four, thirty-five?"

"Thirty-six," Bob says, blinking.

"How old your little ones?"

"Six and nine."

"I'm three years younger'n you and I'm telling you: You're about to make the biggest mistake of your life. You think you're gonna be happier without her. It don't work that way. It ain't even about sex. It's about being connected to somebody. I was married to a girl everybody warned me about and I didn't listen. She drank and ran around and had a mouth on her to make a waterman blush. We got divorced, and I'm still paying for it. But now I'm engaged to a girl with three kids and I love 'em like they's my own." He shrugs his shoulders, sending melted sleet off his poncho, and thinks. "I seen a lot of my family die," he says at last. "Uncles and all. And as they got near the end, all of 'em said the same thing: All you got is family. Not a one of 'em wished they'd had more women or made more money or killed more ducks."

Bob looks down at his hands, watches the sleet beading up on his gloves. But Charlie isn't done. "Look at me. I'm a big, macho guy. Six four, played catcher four years, and I guarantee you anybody ever ran into me at the plate got the short end of it. And every time I talk to my fiancée on the phone, I tell her I love her. Every time. 'Cause you never know when it's gonna be the last." Charlie gazes at a few flecks of pepper wandering across the horizon. "Blacks," he says. "Guys'll come by the house when I'm folding laundry or vacuuming and say, 'C'mon, man, we're gonna go watch the game and pound a few. That girl's leadin' you around by the nose.' I just tell 'em to go on. Because you know what? Every one of them guys is a loser. So the question is, do you love her?"

"Yeah," says Bob. "I do."

"You ever tell her that?"

"Hell, yeah. Say it all the time."

"That ain't what I meant. When was the last time you looked her in the eye and told her she's the most important thing in your life and the only woman you want and you'll do whatever it takes to keep her?"

Bob stares at his feet. Charlie looks over at Scott. "You know him better'n me. You think I'm telling him true?"

"Every word," Scott says. "But he's down to his last card. Bud, you got to do something before it's too late."

Bob looks up, blinking hard. "So what do I do?" he asks in a small voice.

Charlie tells him. "You got to do it your own way. But if it was me, soon as I got off this marsh, I'd buy two dozen roses and get myself over there. You take her by both hands and get down on your knees—I'm serious—on your knees. And you tell her you don't care about your job or your deke collection or how much money she's spending. You tell her you love her and if you're speaking from your heart, I guarantee you'll be crying. And that's okay, you just go ahead and cry."

"I'm half crying now," Bob says. He looks around. "Those black ducks?" he says of birds far out over the bay.

Charlie looks. "Cormorants," he says. Nobody says anything for a while.

Scott says Bob may need to do something dramatic to show his wife he's not just talking. "She knows you love those decoys you got. If it comes to that, you just sweep 'em off the mantel and throw 'em out the front door," he tells his friend. "Decoy ain't but so much wood."

Bob sighs. He thought he'd gone duck hunting to get away from his problems and finds he has walked straight into them. But he knows what Charlie's saying is true and vows he'll try. He looks like he understands what's at stake. He'll chuck the dekes if that's what it comes to.

Two hours later, we're heading for our cars. I feel lucky just to have been here, lucky to have limited out on friendship. "Well," I say to Bob. "I hope it works. You've got three guys pulling for you."

"By the way," Charlie says, "whereabouts you live up that way?"

"Why?" asks Bob.

"I was thinking I might take a drive up there tonight and be standing outside your door just to make sure none of them 'coys gets hurt when they fall."

Scott, Charlie, and I crack up. At last Bob does, too.

ALONE WITH A PRETTY WOMAN
IN A SMALL ROOM
WITH A BIG MIRROR

My dance instructor, Miss Harris, has just introduced me to a move in the hustle called the back pass, a tricky little maneuver in which the beginner must avoid slamming into the nose of his or her partner. Done properly, at the last moment you miss, pass each other, the Lady catches the Gentleman's hand, and he twirls her as if lazily shaking the curl from a ribbon. Just as I am getting to the point where I'm pretty sure that neither of us will disfigure the other, Mr. Dutcher, the head of the studio, brings over an attractive pupil, introduces her to me as Miss Brady and invites me to try the step with her.

"Sure, Mr. Heavey," pipes up Miss Harris. "You can do it!"

At that instant, unbeknownst to the three of them, I am transported from the Arthur Murray studio back in time to the following moment: I am ten years old, sent off from home for the first time to summer camp in the White Mountains. The boys stand in a line on the side of the room nearest the dark pine trees, and the girls face them from the dying light on the lake. There is music playing on a phonograph. A pretty girl, slightly taller than I, with freckles and downcast eyes, dutifully allows herself to be led opposite me by her counselor. One of my own counselors tries to tug me forward by the elbow. I freeze. There is a chaos of music; motion and lights are all around me. In that instant, I know but one thought: I will not dance. They will stick my arm in a fire before I will go out on that floor. I cannot look at the girl. I begin to cry and run out of the building and into the night.

Miss Brady, of course, knows none of this and is waiting politely for me to start breathing again. We do the step, mangle it, I murmur my apologies. Both instructors applaud and say, "Good job."

But I have done it. It is over. And forcing my body to do the back pass in the hustle with a stranger has made me recall a moment I pushed from my memory years ago.

Over the years I have become rather accomplished at not dancing. As early as the tenth grade, I developed a routine where, after my parents dropped me off at a weekly "cotillion" run by a menacingly correct woman named Mrs. Shippens, I would open the door to the building, wave goodbye to the receding station wagon, and spend the hour and a half in a nearby burger joint making chains out of straws. At parties in later years, the sound of furniture being pushed back in living rooms became my cue to fade into the kitchen. I remember actually leaving one party over the back fence rather than face the music.

Then one day, in a fit of righteous self-examination, I decided the time had come to face my fear. I looked up "dancing—instruction" in the Yellow Pages.

At the Arthur Murray studio, a receptionist greets me and introduces me to Miss Sherry Harris, who will be my instructor for my free, private evaluation session. Miss Harris (everyone at Arthur Murray is referred to as miss or mister) is a lively, attractive woman in her early twenties with her hair pinned up in an elaborate comb. She leads me into a small room and shuts the door. My hands are sweating and the cockeyed smile I get when I'm scared pastes itself across my face.

I am alone with a pretty woman in a small room with a big mirror. She puts her arms around me. She puts my right hand on her back and takes my other hand.

"With your hand right on a woman's shoulder blade like this," she says, "you can really control her."

I nod, trying to say, "Yes, I see." What comes out is one word. "Ah-lum."

"Women want you to take control out there," she says. "Remember, the man is supposed to be the one in charge. There is no equality of the sexes on the dance floor."

"Ah-lum."

We quickly go through the basic steps of the fox trot, the waltz, and the hustle. As we move toward and away from each other in the hustle, Miss Harris says, "You have to tell me what's going on with your hands, with the tension in your arms. I won't know how to respond if you just have nude alarms."

Nude alarms? I gauge the distance to the door. If I make my move now, I can get there before she quotes me rates for an all-over massage.

Then it dawns on me. She didn't say "nude alarms," she said "noodle arms."

By the end of the lesson, my anxiety has been halved, and we are both making jokes about my fear. Two realizations have calmed me: that I am in empathetic hands and that the great thing about dancing school is they don't expect you to know how to dance. You need only be able to count to three (sometimes four) and maintain some minimal neural connection between brain and foot. The hardest part is getting up the courage to walk through the door.

Miss Harris, soon to be all of twenty-two, quickly becomes my lifeline in the sea of dance. I begin to look forward to my private weekly lessons and forty minutes of her undivided attention. She seems to sense how vulnerable a new student is, what it is for me to entrust her with my halting box step and my damp hands.

I begin to crave her approval, her giddy, infectious laugh. I try to catch her eye as I leave, but already she has locked her smile on to the next student. I walk to my car alone in the starry night.

Another night, I ask her about the different views men and women have of dancing. "Women tend to see dancing as a way of acquiring grace and poise," she reflects. "Their job is to follow, so a lot of women will just get up and wing it. Men won't."

"Okay," I respond, "but what exactly is it about dancing that's so scary to guys like me?"

"It's because there's nothing out there but your body. And every part of it has got to move."

Ah-lum.

Over the next six weeks, in private lessons, group classes, and Friday night "parties," I learn the basic steps of the waltz, fox trot, swing, hustle, and rumba. At every session, as soon as I sense that there is someone there more scared and unsure than myself, I am at ease. The worst night is at a class in which all the others are old hands, men and women whose bodies know by rote things of which I have no inkling.

The end of my six-lesson package coincides with an Arthur Murray festival, and one event is a night out at a bar with dancing, located inside a Holiday Inn. I arrive after everyone else, having overshot the place and cruised for half an hour trying to find it.

Miss Harris approaches, flushed from the dance floor. "It's that time," she says, taking my hand. We make our way up and start doing the hustle to a Huey Lewis song. I know only three variations on the basic step—back pass, underarm turn, and sweetheart—and keep repeating them, like a traveler who knows only three phrases in a foreign language and must make them mean everything.

I try not to look out at the tables to see who's watching. It is one thing to chip away at your dancing in the safety of the studio, quite another to strut your stuff among the smoothies on a public dance floor.

I sit one out, then dance two in a row—a swing and another hustle— with a woman from Brazil. She dances a very dignified hustle, as if an accident of time has propelled her from some more courtly epoch into the fleshpots of modern America.

Then I dance another with Miss Harris. She is moving with more energy than I have ever felt in a dance partner: She is smiling, radiant, responding with every atom in her body, singing along off-key and not caring who hears. It starts to rub off on me. There are moments when it begins to feel effortless, when I forget to be afraid, when I cease to be her student and become her partner. I can feel that she is dancing for joy.

And for a moment, so am I.

Two months later I am at my cousin's wedding. A seven-piece band is playing "New York, New York," and a friend is urging me to dance. I am remembering that one moment at the Holiday Inn, but my body has its own memories: of a counselor's hand on my arm, of the sound of furniture being pushed back in living rooms, of a grave young girl with downcast eyes. The body's memory is stronger.

"Ah, you go ahead," I say. "I think I'm gonna sit this one out."

BIRTH, DEATH, AND DOVES

One by one, the vehicles pull up on the long grass under the shade trees by a clubhouse that no one has been inside of for years. Tailgates fall open. Boys, buckets, dogs, men, and shotgun cases spill out. It's 91 degrees on the first Saturday in September and the stands of corn and sunflowers out in the fields look to be melting in the heat mirage. But the men are smiling. The hunting year has begun. We are fifteen minutes into legal shooting on the opening day of dove season in the tidewater country of Virginia.

In this part of the world—just up the road from where a historic marker commemorates the harvest in 1611 of the first successful tobacco crop in North America—the dove opener is a sacred thing. Only birth, death, or serious illness could keep a man out of the corn today. And some guys won't even stop for that. One fellow with a beeper next to the bird knife on his belt is shoving boxes of No. 8's into a shooting bag and saying, "Dropped her at the hospital on the way here. She's not due for a couple of days, but the other two kids were both early. I just hope the birds start flying before this damn thing goes off. You see me tearing out of here, you know I got the call."

When a truck with a man who can barely see over the wheel pulls up, all conversation stops. "How you makin' it, Abie?" each man calls to the wizened little fellow with the hearing aid as he walks slowly past.

Abe is eighty-two years old and has been hunting this farm since the days the tractors had long ears and four legs. He lost his wife last winter and it just about undid him. Abe just bobs his head once, gives a general wave, and walks over to shake hands with a man known as the Colonel, who is similarly aged. Abe hasn't seen his friend since the funeral. His jaw works for a moment before the words come out.

"Brung my old Winchester Model 12," Abe says at last, patting a gun whose barrel and stock have been together so long they've faded almost to a single nameless color. "Bought it fifty years ago for a hunnert-and-a-half. A world of money in those days."

The Colonel puts a warm hand on Abe's shoulder. "Well, I'm glad you the one bought it, Abie. 'Cause I know damn well nobody ever killed any birds with it."

Abe smiles. This is an encrypted message, the way two men who've known each other for fifty years exchange affection. The Colonel is saying, *I'm glad you're here; I'm sorry for your loss; I've been worried about you.*

But the dove opener doesn't just belong to the past. Charlie Parrish, all of nine and grinning from ear to ear, is here with his father and grandfather, who take turns bragging on him. Charlie's dad, Woody, tells how the boy killed his first deer two years ago his very first time out. They were walking along a creek when Charlie saw a doe sneaking behind them.

"I didn't even see her," says his dad. "And he threw up that little Green Wing Special twenty-gauge and just folded her. I said, 'Son, I hope you don't think deer huntin's gonna be this easy all the time.'"

Charlie just beams. His grandfather, not to be outdone, tells about how the teacher was grilling the class about various national holidays. "She asked if anybody knew what we celebrate on Labor Day," says Harry Knight. "And ole Charlie liked to fall out of his seat waving his hand. 'I know Labor Day! That's when rockfish season starts!'" Harry laughs and ruffles the boy's hair. Charlie is all of sixty-five pounds of pure boy. And he's got the blood in him.

Finally, we caravan up and head out into the fields. Abe and the Colonel are dropped off in spots that befit their status. They've earned the right to locations that provide shade from the withering heat as well as prime opportunities to pick off birds that cross from the trees into the corn and sunflowers. Younger men are placed nearby to watch over them and retrieve their birds.

The rest of us spread out at least fifty yards apart in the sunflowers and sit on folding stools to wait. It doesn't take long before I hear the distant pop of guns and calls of "Birrrrd!" which means a dove is coming your way. Not yet accustomed to being shot at, most of the doves are coming so low you have to drop to one knee to get a safe upward angle or forgo the shot altogether. I shoot behind one that's right overhead but changing direction with each snap of its wings. It flies past and is neatly dropped by the father-to-be.

"You shootin' over your head today, son," I hear Harry call to the man approvingly. "Got to," replies the fellow. "That's where the birds are at."

Soon the birds are coming in from all directions, and I'm wired, scanning the sky as nervously as a fighter pilot in enemy territory. One of my foam earplugs won't stay put, so I tear a business card in half, suck on it until it's pulpy, and jam it in my ear. It's the best use I've ever gotten out of that particular piece of paper. In two hours, there are four doves and thirty-one shells at my feet. Suddenly, the father-to-be bolts wordlessly from his stand at a dead run.

"Well, I guess we know where he's goin'," someone calls. No birds fly for a while. The sunflower stalks clatter in the hot wind. The down-turned faces of the flowers look like every girl who never got asked to dance.

At four o'clock, with just an hour of legal shooting left, I see Abe standing at the edge of the field and beckoning me with one hand raised over his head. I rush over, afraid the heat has gotten to him. It turns out he's looking after me, instead of the other way around.

"You getting any birds over there?" he asks.

"Yessir, some."

"Well, I got my limit. You come shoot in here for a while. They flying thick as thieves. Sit on my bucket. One a these boys gonna drive me back to the shade."

With that he turns and moves away. In forty-five minutes, I've downed six more birds and shot an entire box of shells. Mostly I'm shooting holes in the air. But a couple of times, my body takes over, bypassing my head. I see the bird, mount the gun, and roll a dove out of the sky in a single motion. It's a sweet, addictive feeling, something that'll keep you coming out even on days when you don't see a single bird.

At five fifteen, we're all back under the trees by the clubhouse.

"You get your limit?" Abe asks me.

"Just about," I tell him. "And I sure enjoyed it."

"I tell you what," he says, lowering his voice and putting a hand on my shoulder. "Gettin' old's hell on a man. But the boys do put me in a nice stand when dove season rolls around."

He turns and walks back to his truck, raising his hand silently to acknowledge the goodbyes from the assembled. His tires hiss on the long grass as he pulls out.

TRUCE AND CONSEQUENCES

My father is coming over to help me put in a new disposal in my condo. Actually, I'm helping him. His mechanical gene passed over his only son without even looking down, winging its way toward some future generation. I've made my peace with this. At thirty-nine, I'm content to pull out from a self-service gas station without having had to threaten the pump with my ice scraper.

When my father rings, I hurry down to the front door of my building. There he is, in corduroy pants with all the tread worn off the knees and a shirt I outgrew in tenth grade, carrying enough stuff to service a locomotive. He has brought enormous pipe wrenches, screwdrivers that look like bullfighter's lances, a set of metric and standard socket wrenches, a rust-scaled twenty-five-foot plumber's snake coiled tightly and tied off with rope in a paper bag. He has brought fresh plumber's putty, new electrical tape, a six-battery flashlight that was old when I was a kid, strange bits of old motors we can cannibalize if need be.

He sees me shaking my head at all this stuff but is undeterred. "Never know what might come in handy," he says brightly. "Yep," I answer. Heck, if we can't do the disposal, we can always put a turbocharger on the dishwasher.

We carry it all up. He hasn't been here since he helped me paint when I moved in, four years ago. The truth is, I'm often not sure how to talk to my father. But this time it will be easy. We have a job to do.

In minutes he has taken over the whole enterprise, lying on his back under the sink at an uncomfortable angle and squinting up into the machinery. And suddenly, like an iceberg rolling over, I am once again twelve years old, watching him fix things and feeling as if my brain is turning into Hamburger Helper.

"Listen," I tell him suddenly, surprising myself with my own boldness. "This is how it's always been. You do the work and I hand you the tools and I don't learn anything. Why don't you sorta look at it and show me what to do?"

The question hangs in the air between us. It seems so straightforward to me, but it glances off him. He doesn't come out from under the sink right away. "I gotta find out how it unhooks first," he says. But he detaches the old one fairly quickly and when he finally comes out, I see my chance and move in under the sink. Only I have to come out again because we haven't even read the directions about putting the new one in.

As a child, I identified so strongly with my mother that for a few years I thought my father was just a long-term houseguest with spanking privileges. She and I are bookish, introverted worriers, the kind of people who go through life expecting to be decapitated in air crashes and knowing it's just a question of when. My father is a gotta-be-a-pony-under-all-this-crap optimist who has never had a sleepless night in his life. His literary tastes run the gamut from military history to military mystery, including all of Tom Clancy. For a number of years, he routinely invited people he'd just met standing at a bar or in the grocery store home for dinner. Finally, my mother told him if he ever did it again, she'd throw out his old newspapers. That threw a scare into him.

Like most fathers and sons, we fought. But there was no rhythm to it, no cooling-off period between rounds. It was a cold war lasting from the onset of my adolescence until I went off to college in 1973, the same year we pulled our troops out of Vietnam. I hated him. He was a former navy fighter pilot, a fifth-generation military man with an Irish temper and a belief that all the problems of the world—including an overprotected, mopey son who never saw anything through to completion—could be cured by the application of discipline. If discipline didn't work, it was only because you hadn't used enough of it.

My parents were divided over how to deal with my sister and me. My mother was the only child in an aristocratic southern family, the idol of her parents, the kind of daughter who was so naturally good she needed no correction. My sister and I were cut from different cloth. Olivia was only sixteen months older than I, resented the intrusion, and began referring to me as Mean Ol' Billy before I learned to crawl. She and I fought, too. We both played Mother off against Dad as best we could, but it only went so far.

I got the worst of it from him because my sister had the good sense to claim the high ground of being totally uncontrollable, while my rebellion was interspersed with moments of tractability. Also, I was the main event, the boy. I am firmly convinced that all families require redemption of some sort, and it was osmotically communicated to me (no language was needed) that I was to do the heavy lifting in the Great Expectations department. I especially dreaded report cards, when he would look at the C's and shake his head. "I don't get it," he'd say ruefully. "If I had your brains, I'd be setting the world on fire." To which I wanted to answer, "If I had yours, I'd move out," but didn't. In fact, I didn't say a word. How could you win against someone who would have been a better version of you than you were?

At a time when an eighth grader's social status was measured in the fraction of an inch of hair spilling over his ears or kissing his shirt collar, my father would (on Saturdays when my mother was out) march me down to the barbershop and triumphantly tell the man with the scissors, "Just leave him enough to comb." I would close my eyes, determined not to give him the satisfaction of seeing me cry.

Without even thinking about it, I froze him out of my life with even less mercy, volunteering nothing, speaking only when spoken to, my one communiqué for an entire dinner eventually reduced to a sarcasm-drenched "May I be excused now? I have homework." I lay awake at night imagining him being transferred by the gas company he worked for to an oil rig in the North Sea. But it didn't happen, and soon all that remained was the contest of wills, a reflex so conditioned that if he'd told me I should try smoking dope, I'd have been on the next bus to Utah to become a Mormon missionary. I learned how to use silence like a knife. It became a standing joke among my friends that if they called and didn't get me, it was no use asking when I would be home. Nobody at home would know.

He could be, I thought, unbelievably obtuse. I remember the family going to a very fancy restaurant for some occasion, the painfully beautiful blond waitress with big hoop earrings telling us the specials. "As appetizers, the chef has prepared a smoked mozzarella and tomato salad, clams casino, and seviche."

"Beachhead?" my father asked loudly, his voice audible to everyone in the place. "What's beachhead?"

"It's raw fish," I told him. "They bring it still flopping to the table and kill it in front of you. You might enjoy it."

I went off to college, which meant that we only got to fight irregularly, but already it was less vehement. He was still in my head, I could hear his voice every time I fell short in anything, but I was no longer under his roof. I got a job working as a reporter for the Saudi Press Agency, attending briefings at the State Department and sending summaries and editorials back to Riyadh, never to know what happened to them. I began seeing my freelance articles in print (and, strangely, it didn't trouble me that they appeared under the name I share with him). At last it seemed that I was slipping beyond his reach and into my own life. Then bits of him began popping up in me. I was horrified. But there was no denying it. I was my father's son. Blood, it seemed, was thicker than sarcasm.

I took a personality test, which said I succeeded not because of my enormous God-given talents, but mostly because I refused to give up. I had never been a snappy dresser, and found in adulthood that I could go several years without seeing the inside of a men's store. (At this point a submerged early memory came up, of watching him putting on an undershirt so full of holes I thought it must have been designed that way and my mother groaning, "Honestly, Bill, I know the Naval

Academy issued you wonderful underwear. God knows it has served you well. But I don't think they meant for you to wear it into retirement.") Like him, I thought only people with money to burn put it into snazzy automobiles. I found myself buying used subcompacts, changing the oil every three thousand, and deriving a certain pleasure from pushing them until their engines gave up the ghost. I recalled his exhortations to me as a child: Squeeze the toothpaste from the bottom, flatten the tube as you go, screw the cap back on tight.

There is no anti-inflammatory agent like time. Could this be the giant who had once thundered up the stairs to spank me, of whom I was so afraid that I wet my pants? In his place was someone I worried about, whom I dressed in my down hunting jacket with the enormous hood for his annual pilgrimage to Philadelphia for the Army-Navy game. My writing, which he had once ridiculed, saying, "Gee, do you really think there's any money in it?" now became a source of pride. His face would light up when recounting how people at Rotary had mistaken him for the Bill Heavey who'd written of his adventures kayaking in the Everglades. It was as if now that I no longer needed so desperately to please him, I had succeeded. We had become two old veterans from opposing armies, shaking hands years after the fighting, the combat so distant as to be a dream.

It turns out that before we can install the disposal we have to snake out the pipes. They have been receiving partially chewed-up organic matter for at least four years, which is how long ago I moved in.

Slowly I feed the snake in. It has a handle you turn, sort of like what shopkeepers use to furl up their awnings, that makes it screw its way deeper into the pipes. The damn thing is so long that the unused portion sticks out into the hallway, where my father has to turn it so it doesn't kink up. Every so often I pull it out, loaded with black pipe gunk that clears your head out marvelously. It's so Freudian it almost cracks me up, my father and I pulling up all the stuff that went down the drain so many years ago. I don't mention it to him. He is not versed in psychological theory. All he knows is that when somebody mentions Freud, they are usually trying to make him uncomfortable.

Clearing the ancient muck out takes a long time. We spell each other under the sink, remarking how gross it is. He knows more about this stuff than I do, but it's not the same as being a plumber. At a certain point we get stuck trying to figure out how a gasket fits. "When all else fails," he announces, "refer to the directions." "Gasket sleeve must fits way showed," say the directions, which seem to have been drawn in charcoal, smudged, and then photocopied.

There are only two ways it can go on, and we opt for the lip facing up. We connect the wires, black to black, white to beige. But I torque down too hard on a wire nut and snap the entwined copper wires. I'm afraid I have ruined the whole project, but he seems almost pleased by this accident because he knows exactly what to do. Pulling wire cutters from the magic tool chest, he strips the insulation in one movement and we're back in business. We reconnect the wires but finally run out of expertise when it comes to actually fitting the thing up through the drain. We both try every configuration we can think of, but it's not happening.

"Ah," he says finally. "We're going to have to call in a plumber."

This is not how I remember him. He used to be so stubborn, the kind of guy who could make IRS examiners throw up their hands in frustration and let him off. Now that I have his mind-set and don't want to give up, it's as if he's acquired mine. We've somehow circled each other.

"I gotta get home," he says. "Your mother and I have to be at a dinner party at seven thirty. I'll get hail Columbia if I'm late."

I don't know anybody else who uses this expression, but he's been saying it all my life.

"Don't you pay for the plumber. Putting this thing in is part of my Christmas present to you."

When he finally stands, he lets out a little yelp. His legs are cramping from being in one position so long and he crouches reflexively, grimacing. It's strange. My reaction is as much annoyance as compassion. He's seventy-four, for chrissake, he should know that he has to take better care of himself. Is he getting enough potassium? Is he doing his stretching exercises? Maybe it's because he's always insisting that he doesn't feel old and I want it to be true and the fact that it isn't is now staring me in the face. The Oedipal giant of my childhood is now an old guy in blown-out corduroys with muscle cramps.

I take the heavier of the tools, walk him to his car. We shake hands again and he drives off, one hand rising as he sees me standing there in his rearview mirror. Though we've failed to install the disposal, it's been strangely satisfying, this time among the parts. At last we're on a kind of even ground. I feel as if we're two old warriors who somehow got thrown together by circumstances. Maybe he wasn't the best father. Maybe I wasn't the best son. But I could have done worse. And now I realize that there will be a day when he dies and leaves me behind. I know that I'm luckier than some of my friends, whose fathers died while they were still locked in the battle that neither really wanted. But I will never be ready to cope with his leaving.

The plumber comes two days later. He lifts the disposal into place and secures it as easily as I buckle my belt. When he turns it on, there is an empty pop and a cloud of smoke bellows up out of the InSinkErator like a miniature volcano. He checks the wiring. We had actually done it correctly, only stuffed it back in such a way that two of the wrong wires touched.

There is no permanent damage, however, and I spend the next twenty minutes joyfully inaugurating it with a meal of stale carrots. I would like my mind to work that well: processing each thing as it comes in, washing it away, and retaining no memory of it whatsoever.

Christmas. My father and I are driving over to my sister's apartment, carrying a table in the station wagon. We pull into the lot and start to unload. "It's not so much that it's heavy, it's just awkward," he says. This is one of his axioms, a sentence I have heard ever since I first helped him move anything. Also in this category are "Well, we want to see ya," used to close out phone conversations, and "It'll make your hair curly," said of anything on my plate I didn't want to eat.

The table is light. It's faster for me to carry it and just have him hold the door. He looks a little bewildered now that I'm the strong one. We fuss with the arrangement. He thinks it should be perpendicular to the wall with the leaves extended, as if the table's usefulness is in direct proportion to its surface area. "Dad, she won't be able to get around the damn thing like that. Let's just turn it next to the wall and leave the leaves down. They're easier to put up than they are to take down."

We debate this for a couple of minutes, as if it were our solemn duty as men to leave it in the proper configuration for my sister, who could not possibly do it on her own. "Well," he says on the way back, "that's taken care of."

"Yep."

As so often happens, once the work is done I don't know exactly how to talk to my father. It's Christmas night and a fine drizzle is falling. I have the wipers set on delay, and there is almost no one out on the road. Minutes pass.

"I didn't tell your mother this," he finally says, "but I was afraid you were going to be cashing in on what little insurance I've got on that sail back from Bermuda."

Sailing is my father's biggest passion in life. He built a simple rowboat when he was twelve. Last year he and five other guys flew down to the island to ferry a big racing boat back to Newport. The crew ended up being two men in their forties, a seventeen-year-old boy and three guys in their seventies. The weather report was good, but they ran into a storm one day out of port that didn't let up for four days.

The boat was forty-four feet long, but built for raw speed, with the thinnest possible hull, no pumps aboard, and a 110-foot mast. A man on a boat nearby was swept overboard and lost at sea when a wave washed over at the instant he unclipped his safety line to go below. The same thing happened to one of the men on my father's boat, but the others managed to grab him by the ankles. The boat's mainsail blew out like a paper bag when the wind hit 52 knots.

"I really didn't think we were all going to make it back," he says. "Boat like that, it's pretty easy to bury the bow into a wave and broach."

There is no drama in his voice. On the contrary, he sounds almost sheepish, as if he knows he would have gotten in big trouble with my mother if he had died. His own death has never particularly interested him. But I'm glad he's told me. I like the feeling that we are the men of the family, that we have our secrets, too. And I vow he's not going to be allowed to do anything like that again.

Not long ago, I started badgering my parents to get their estate in order. They simply didn't want to deal with it. To them, it was as if a cabdriver had pulled up and asked if they wanted to go straight to the cemetery or drive around a little first to get used to the idea. I finally wrote them a letter saying that if I were a parent, I would want to make damn sure that the IRS got as little of my money, and my children as much, as possible. I knew this would push my father's buttons, but felt it was necessary. It worked. They met with a lawyer.

My father and I arrange to have lunch near my office one day so he can fill me in on the details. We end up at a restaurant full of air kisses and men with hair like Prince Valiant. We are the only guys in the place not in suits with shoulder pads.

My father says that during the meeting with the lawyer, they also drew up some funeral plans. "One thing I don't want you to worry about is what'll happen to me," he says, with the satisfied air of a man who has taken care of business. "The navy will cremate me for free."

"And what about the ashes?" I ask, unconsciously slipping into our male mode, concerned only with practical things. It was if we were talking about how to get rid of the old disposal.

"They scatter them at sea." He turns away, looking around for our waiter. Something breaks inside me. When he turns back, I am crying, hot tears springing up in my eyes so suddenly I'm almost choking.

"I don't want you to die," I finally manage to say. "I don't want them to scatter your ashes. I'll scatter your ashes."

"Oh, Bill," he says, taken aback, totally at a loss about what to say. "I don't plan on dying anytime soon. I just didn't want to burden you with it."

I have no way to tell him that I want to be burdened with it, that it is my birthright to be burdened with it. "I know," I say. I don't even look around to see if anybody is watching us. I don't care. I reach across the table for his hand and hold it, trying to stop the tears.

II

IT'S ALWAYS NOVEMBER SOMEWHERE, 2000–2004

WORTHY

November 9, 8 A.M. Even twenty-eight feet up, I hear the buck before I see him, a shuffling of leaves no louder than the squirrels, but slower. Then there are eight points and his bulk ghosting down the hillside. The adrenaline gatekeeper decides he's open for business. Now I see the buck's swollen neck, the heavy swagger in his gait. Shaking, I clip my release to the bowstring and rise. (Taking the life of a deer is many things, but if you think trivial is among them, it's time to put down your bow and take up badminton. Come to your feet. Honor the animal whose life you seek.) He's moving like he knows where he wants to go, not fast but purposeful. On his current course, he'll stay out of range.

My grunt fails to stop him the first time. The second stops him momentarily before he shrugs and resumes course. The estrous call is the ticket. When he stops, partly shielded by a tree all of twenty feet from mine, I'm at full draw and forcing myself to breathe regularly. Half a step more—even four inches—and I'll double-lung him. It never happens. In a single movement, he snorts, pivots, and is gone, the heavy body now weightless in flight.

November 15, 10 A.M. Same hillside, different tree. Three does wander into view. They're grazing, moving in and out of the dappled sunlight of this oak woods. I rise to my feet as they drift closer. Well within range, the biggest turns broadside with her head down, nuzzling acorns beneath the yellow leaves. I draw, squeeze, and watch the arrow hit a full foot right of where I aimed. A paunch shot. She kicks her hind legs straight up and in five seconds has scrambled down the hill, through the creek, up the far hill . . . gone.

Nothing registers at first: neither frustration, sorrow, nor remorse. Slowly, all three do. And remorse packs the longest blade: *How do you think that deer feels about your potshot, big boy?*

On the ground, I kneel to finger the light belly hair, the green slime of partially digested acorns, and too little blood coating the arrow shaft. Her path yields no sign. At the place where she disappeared over the hill, I drop my fanny pack and begin walking ever larger circles. Soon there is a tablespoon-size splotch of blood on the leaves. Ten yards distant is another, then irregular droplets. I search for two hours, tracing and retracing her path, sometimes crawling on hands and knees to tell if the red drops are blood or leaf mold. The blood is oily and smudges when you roll the leaf between your fingers. Then the droplets stop. The wound has closed up. I search for another hour. Nothing.

On the ride home I distract myself by thinking of aboriginal cultures and how we've taken their beliefs and stood them on their heads. Where bringing home meat is a matter of life or death for a whole society, it is taken for granted that the hunter succeeds not so much because of his skill, but because the animal chooses to make a gift of itself. The hunter's main job is not to kill but to live in such a way that he may be judged worthy of the gift. We don't believe that anymore. We're not even sure what it means to have hunting success tied to the hunter's character rather than an acquired set of skills. But it suddenly comes to me as I fight the hollow feeling in my stomach that what I want above all else is precisely this: to be found worthy.

December 2, 4:30 P.M. A brushy funnel above a creek in a neighboring state. I've been sitting up here for three hours, busy *not* thinking about the deer I wounded. As the red sky begins to fade and the shadows gain heft, a doe wanders down the path. I rise and clip on. She stops in a shooting lane as if it had all been agreed to beforehand. The arrow shoots. She jumps, settles, takes nine wobbling steps, falls, kicks once, and lies still.

Holding a flashlight in my teeth, I ratchet my stand down the tree and walk to her. I lay a hand on her flank and stroke her hair. Wisps of steam from her body curl upward in the flashlight beam. I've read how native hunters believe that an animal doesn't die all at once, but slowly, its spirit finding its way out of the body and up to the next world. I stay there another five minutes, stroking her coat, feeling the interlocking elation and regret, the gratitude and sorrow that only hunters know. With every stroke, I discover I'm mouthing, "Thank you, thank you, thank you."

AMERICAN SCENE:
ROD AND REEL REPAIR

The record player clicks and another platter drops while he's writing up your ticket. A moment later Phil Evans's microscopic shop, crammed between a Latino grocery and an electrical parts store in Arlington, Virginia, fills with the Sons of the Pioneers singing "Cool Water." The music sounds as if it's welling up from somewhere deep inside your own memory—a song you forgot you even knew. "Nineteen fifty-nine," says Phil, his blue eyes lighting up to see that you recognize the tune. "Cowboy music. Outta style, outta print. Can't buy these records for love or money today." He grins, lifts a spaghetti colander holding the guts of a spinning reel out of a bucket of solvent, and hangs it from a bent coat hanger hook to drip.

Around here, just like everywhere else in America, the megastores have sucked the life from your neighborhood tackle shop and turned the space into overflow parking. Their wildly successful strategy is pure sales volume, zero service. Rod and Reel Repair, with a square of carpet inside the front door that will accommodate up to four patrons and the rest of the place given over to a workbench and old file cabinets holding a universe of parts, is their opposite.

Phil sells almost nothing. He doesn't even advertise. But over the years, the word has spread among the fraternity of hard-core anglers for thirty miles and more in every direction that if you want your gear fixed and can't wait three months for the factory to do it, bring it to Phil. He can fix any reel ever made. If he doesn't have the part, he'll make it for you.

74

And the prices aren't just good; they're damn near ridiculous. Phil charges $1.50 for a new rod tip, $8 to rewrap a guide. Don't get the wrong idea, though. Phil tries to change with the times. He just does it at his own speed. Just this year, he bumped the minimum charge to work on your reel one whole notch, from $5 to $6. I ask when he last increased the price, and the blue eyes narrow as he thinks back. "In 1988," he says after a while. Then the eyes crank up again, and he grins like an unindicted coconspirator. "But you oughta come in here on a Friday afternoon. Hundred-dollar bills all over the place. Have to get the snowblower out just to round 'em up." It's as if his lack of material success amuses him. As if he knows something you haven't figured out yet.

Even the guys behind the tackle counter at the sporting juggernauts have a soft spot for the guy. Bring an unhappy reel in, and some of the nicer ones will palm you Phil's phone number.

Once I was out fishing with a buddy who sands floors for a living and whose philosophizing seldom goes deeper than a theory that canned beer causes tooth decay. "Hey," he said, "sounds like you lost the squeak in that reel."

I told him I'd just picked it up from Phil. He nodded, cast out, and said: "Phil's as close to being in a state of grace as any man I've ever met."

Then he didn't speak for an hour. I was stunned. He'd found the exact words to describe the guy. Phil, who quit school in the eighth grade ("Oh, I was a bad kid" is all he'll say) before going back to get his GED and take some college courses, is the most unprepossessing man I know. He's unfailingly upbeat, owns and eats little, covets nothing. In the winter, he wears a brown sweater with a hole under one arm. In the summer, he wears shorts and dark knee socks.

Behind his counter is one of those hokey signs: AN OLD FISHERMAN LIVES HERE WITH THE CATCH OF HIS LIFE. Only it doesn't seem hokey with Phil. The woman is Pearl. They live together in a few rooms above the shop. The two of them go out on the river in his canoe on a nice evening and fish. What does a guy who fixes tackle all day fish with? A five-foot, make-do fiberglass ultralight he cranked out one afternoon from spare parts. It's devoid of ornamentation, has four different makes of guides, and carries an aged Mitchell 308 that ticks like a foot-powered sewing machine. "Love that big face on those old reels," he says. "The line really behaves."

Tacked to a bulletin board above the desk in the back of his shop is a yellowed newspaper clipping, his mother's obituary. And, in tiny handwriting where he can see it without raising his eyes, a quote from Pindar, the Greek philosopher: "Deeds of No Risk Are Honorless."

A guy in a Stetson and a nylon jacket comes in with an old Abu Garcia 5500 D on a rod with frayed guide wrapping that he picked up at a yard sale for two bucks. "Like to fix 'er up," the guy says. "But . . . I dunno, maybe I got more money than brains." Phil cranks the reel a few times to get a feel for where she sticks. "Well, most people do," says Phil. "Maybe I can help you balance the two out." The guy looks dumbstruck for a moment, then starts to laugh. He's apparently just met Phil. But already he knows he can trust him.

It's a joke only an honest man would make. In the background, the Sons of the Pioneers are singing "Tumbling Tumbleweeds."

TREE-STAND DAY

Don't ask me how, but the moment Snoop sees me padding downstairs in slippers and bathrobe she knows that today's the day. Erupting into pure dog joy, she does twenty seconds of rapid-fire tap-dancing on the kitchen linoleum, dashes into the living room for a victory lap around the coffee table, then roars back into the kitchen. Forgetting that dogs can't stop on linoleum, she runs headlong into the trash. It's an ugly one-dog pileup: yesterday's coffee grounds, old salad, a long smear of strawberry yogurt. She tries to look sorry but is too excited to hold the expression for more than five seconds before breaking back into her wolf grin. "I guess you're right, girl," I tell her. "I guess it's Tree-Stand Day."

My particular dog's version of Christmas comes in midsummer, nearly three months before the start of deer season. For Snoop, the brown-and-white foxhound mutt who adopted us at the animal shelter, it's a triple play. She gets sprung from the prison of the backyard for a whole day of following scent streams in the woods. She gets to stink up my car and ride with her head out the window down Route 66. And tradition dictates that she gets a Double Whopper for lunch.

Tree-Stand Day generally falls in the second half of bass season. Its exact date is a complex calculation involving moon phases, how my back feels, and how willing I am to get a good dose of poison ivy. I descend into the basement to gather two hang-on stands, gloves, a backpack full of screw-in steps, a safety belt, and a folding saw. Forty-five minutes later, high on expectation, we glide into the Burger King. Less than a minute later we're back on the road with Snoop's head out the window.

Then we are in the woods, loud with bees and mosquitoes, choked with honeysuckle and briers, full of hunting potential. I actually hunt more from my climbing stand than from these fixed ones, but deer season starts long before opening day, and this ritual is as important as scouting or sighting in a bow. Your choice of fixed-stand locations is your annual declaration of who you are as a hunter and how you interpret the lay of the land—your feeling about where the big one can be ambushed this time. You fix your stand and your heart high in the very same tree.

The first stand goes up in a logical place: an oak stand, interspersed with pines, set on a gentle hillside. I find a pine tree with good covering branches twenty yards downwind of the biggest oak.

The second stand's placement is more complicated: an ancient tulip poplar near a cedar bottom where the deer love to hide. The textbook says bottoms mean swirling winds and a place for your scent to collect. But the idea has been worming its way into my head for better than half a year, and I'm giving it a shot.

The place is so overgrown I have to cut brush for ten minutes just to get to the base of the tree. Snoop watches from a makeshift lair under a bush as I ascend into the sky, probably wondering why I'm wasting my time in a tree with no squirrels in it. I'll have to hunt high here to have any chance, and it takes me forty minutes and fifteen steps to get to thirty feet. Finally I get the stand in, sit down, and practice drawing my imaginary bow.

By the time I wade back to the trail, I've ripped a gash in my nose on a brier, several kamikaze bugs have flung themselves deep into my ears at full speed, and there's a tear in my pants in a spot that will keep me from stopping in public places on my way home.

Snoop raises a rabbit on the way back to the road and takes off. A minute later, she's again at my side, grinning proudly. I know she came nowhere near catching the animal, but she seems proud to have reaffirmed her standing as a dog. She grins encouragement at me the whole way home, as if to say, *We're gonna get 'em this year, pal.*

The season has begun.

FINALLY . . . UNCLE DANNY

"Least experienced" was an understatement about where I stood in relation to the other hunters in camp that year down in Mississippi. Uncle Danny had persuaded my father to send me south in late March to begin my indoctrination into the manly art of turkey hunting. Nobody there enlightened me when I talked about a gobbler's beard hanging off his chin, the way mine might in a few years. It wasn't until one of the older hunters showed me a gobbler laid out in the bed of his truck with nine inches of coarse hair sprouting from its chest that I knew the truth.

"You guys've been having a real good time playing me for a fool," I blurted out at dinner that night, my lower lip stuck out so far I'd have tripped over it had I not been seated.

"Heck, Billy, you played the fool on your own," drawled one of my elder cousins (he must have been all of sixteen). "We just been enjoying the *puhfomance.*"

Everybody laughed that much harder. I was thirteen, something of a mama's boy, and teetering on the high, narrow bridge between childhood and the unknown territory beyond. It seemed nothing short of stupefying to me that, far from being sorry, they actually seemed to be enjoying my anger. Clearly hunting camp rules were different from those governing the other parts of my life. It took every ounce of determination I had to squinch back the tears.

Uncle Danny was my lifeline in that camp. He had longish white hair and blue eyes and looked pretty much the way I imagined God would if He had a potbelly and one bad leg. The first was the result of too much Cajun cooking, the second from his last bull ride back in his rodeo days. It was well known that Uncle Danny had a seven-foot-long necklace of turkey spurs. His own father had started carrying him into the woods at the age of five, and there was nothing he didn't know about hunting and fishing.

Uncle Danny and I hunted together. His approach was to set up, call sparingly, and wait the bird out. My job was to sit absolutely still while he called. It was the hardest possible way for an overeager boy to hunt, but the image of that spur necklace was burned into my mind. Uncle Danny had said that you never knew when a turkey might come in, and missing a bird because I'd yielded to an itch or an ache was a fate to be avoided at all costs. More than anything else—even, perhaps, more than a big gobbler turkey—I wanted to go home carrying the trophy of Uncle Danny's approval. Sometimes I'd set up comfortably, only to find after five minutes that I'd committed myself to having a tree knob in the small of my back or an acorn under my thin foam pad. No matter.

By the morning of the last day, we had not seen a turkey. We set up with our backs to a tree commanding a clearing of clover surrounded by pine trees, and he began calling. Twenty minutes in, a yelp came back to us. A minute later, a male came hesitantly into view fifteen yards out, and I began to shake.

"Wait," he breathed. "Might be a jake." The bird turned, and I could see its short beard jutting out almost perpendicular to the ground. It was indeed a jake. It didn't see us, but it didn't see a hen, either. The bird reversed direction and left. We didn't see another all morning.

Back at camp, as I sat inside stuffing clothes into my suitcase, I heard one of my cousins ask, "Well, Dan, how'd the boy do?"

"I wouldn't say this to his face for fear of spoilin' him," answered Uncle Danny, "but that boy sat still as a cigar-store Indian. Never saw anything like it. He's gonna show us all up someday."

I was airborne on praise long before the plane took off. And it was years before I figured out that Uncle Danny had meant me to hear every word.

We never got to hunt together again. He went to bed one night the following July and never woke up. But I still love that man. And every time I take a child hunting or fishing, I find a way to praise that kid to the skies.

SUDDENLY, SHE WAS GONE

It is the unthinkable, every parent's nightmare, the world turned upside down. The death of a child plunges you into a parallel universe of loss where the old assumptions about everyday life—that a spouse going to the store for milk will return, that a teenager headed off to school will still be alive when school lets out, that a child put down for a nap will indeed wake—no longer obtain. You can't stay in this place, of course. Your new knowledge is simply too horrible to bear. Eventually, after much despair and grief, most of us claw our way back to normal lives. We learn to forget some of what we know to keep going. But we never forget and we're never the same. For the rest of our days, an otherwise arbitrary date cuts our lives into "before" and "after." For me, that date is June 16, 1999.

When the plane had reached the gate and the captain had turned off the seat belt sign, the stewardess came on the intercom and said. "Mr. William Heavey, please see the gate agent for a message." I was impressed. Jane had said she would try to pick me up at the airport when I returned from an editorial meeting of a magazine I write for, but didn't know if she'd be able to get the baby from daycare in time to make it. I figured she'd gotten someone at the airline to have me paged with the news I should get a cab home, no small feat of persuasion. But when I introduced myself to the woman with the clipboard, she said, "Follow me, please." After four days of meetings and hotel food, I wasn't in the mood to follow anybody; I just wanted to get my damn message and see Jane and Lily. When I asked her what it was, she glanced back over her shoulder and said, "I don't know."

She opened a locked door to a cement stairwell and began to lead me down. After the first set of stairs a beefy guy fell in two steps behind me. He was wearing small gold insignia on the shoulders of his white shirt. I thought I caught a glimpse of a badge. I glanced back, and he nodded once, his eyes noncommittal. We went through another door to what seemed like a secure area with a series of small offices. He began poking his head into one after the other, evidently looking for an empty one. At last he said, "Could you give us a minute here?" to the guy inside one. He slipped out past us and disappeared. The man led me into the tiny space, motioned me into a wooden chair, and shut the door. I was scared. I couldn't remember having committed any crimes recently, but this was not where they took you for good citizenship awards. I still can't remember what he looked like, though I realize now I was staring him in the face the whole time. He told me a name and said he was with the Arlington Fire Department. Sometime that afternoon at daycare, my daughter had gone into cardiac arrest. They had called an ambulance and rushed her to Arlington Hospital. The doctors had done all they could, but they couldn't get her heart started again. Lily, my baby girl, the perfectly healthy child we had adopted just ten weeks ago, was dead. My wife and stepdaughter, Molly, were at the hospital now. He would drive me there to be with them. Someone would collect my luggage and take it home.

Jane and I were in our forties when we met in 1995. Like most single men of that age, I had definite ideas about what I wanted: someone a few years younger, never married, certainly without a child. Then I met Jane, who was none of these things. But she was beautiful, hardheaded, honest, and scrappy. I fell in love and gave Jane the engagement ring that my great-grandmother had bought in Paris in 1901. Molly—then nine—was part of the package: a bright, affectionate girl with dark hair and her mother's will. I fell in love with Molly, too. Two years later, she was the flower girl at our wedding. When Jane and I watched from the altar as she walked down the aisle of the Bethlehem Chapel in the National Cathedral, smiling at friends and family on both sides, we had marveled at how luminous she looked. Jane and her ex, John, have worked hard to have a good divorce and remain friends. Molly sees both of them nearly every day and spends half her nights at his house and half with us. I love Molly like a daughter, but she already has a dad and the two are immensely loyal to each other. Besides, I wanted the full taco platter of fatherhood—baby giggles, a tiny fist tight around my little finger, baby puke on my shirt, the sound of "da da" spoken for the first time.

Like many parents who eventually adopt, Jane and I first spent a couple of years and tens of thousands of dollars trying to have our own biological child. We'd traipsed through the well-appointed offices of cheerful area specialists who rattled off success percentages for various procedures as if handicapping hedge funds. I'd learned to make love to plastic cups under the fluorescent lights of clinic bathrooms so my sperm could be clocked for speed and endurance in the 40-micron dash. I'd jabbed needles dripping hormones into my wife's purple-bruised backside every night for a month on three occasions to ready her womb to receive an egg fertilized in a petri dish. A guy so cheap he tries to haggle with the ladies at Goodwill over shirt prices, I'd willingly written the biggest checks of my life outside of buying a house in hopes of fathering a child. The doctor had told us the odds of Jane getting pregnant with the procedure were 43 percent. I'm not a gambling man. I look at a casino and see a well-oiled machine founded on human weakness that separates people from their money the way Eli Whitney's cotton gin separated cotton and seeds. But when it came to my dream of fatherhood, I was a willing mark. I thought that Jane and I were somehow special, different, that we'd beat the odds. Well, we weren't. We didn't.

When the first transfer failed to take, I'd burst into tears after getting the news. After the second, hardened by disappointment, I'd shrugged. After the third, the doctor had called us in for a consult. "It's unusual," he mused. "You should have gotten pregnant by now." It was an abstract problem for him, an equation that should have worked out. He pointed out that we could always try again. But the drugs were an emotional roller coaster for Jane, each failure added another layer of despair to our search, and I was running out of money. It was his detachment that I resented the most. Standing in his office with the framed photos of babies and gushing testimonial letters, I imagined punching his stylish little eyeglasses down his throat.

In the firefighter's car, I was vaguely aware of the highway rolling by and the hazy June light outside. The highway was jammed with people jockeying for position as if it were just another day. I heard the man's voice saying something about how he'd talked to the people at the hospital and heard that my wife, like me, was bearing up. An involuntary hoot of laughter started to rise in my throat. I wasn't bearing up; I was disappearing. This was happening to my stand-in, my stunt double. I had gone off some distance to watch. I noticed tears and that my vision seemed to be collapsing around the edges. I thought I might keep the world from dissolving entirely by focusing on its navel, which at the moment happened to be the glove compartment latch, two feet away. Lily, the child who cooed in delight when slung round my shoulders and twirled while I sang her nonsense songs in the dining room, was dead. Tomorrow was to be her four-month birthday. Say the magic word and a baby appears. Say it again and—poof!—she's gone. It couldn't be true. It was true.

A statistic I didn't know I knew popped unbidden into my head like some magic flash card. More than three-quarters of marriages in which a child dies do not survive. It occurred to me that in one stroke I might have lost not only Lily, but Jane and Molly as well.

Jane and I had long talked about adoption as our backup plan if the fertility route failed. We'd done some research and decided that we preferred a private, domestic adoption, rather than going through an agency or adopting from overseas. We didn't like the idea of seeing a photo, taking a trip to China or Korea, and then having to decide yes or no on the spot. We wanted to meet the mother, get to know her, make sure it felt right. It was more work and would probably take more time than an agency adoption, but it offered more control. At this point, we were big on control. We got involved with a local group, Families for Private Adoption, that offered advice and support. One of the first things we learned was that everyone you know or meet is a potential lead: friends, family, the checkout girl at the grocery store, the attendant at your health club, people at parties. "Get over being self-conscious," one woman who had adopted three children told us. "You're on a mission. Do at least one thing every day. Post a card on a new bulletin board, research a new place to run an ad, buttonhole a stranger. Most people are happy to help. If they're not, that's their problem." You give every contact at least one business-size card with your pitch. The rule of thumb about the pitch is the simpler the better. You also have a separate, toll-free line installed in your house to receive the calls, ensuring no busy signals and a level of protection against scam artists (people desperate to adopt are notoriously easy to con). The toll-free part means a prospective mother doesn't have to talk to the operator and can leave a message whether you're there or not. "You want to make it as easy for a mother to contact as you possibly can," we were told. We pared away the language on our card until it was bare-bones: "A very warm, loving couple unable to have second child seeks newborn to love and nurture. Can pay medical, legal expenses. Call toll free." And listed the number.

We passed out cards diligently. We ran ads in newspapers all over rural Virginia. (A baby is a commodity subject to the laws of supply and demand, just as soybeans are. In metropolitan Washington, D.C., with a high number of career women who sometimes wait too long to have babies, the demand is high and the supply is low. In southern Virginia, the situation tends to be somewhat reversed.) We checked the message machine every time we walked in the door. And nothing happened. Months dragged by. We had been warned about this. We knew that all it takes is one phone call. "If you stick with it long enough, you will find a baby," we had been told again and again. When we got lucky, after just five months, it wasn't an ad or a friend-of-a-friend, it was our neighbors, Kevin and Ellen Bailey, who led us to Lily. Ellen had been having her hair done when she dutifully mentioned to a manicurist that she knew a couple who were looking for a baby. The woman had a friend, another Vietnamese manicurist, who might be a possibility. She would check.

The car came to a stop. Someone opened my door. Inside the emergency room was a clot of people. In the middle were Jane and Molly, wild-eyed, their faces flushed and streaked with tears. The three of us ran and clutched at each other, the sobs at last finding their way up in my throat. Some nurses shepherded us into a private room. Jane had been there for more than an hour, had already done the unthinkable, gone in to see Lily's body alone except for a nurse. She had pleaded with the nurses not to take her to the morgue before I got there. A nurse came in to talk to us. She said that Hien, the woman who ran the daycare center in her home, told them she put Lily down for a nap, then checked back to find her blue-lipped and still. She had tried CPR, had called 911. The paramedics had worked on Lily in the ambulance. At the hospital they had worked on her as well, but she had probably been dead when she arrived. It sounded to the nurse like sudden infant death syndrome, SIDS, also known as crib death. Doctors didn't know why, but each year about one in a thousand babies in the United States, most between one month and one year old, simply stop breathing and die. There is no telltale sound, no warning, no sign of a struggle. SIDS is unpredictable and, currently, unpreventable. I could see Lily, though the woman warned I might not want to, as they'd had to stick tubes down her throat and in her leg. In a voice so enraged I could barely control it, I bit off the words: I would see my daughter.

Jane and I held each other as a nurse led us into an examining room cluttered with medical equipment. A uniformed cop stood off in one corner absently, as if a bus he wanted to catch might be passing through soon. I scarcely noticed him. My daughter lay swaddled in a blanket on a table, wearing only a diaper. The tubes were there, but otherwise Lily was unblemished. "She was warm before," mumbled Jane, stroking her cheek. "She's . . . cold now." I picked her up, felt her smooth baby skin, cradled her head in my neck. I recognized everything about her: her small heft, her black hair, her brow, her cheeks. But this was not

Lily; this was just the doll that death had left behind. Her cheek was cold against mine. I couldn't seem to breathe. My vision started to go again, the sides of the room caving in. "She's ... so ... cold," I finally managed to croak. The police officer shifted once on his feet. What was he doing here? Then it dawned on me that they might suspect us, the parents, of having killed our own child. As long as the world had turned into Hell, why not throw in a murder charge as well?

I started to dissociate again, to feel like I had a part in some strange play, that I was performing for the cop. But the fact of her body in my arms was too real. Then I felt a tiny bit of warmth in her back, the last spark of life that was even now on its way out of her body, this room, this earth. "Still warm!" I blurted out to Jane. "I know," she wept. "There was more before." I held Lily tight and rocked, long swings forward and back as if I might somehow wake her. I was aware enough to be terribly scared. I was numb now. What would happen when the numbness wore off? The nurse came in and put a hand on my shoulder. I understood the signal. I was a good boy. I obeyed.

We had met Lan (not her real name) on a Wednesday morning at her friend's house over cups of mint tea. She was in her early twenties, with a round face, shoulder-length black hair, and, of course, impeccable nails. Our first impression—of a reserved, serious young woman—was just the armor she wore until she felt comfortable. Underneath, she was a strong-willed, jovial girl who liked to laugh. She was unmarried, worked seventy hours a week at a salon in D.C., already had two toddlers, and had just had another baby. We liked Lan right off the bat. She hadn't brought the baby, but one of her two other children, a four-year-old named David. He was a happy, well-cared-for boy. When I shook his hand and kept shaking it as though he were the one who wouldn't let go, he giggled.

Lan had come to the United States in her early teens from South Vietnam, dropped out of high school when she got pregnant for the first time, and had been working full-time ever since. Her parents were divorced, her siblings scattered all over the country. She was pretty much one her own. "It's just too much," she said. "I can't take care three children." We stayed for an hour, drinking tea and making small talk. We showed her pictures of Molly, our house, the Christmas card at the animal shelter with the three of us standing around Santa's sleigh and Snoop, our adopted dog, looking forlorn in a red stocking cap with a snowball on the end. We said we would love to meet the baby. She told us to come to her apartment in D.C. on Sunday, her day off.

The next Sunday was Easter. Jane, Molly, and I drove into D.C. and stopped at a bakery in Adams Morgan for a cake in the shape of an Easter bunny with white coconut fur to bring as a gift. Lan lived in a tiny apartment in a building apparently occupied exclusively by Vietnamese. Lying in a baby carrier and wrapped up so that all we could see was her face was a six-week-old baby girl with black hair and brown eyes. She did not look particularly impressed to see us. I did not know then that at six weeks, a baby sees anything more than a couple of feet away as a blur. We sat on Lan's bed and fed cake to her son and daughter, a two-year-old who was instantly fascinated by Molly. Jane and I took turns holding the baby, whom Lan had named Stephanie. She was small but solid and seemed remarkably self-contained, as if accustomed to spending time on her own. At six weeks, babies are not particularly concerned with how they are coming across to strangers. As I held her I wondered, Are you the one? How will we know? Jane, however, was smitten instantly. "Oh, she's so charming," she told Lan. "She's beautiful." I looked at Jane's face. It was glowing with the look of a woman who had already begun bonding with her daughter, a process that bypasses the brain entirely. That was how we knew.

Lan had a boyfriend upstairs, whose mother lived with him or in the unit next door, we never did decipher which. The mother took care of all three children while Lan worked. Lan told us to wrap Stephanie tightly and not to hold her too much. "She smell you," Lan said. "Then you can't put her down easy." We nodded. We didn't say that having the baby smell us, bond with us, and demand to be held was exactly what we wanted. Lan's face never changed, but tears began to invade her face. "You good people," she said. "You take her." Jane and I exchanged glances. We had discussed that we might be coming home with a baby today, had even hauled Molly's old crib out of the attic against that possibility. Suddenly, it was actually happening. Lan insisted on loading us up with diapers, formula, clothes, a car carrier, and a few toys. She refused any money for these things. We explained a little about how the adoption process worked, that we would get her an attorney, as well as a social worker who spoke Vietnamese to do the required counseling, and that eventually she would go to court with us in Virginia to make the adoption final. We told her we would take care of Stephanie and that she could visit her anytime she wanted, that we wanted the child to have the opportunity to know her biological mother when she was older if she wanted. Her face was losing its composure now. "Please," she whispered. "Take her now." And suddenly we were on the sidewalk blinking in the bright sunshine of Easter morning with a baby in our arms, feeling a strange mixture of elation at our good luck and sorrow for the heart-wrenching loss Lan was going through. It was as close to instant fatherhood as a man could get. I did not know then that in ten weeks it would be over.

I had told my sister, Olivia, about the baby, but not my parents. They'd already had three rides on the fertility roller coaster with us and I wanted to spare them more disappointment if possible. But we were due to have lunch with them and a family friend at the Morrison House in Alexandria, where Olivia worked, and we intended to surprise them with the good news. My mother had never said anything about it, but it was obvious she wanted nothing on earth so much as a grandchild. Our plans were foiled when Jane went into the ladies' room at the restaurant to change the baby before our triumphal entrance and ran smack into my mother. Baby, mother, and grandmother proceeded into the restaurant, where Lily was officially welcomed into the family with laughter, tears, and champagne. Olivia took the baby back to the kitchen to meet the staff. Photos of the occasion show me looking like a man who has just been hit in the face with a frying pan. We had already decided on a name. Elizabeth, after my mother. Ashley, Jane's maiden name for her middle name. And Heavey.

I wish I could say she came home with us and fell sound asleep. In fact she was up all night, crying. "I think she's terrified," said Jane. "She doesn't know why she's here or who we are." Jane stayed up all night with her, alternately walking the living room and massaging her back as the baby lay sobbing in her crib. I opted for the only constructive thing I could think of: a massive anxiety attack. Staring at the ceiling in bed, I suddenly wondered if we had done the right thing, whether I was ready for this, what business I had accepting another woman's child to raise. I called a good friend who had also adopted. "I'm just freaking out," I said. "I'm so anxious I can't think straight." "Enjoy it while you can, pal," he said laughing. "You're gonna be too busy to freak out soon."

We got through that night. And the next, and the next. My friend was right. I learned to change a diaper one-handed while pinning a squirming child to the changing table with the other. To always wipe down, in the direction of the feet, instead of up during changing, to heat a four-ounce bottle precisely twenty-seven seconds in our microwave, to transfer the napping baby from my arms to her crib with the dexterity of a bomb disposal technician. I learned to sing lullabies I didn't know I remembered as I stroked her stomach to put her back to sleep after a feeding in the middle of the night.

Some nights I would linger after she had gone back to sleep, watching over her as she slept, and just listen to her breathing. She began to smile when I approached her crib or picked her up. "It's Daddy," I would say as I tucked her up in the hollow of my shoulder. "How's my girl today?" She especially loved it when I stretched her arms and legs on the changing table, yoga-style. She was yielding but quite strong and the harder I tugged the more she smiled. Sometimes she would gurgle in delight. "Little Buddha girl," I cooed at her. "The perfect being." The happy sounds she made seemed as close to pure joy as humans are permitted. I was becoming a father. I was learning what all adoptive parents know: It's not DNA that confers paternity. It's baby poop.

We always called her "the baby" until we took her for a visit to my father's mother, Granny, ninety-nine years old and living in a rest home on the Eastern Shore. "Elizabeth," mused Granny, when we told her the name. "You know, Queen Elizabeth was called Lily when she was a girl because she couldn't pronounce her own name. She could only say, 'Lilybeth.'" Jane and I looked at each other. Lily. That was the name we'd been looking for. Thereafter the baby was Elizabeth on legal documents, but Lily for all other purposes.

Jane and I quickly arrived at a wholly unsatisfactory arrangement for baby care. Since my wife sees clients at her psychotherapy practice mostly in the afternoon, she would take the baby in the mornings, leaving me free to write. In the afternoons, we would switch. In the evenings, we would share duty. For reasons I cannot now fathom, I expected to be a natural at baby care. Jane said I was better at it than most men, but she said this in the same way you might note that horses are better at needlepoint than most fish. I only knew three things to do with a crying baby: feed it, change it, or burp it. If none of these worked, I generally repeated the sequence until overwhelmed by anxiety, frustration, and crankiness, not unlike Lily herself.

Jane, having already raised one child and coming from a large family overflowing with nieces and nephews, had not only more experience, but another quality I seemed to lack entirely: baby intuition. She could tell what Lily wanted just by looking at her, a feat bordering on witchcraft. "She wants water, not formula," she would say, based on a look. Or that the baby would stop crying if I a) took her for a walk, b) put her on her stomach, or c) sang the theme from *The Sound of Music*.

The arrangement was supposed to be fifty-fifty, but wasn't. Jane ended up doing far more than her share. It was the source of more than a little friction in the marriage. Three hours alone with the baby would leave me feeling exhausted. "You don't get it," Jane would say. "You have to surrender to her." I come from five generations of career military. My father was a fighter pilot. Surrender was not on the curriculum. When I had to travel, we figured we'd need extra help. We turned to a local Vietnamese woman who offered daycare in her home nearby and came highly recommended by dozens of parents in the area. We inspected her house one afternoon. It was clean and bright. Hien picked Lily up and the baby beamed at her. We told Hien we would be irregular clients, and she said that would be fine. She asked us to try to give her a couple of days' notice since she only took one or two infants at a time.

When we got home from the hospital, I began the grim job of notifying family and friends. The protective dissociation was beginning to wear off. I would compose myself to make the call, but the moment it went through—even to an answering machine—I fell apart. I can't remember most of the calls. I know I talked to my mother and managed to blurt out the news, but that's all. I left a message on the car phone of my friend who had adopted, several more locally. There weren't that many people it felt right to tell. My friend got the message while driving. At first he'd thought it was a terrible joke. Then he'd pulled onto the shoulder, listened again, and broke down crying, too.

The bottle Lily had drunk this morning was still lying unwashed in the sink when we got home. Her clothes were still on the floor and the changing table. Her favorite toy, a cloth butterfly with big red wings with mirrors in them and long blue antennae, lay in her crib. I pressed my face into the mattress and smelled the baby smell lingering in the sheets. I fell to my knees, clutching at the bars of the crib. She was dead all over again. It was still happening. The unthinkable had invited itself in as our houseguest. It would be here for an indefinite stay.

My parents and Olivia came over. Friends of Jane came by. Around eight o'clock, it suddenly occurred to me that while the family was embracing each other and saying that we would get through this somehow, my daughter was alone and lying on a stainless steel table in the morgue. I wanted to be with her, to watch over her one last time. I made frantic calls to the emergency room and was turned down at every turn. It was, I was told, impossible. Once again, I obeyed. (Months later, in a SIDS support group, I met a single mother who had experienced the same feelings, made the same phone calls. Only she wouldn't take no for an answer. She had gone and sat on the steps of the morgue building and refused to leave. She hadn't been let in, either. But she had made the attempt, had made the people who told her no look her in the eye. I was filled with admiration for her tenacity. And I will always regret that I didn't find out exactly where my baby was, go down there, and beat at the door until they let me in to sit by Lily or had me arrested for trespassing. I owed my daughter that much.)

There was one more call to make. Lan had to be told. I got her about ten o'clock. She seemed happy to hear from me. "How's the baby?" she asked brightly. "Lan, I have bad news," I said. I told her to sit down. I told her just as the firefighter had told me: Lily had stopped breathing at daycare, the ambulance, the doctors working on her, that she had died. I heard gasping for breath on the other end of the line. "Lan, is there anybody there with you? Any friends?" She said there weren't. I asked if she wanted me to come down. Five minutes later, I was headed her way. I stayed for the better part of an hour in her tiny apartment with the two children lying on the bed. She didn't let them know what had happened. She left the door open and people from the apartment filtered by in the hall, talking among themselves in Vietnamese but not coming in. I had no idea what they were saying, but I could imagine it well enough: You see. Give your baby to one of them and it dies. I tried to comfort Lan, telling her that Lily hadn't suffered, that no one understood why some babies simply stopped breathing in their sleep and died. After about an hour, I found myself back out on the very same sidewalk as on Easter morning. It was after midnight. There were knots of people moving about in the shadows, cars cruising slowly by. I drove back to Arlington. Molly had gone to sleep. Jane and I held each other and took turns crying. I drank rum and tonic until I couldn't stay awake any longer.

The next morning Olivia called early. "Everything's okay, but Mom and Dad's house burned down this early this morning," she said. "I didn't want you to hear it on the television news." I realize now that she had chosen her tone carefully, the way you do with anybody in shock, so as not to upset them further. Surprisingly, it worked. The house my parents had lived in for thirty-five years was mostly cinders? Most of what they owned up in smoke? No big deal. At least they weren't dead. I found out later that a passing newspaper carrier had seen the fire, which had apparently been started by some faulty wiring in the basement that took decades to burn through its insulation—and just happened to finish the job about fourteen hours after Lily's death. The man had thrown rocks at the bedroom window, waking my father and almost certainly saving my parents' lives.

Initially, still too stunned to take in new information, I accepted the destruction of the house I'd grown up in as a minor distraction, sort of like losing your credit cards. A baby's death, a house fire the same night. The surreal was suddenly becoming commonplace. These things are supposed to run in threes, I thought. What was next? A swarm of locusts picking out our house from all the others in the block? Close enough, as it turned out.

Flowers began to arrive. The phone rang as the news spread about Lily. Then the police showed up. The Arlington detective asked if he could come in, then told us that Hien, the woman running the daycare home where Lily died, had had thirty-six children in the place. Thirty-one children were in the basement; five infants were in the room with Lily. She was licensed for no more than five children. "These people, they come over here and get used to nice things," the detective said. "Sometimes, they get greedy." He told us Hien said she had put Lily down in a portable crib for a nap and checked back on her once in ninety minutes. They had raided her house, removing even her son's computer to look for evidence, yanked her license, and shut her down. She was being charged with violating state licensing rules and taking money under false pretenses. There might be more charges later.

The whole thing stank. She had lied to us. She'd told us she never took more than two infants and there were six in the room, plus all the kids downstairs. Jane and I had never asked Hien exactly how many kids she took care of, a ludicrously obvious question in hindsight. It flashed through my mind that her neglect might have led to Lily's death. But if she was guilty of neglect, then so were we for having hired her.

And it definitely seemed like the cops were out to get her, in no small part simply because she was Vietnamese. I was angry at Hien for lying, the police for their bigotry, myself for trusting her so readily.

The detective told us that although Hien had too many kids for her license, she did have the proper number of helpers. He asked some follow-up questions, told us he'd be in touch, and left. After he left, Jane was quick to defend Hien. I was less convinced. I felt she at least she had lied to us about the number of infants she took in. Who knew what else she might be lying about?

The funeral was held on Saturday, just three days after Lily's death, at the Unitarian Church in Arlington. I put aside my lifelong fear of speaking in public to bid my daughter goodbye, but didn't know how to say it. I was raised Episcopalian but it never really took. Jesus and I are still looking for each other. Instead, I called my old yoga teacher, Victor, who runs Shanti Yoga in Bethesda, Maryland. Over the past ten years, I've taken lessons from him off and on and come to regard him as a sort of unaccredited holy man. He said he would write something that I could adapt as I saw fit. I don't know that I believe Victor's take on the cosmos any more than the church's, but I trust him. Standing before several hundred people and trying to breathe, I knew I would break down as soon as I started talking. But I no longer cared. I unfolded my notes and read my teacher's words:

"Lily didn't stay long on this earth. Certain beings need only a brief time here to complete their work before moving on to a higher place, a place from which they will both continue their own journey upward and help those who stay behind. I believe that Lily was, and is, such a soul.

"The relationship that Lily formed with those who loved her is an ongoing one. Those bonds of love created a channel of communication that never closes. I believe the departed soul of this child is making a great effort to soothe the pain of those left behind. Her compassion compels her to stay close to those who loved her so strongly and to help them through this time. The compassion of such souls is so great that they will do this even if it means inhibiting their own soul's upward journey.

"Let us return her sacrifice by releasing her spirit and not hindering her journey with our suffering. Let us draw on our courage and faith in God to overcome our pain. I ask us all to take a moment to open our hearts and imagine Lily's soul entering the holy assembly of spirits, those beings who vibrate with a love so pure as to be inaccessible to human experience. Let us give thanks to her and all those involved in her time on earth for allowing us to partake in her miraculous journey."

Jane spoke. Molly spoke. A minister spoke. Two hundred people, more than I had ever imagined would show up, stood in silence as a violinist played "Over the Rainbow." It was a beautiful moment, the instrument's clear tones ringing through the church, the melody searching for a way up and out of this world. I had thought I was all cried out. That violin found a whole new reservoir of tears.

In the days and weeks after Lily's death, Jane and I paced mechanically through our lives, stopping several times a day to cry, while Lily's ashes, amounting to a single handful, rested in a blue urn on the mantel. Jane seemed more tortured by doubts and "if onlys" than I was, turning over in her mind all the things that we might have done differently: kept the baby at home until she was older even if it meant going into debt, hiring someone to come to the house when needed instead of taking Lily out for daycare. It's hard to elude the belief—however false—that you might have somehow saved your child if you'd only been there. Jane recalled playing with Lily on her bed for the better part of an hour that final morning. She remembered telling Lily she'd never met a more charming baby.

For whatever reasons, I escaped the worst of this cycle of second-guessing. The separation had been so swift, random, and horrifying that it seemed—at least in the way insurance companies use the term—an act of God. To apportion blame or wonder what might have been done differently supposed a rational universe, a place where there were reasons for Lily's death. But making sense is not among the universe's higher priorities. Its workings are hidden, perhaps random, and Lord help you if you get in its way. I imagined Lily's short life as a plane coming in for a landing on an aircraft carrier in rough seas.

My father had often told me that when a pilot sets his craft down for a carrier landing and finds that he's not going to make it, his best option is to power up, take off again, and circle around for another attempt. Maybe that's what Lily had done: come down to earth for a landing and taken off again just as we thought she'd come to rest in our arms. Maybe she was up there right now looking for a safe place to land. I didn't believe it. But it comforted me to imagine it that way.

Life went on. The paper landed on the lawn every morning, the dog still hurled herself at front door when the mail lady opened the storm door, the shouts of the kids at the Catholic school across the street still penetrated our walls. It was then I realized that just as the world was oblivious to my loss, so had I been oblivious to others' losses until Lily's death. How many faces had I blithely passed on the street who were inwardly unmoored by the recent loss of a child, wife or husband? They had always been there, peering back at me from that parallel universe of loss. I just hadn't seen them. And now I was one of them. Every morning I woke and moved once more through my own life like a ghost.

I went fishing a lot that summer. I would drive up to Violette's Lock on the Chesapeake & Ohio Canal out past Potomac, Maryland, and wade the river with a spinning rod for smallmouth bass. My hands were practiced at the motions—tying on a lure, casting, retrieving—and I was content to let them. Wading deep into the water, I fished in 100-degree heat and in lightning storms, half hoping that a stray volt would arc down my graphite fishing rod. Whenever I caught a fish, bringing it up into the world of air before releasing it, I wondered if this was what dying was like, passing from the world where you could breathe to one you couldn't. Only maybe death was the discovery that you finally could breathe there after all. What was life that made it different from death? What slender thing separated the lively baby I'd known from the doll in the emergency room? It did seem that her tiny spark must live on somehow, that matter may be changed but not destroyed. Maybe it had been absorbed into one of the lightning bolts I was half wishing would come my way. Maybe it was just circling. Out on the river, I began to talk to Lily. I told her how much I missed her and loved her and that I hoped she was safe. That I would always be with her. I felt the water sliding past my legs. At dusk, birds came out to wheel and loop in the heavy air to catch insects. No lightning came near me that summer.

Jane and I never resolved our fundamental difference about Hien. For whatever reason, Jane forgave her totally and almost instantly. She said that Hien was nearly as devastated by the loss as we were, that she had complied with the spirit—if not the letter of the law—by having the proper number of helpers, and that a zealous Arlington prosecutor might well want to make an example out of her. She pointed out that Lily might just as easily have died in our own home, in which case she and I would be blaming each other. All of this was true. But I felt that Hien had misled us, if not lied outright, about the number of infants. And I couldn't get past the fact that we had entrusted our daughter to her care and Lily had died in her care. Some ancient code had been violated. Maybe I felt Jane was being compassionate enough for the two of us. Maybe I'd simply allowed my anger and grief to harden my heart. I'd taken my lumps, I thought bitterly. She could take hers.

There was one thing Jane and I did agree on. We still wanted a baby. I think we decided that almost before the funeral home had turned Lily's body to a fistful of ash. We agreed not to start for at least a few months, maybe longer. But we knew if we didn't get back up on the horse soon, we might not have the courage to try again. And then we'd spend the rest of our lives looking back at what might have been had Lily lived. I knew she was irreplaceable. I was terrified of again being responsible for the life of another child. But I needed some kind of hope in my life. And somewhere, there had to be a baby who needed us. Then Jane said something I will never forget. "Someday, we'll look back at this and realize that we had to go through Lily's death to find the baby we're supposed to be with." I loved her for saying that.

Some weeks after the funeral, I heard about the Northern Virginia SIDS Alliance from a woman who had a daughter on Molly's soccer team and whose sister was president of the chapter. "You might want to give them a call," she told me. I did. A few days later, Judy Rainey knocked on the door, introduced herself, and handed me an envelope. She was backing away almost as soon as she had come. (I thought she was being careful not to intrude; much later I found out she was late for an appointment.) Her number was in the envelope, she said. I could call anytime. Inside was *The SIDS Survival Guide*, a book filled with the raw stories of parents who had lost babies and their struggles through horror, anger, and grief to acceptance.

It helped to know that other people had been through the nightmare and come out the other side. There was advice from grief counselors, chapters on planning the funeral, chapters on the different ways men, children, and grandparents deal with the death. There was one about being a friend to a SIDS survivor (do use the baby's name; don't say it was God's will; do say "I can't even begin to imagine your pain") and even one called "When a Baby Dies at the Child Care Provider's."

I wanted to talk to Judy again, to someone who had taken her own tour of the universe of loss. Jane, Judy, and I finally went out to lunch one day. Judy apologized for bringing along Sarah, her ten-month-old. Some SIDS parents can't bear to see another's child. But we were hungry for a baby's smile, any baby's. Over pizza, Judy told us about her son, Joe, who had died in 1996. Like Lily, he had died at his babysitter's. And like me, Judy had her own unresolved issues about the sitter. Because she worked right across the street, Judy had arrived at the house within five minutes of getting the call that Joe had stopped breathing. But for some reason, the woman hadn't dialed 911. Judy had been the one to do that. "I don't blame her for Joe's death. But I never understood why she didn't call for help sooner. And I've never really found out why."

I don't remember much of our conversation, but I remember feeling tremendously comforted to be in the company of someone who understood my isolation, the fear that I would never get over Lily's death. I told her how waking each morning was like the movie *Groundhog Day*, her death happening all over again. I'd gotten used to suddenly tearing up in public places. I could now do it over lunch and not even look around to see how people seated two feet away were reacting.

Judy was eager to hear everything about Lily: how we'd found her, how strangers would see her smile from forty yards out in a super-market or playground and come over to make her acquaintance. She told us how she and her husband, Terry, had also been terrified to have another child, but had been even more terrified not to. "My arms just ached for a baby," she said. She'd been so fearful of SIDS by the time Sarah came along that even at ten months, the child was still sleeping strapped into a car seat placed inside her crib so that she couldn't turn onto her stomach in the night. Judy, the unpaid president of the Northern Virginia SIDS Alliance and a dynamo of a woman, was on a crusade to save as many babies from SIDS as possible. She told us the "Back to Sleep" campaign had helped reduce SIDS 40 percent since 1992, but that less than half of all parents knew that putting a child down on her back reduced the risk of death. That a child accustomed to being put down on her back who was put down prone at daycare was something like eighteen times more likely to die of SIDS. That though SIDS is not totally preventable, thousands of children could be saved simply by getting parents, daycare providers, and grandparents to put them down on their backs and remove from cribs the fluffy bedding and bumper pads that babies can nose their way into and suffocate in.

"All I can tell you is that you will get through this, it will get better," she said. "But don't listen to anybody who tells you it's going to take a year or eighteen months. It takes however long it takes."

Hien's case finally came to trial in January. She had pled guilty to three misdemeanor charges, including exceeding the Arlington County limit on children at a family daycare home and not reporting all the income she had made. Jane attended the trial. I did not. I just wanted it all to go away. I read in the paper that dozens of parents showed up to try to convince the judge that she should not be sent to jail. One mother said that Hien had saved her child's life by administering CPR during a seizure. Another showed a special chair that Hien and her husband had made for her disabled child. "Sometimes we think [she] did a better job than we did," a lawyer who left his daughter in her care said. Jane did not speak at the trial, but she had agreed to let

Hien's attorney point out privately to the judge that she was in the courtroom and didn't hold Hien responsible for our child's death. The judge ruled that there was most likely nothing she could have done to save Lily. He upheld the suspension of her license and gave her probation on the charges she'd pled guilty to. After the ruling, Jane said Hien's mother, a tiny woman, came over, stood before her, and made a deep, wordless bow of thanks. I realized later that I should have been there. Not necessarily in support of Hien, but to support my wife. I'd let my anger blind me to the person who needed me most.

Jane, Molly, and I developed rituals for Lily. We'd light a tiny candle next to the taller ones at the dinner table. We'd light one each Sunday we went to church. At Christmas we perched an angel of golden foil on the urn on the mantelpiece that held her ashes. At Christmas dinner, we counted our blessings: My parents had been spared their lives in the fire; Molly was doing well in school and had a lot of good friends; Jane and I had not fallen apart. In some ways, the year had been hardest for my father. He'd lost his house and only grandchild. Then his younger brother and only sibling, John, had died a few months later. Then Granny had finally let go. She'd lived to be ninety-nine. My father was eighty. But losing your mother makes you an orphan no matter how old you are. His doctor had suggested Dad have no more than one drink a day to cope with low blood pressure and the fainting spells he sometimes had when tired. Never one for half-measures, he'd stopped drinking entirely. At Christmas dinner in my parents' rented apartment, we spiked his eggnog with rum. About halfway through dinner, his face lit up for the first time in months and he started telling stories. My sister and I looked at each other and winked. Liquor, in controlled quantities, can be a wonderful thing.

Before Christmas, Jane, Molly, and I also went to the NOVA SIDS Alliance memorial service, preceded by a potluck dinner, at a local church. There must have been two hundred people crammed into the downstairs activities room at dinner, some still raw and tearful from losses only a couple of months old, others commemorating children who had died more than fifteen years ago. It was like a civilian version of the survivors of D-Day, whole families who had been through the fire and lived to tell about it. It was all right to cry, to laugh, to hold the babies of people you'd never met before but who knew how badly you might need to hold one. At the service upstairs, the name of every child who had died was read aloud as each family came up to receive a glass Christmas tree ornament with the baby's name on it. There may have been a dry eye in the house. I don't know. I couldn't see well enough.

Within three months after Lily's death, Jane and I had gotten back in touch with Families for Private Adoption groups, reactivated the phone, and started running ads again. I was surprised at how much better the simple act of calling newspapers and dictating the copy felt. At an FPA meeting, I talked to a woman who had adopted through an agency in Oklahoma City run by a woman lawyer who herself had adopted two children. We called them and got the information packet. It was an agency, which meant less control. But we'd learned a lot in the past year about how little control one really has in life. Besides, if you didn't adopt, you paid only the $150 registration fee. The deal with the agency was that you made up two booklets about yourself—a brief family story with pictures—and left it on file with them. When prospective mothers came in, they looked through the books and selected the ones they liked. By November, we had ours on file, complete with pictures of us, Molly, the house, and Snoop. We said we favored an open adoption, in which the child would have the option of contacting the mother when he or she was old enough. We figured Molly was our strongest card and played her up big-time.

Once the books were gone, I pestered the attorney, Julie Demastus, with phone calls every two weeks. Had anybody looked at our book? Did they seem interested? At FPA meetings, I kept hearing of couples whose ads in the newspapers had paid off. How had they gotten lucky and not us? You just have to hang in there, we were told. Then one morning, the phone rang. It was Julie. "I think we've got you a mom," she said. Pam (not her real name) was thirty-three, seven months pregnant with a girl. Every adoptive parent hopes for that dream candidate, the honors club cheerleader who got too friendly at a keg party with the captain of the football team (who was also the winner of the science fair). The actual women putting children up for adoption tend to come from grittier circumstances. Many grew up in single-parent homes, have low-paying jobs, and have histories of medical or substance abuse problems. None of this necessarily means there will be any problems with the children. We had seen proud parents showing off impossibly healthy, beautiful babies at Families for Private Adoption meetings whose biological mothers sounded like rejects from *The Blair Witch Project*. Pam was a good candidate. She'd kept all her appointments with the adoption agency (a good sign), had a steady job, and was healthy. "She just doesn't think she's mommy material," Julie told me. "She picked your book and wants to talk to you all."

The conversations went well. Pam was an unassuming woman of Italian-Irish ancestry, five foot four, 120 pounds. She had a smoker's voice but said she had all but quit once she found out she was pregnant. She'd been in Alcoholics Anonymous for years and worked in a coffee shop at a hotel. She'd hooked up with a guy briefly, decided he was trouble, and dumped him. He had red hair and was of middle height. She didn't know where he was now and didn't want to know. She'd never really considered abortion. She was looking for parents who would expose a child to religion but not shove it down her throat. The Unitarian Church sounded good in that department. She liked how happy Molly looked. Pam had grown up with four different stepfathers. She especially liked that Jane and John had worked things out around Molly so well after the divorce. It sounded like she had limited faith in the institution of marriage.

The baby, a girl, was due in February, less than three months away. There was a lot to do before then: letters of reference, fingerprints, an updated home study, copies of our criminal and child abuse backgrounds from the state of Virginia. After two attempts at fingerprinting, the authorities gave up on Jane. Her prints were so light they didn't show up on the most sensitive electronic equipment. "There are criminals who'd kill for your hands," the guy operating the machine said. The baby was scheduled for Caesarean section at Mercy Health Center in Oklahoma City on February 25. Pam said it was okay if we wanted to be at the hospital. Jane could even be in the delivery room. We could take the baby immediately and spend the night in the hospital with her. Then we'd need to stay in Oklahoma City for two weeks while the interstate compact was completed, allowing us to take the baby back to Virginia pending final adoption.

We made plane reservations, found a cheap hotel with a kitchenette to save on restaurant expenses, and started throwing baby names around. We liked Emma. I told Jane I was almost afraid to get too excited about this. I was afraid it would somehow backfire, that Pam would change her mind. "I know what you mean," she said. We called Julie Demastus for reassurance. "Look, nothing's done until it's done. But I wish all the girls we got in here were as stable as Pam. I think you've got yourself a daughter on the way."

The baby decided she wasn't on anybody's schedule but her own. On the morning of February 18, 2000—a year and a day after Lily had been born—the phone rang. It was Julie. "You better get on a plane and get down here. Momma's water just broke. We'll be at the hospital with her. See you there." Jane had commitments she couldn't cancel and couldn't get away until the next day. It took me four hours and a lot of pleading to ticketing agent supervisors, but I found a flight out that evening at five o'clock.

At 2 A.M., a cab brought me to the hospital. Five minutes later, I was holding a tiny baby girl, a pink bow in her bright red hair. A photo taken by one of Julie's staff shows a man suddenly plucked from a sea of grief, smiling and almost crying at the same time. Pam lay in bed, exhausted, with tubes in her arm. I gave her a kiss on the cheek and she smiled. "I am so happy to meet you," I told her. "The baby's beautiful. We're gonna take the best care of her we possibly can. Jane's flying in tomorrow." We talked for about half an hour. The baby had been born about five o'clock and weighed five pounds, ten ounces, just two ounces above the official cutoff for "low" birth weight. She was almost as big as a loaf of bread, but squirmier, quite red in the face, and not at all pleased to have been kicked out of the womb. Finally a nurse said Pam needed to get some sleep. "I'll come see you in the morning," I told her. I wheeled my new daughter down the maternity ward in a sort of plastic tub on a trolley and into a room with a bed for me. The nurse showed me how to fold and tuck the blanket to bundle her up tight and warm, gave me some bottles of formula, and closed the door. "It's just you and me now, honey," I said to the baby. "You and your daddy." I curled up on the bed in my clothes and moved the trolley so she was just inches away. Every two hours, Emma woke, her thin cries signaling hunger. She was so tiny that half an ounce filled her stomach and sent her back to sleep. I had never really seen newborns. Her vulnerability was heartbreaking. I was hooked. With Lily, who had come to us at six weeks of age, the bonds had taken some time to form. But Emma was mine from birth and I was hardwired to her cries. I had the feeling that the smallest sound from her would wake me from any sleep. She managed the trick that all newborns do, looking ancient and brand-new at the same time. I woke again and again to inspect her in the night. "Emma," I said. "Do you like that name?"

Everything went fine until I saw her first bowel movement and went running down the hall for help. "Come quick," I panted. "Something's wrong. She just crapped and it looks like coal tar." The nurse followed me down the hall, inspected the diaper, and cooed at the baby. "Good girl!" she said. "Your first poop!" She explained that all the stuff that accumulates in the baby's bowel during its stint as a fetus is called meconium and that it's supposed to look like that. That's fine. But somebody should give fathers a heads-up. I'd thought she was defecating something EPA would have to dispose of.

The next morning, I took the baby in to see Pam, who was daubing at tears when we showed up. "I'm a mess," she said, smoothing her hair. I told her she looked fine. Just then a nurse came in. "Stitches hurtin' you, hon?" she asked. Pam nodded. "We'll fix you up," said the nurse. A minute later she emerged with a shot of Demerol. Pam rolled her eyes. "What I really want is a cigarette," she whispered to me. I waved the nurse off and took her aside, explaining she was about to administer the wrong drug. "Gotcha," she said. Then she went over to Pam. "Darlin', I can't let you smoke in here." Pam's face fell. "On the other hand, if you were to light one up when I walk out of here, there's nothing I could do about it." She winked and left. I rummaged in Pam's purse, lit a Marlboro Light for her, and opened the window. After that she calmed down. I told her about Jane and Molly and the dog, about my work and the neighborhood and my parents. She said not to worry about her changing her mind. She was sure. "I knew as soon as you picked her up last night that you'd be a good dad," she said. She was still crying, though. I didn't pry about why she wasn't keeping the baby. I figured she had her reasons.

Jane came late the next day, Saturday. The hospital wouldn't release Emma until she downed an entire ounce of formula at a sitting. That didn't happen until Sunday, so Jane and I spent a night with her in the hospital room before the three of us moved to the hotel we'd found out near the airport. We went to every Kmart in the greater Oklahoma City area looking for a certain baby sling that Jane had seen and wanted. We never did find it. We watched TV and took videos of the baby and tried to get her to smile at us. But Emma was tired from her journey into the world and mostly wanted to sleep. That was fine, too. We were exhausted, elated, anxious to go home and show Emma off to everyone. Her birth had delivered us back to the world of the living. It was a good place to be.

SIDS parents are understandably anxious about their subsequent children. Some of us spend thousands on high-tech monitors for our babies to wear that go off like car alarms when the child's heartbeat becomes irregular or the child fails to breathe for a certain number of seconds. Some of us virtually put our lives on hold—not letting the child out of our sight—until that first birthday's deliverance from the danger zone. What Jane and I learned from SIDS is that the world is a dicey place where calamity tends to blindside you. "I just figure lightning's not going to strike twice in the same place," Jane said not long after we got Emma home. "Otherwise, I'd go crazy with worry." We do put Emma down on her back, though she tends to roll over almost immediately onto her stomach. We don't put blankets, pillows, bumper pads, or anything else that she could suffocate against in her crib. Instead we bundle her in sleepers against cold nights. And we bought a two-hundred-dollar HALO mattress that has tiny holes in it and a fan that circulates air continually (it's the only anti-SIDS product endorsed by the National SIDS Alliance). We've hired a wonderful woman named Nancy to come into our house and take care of Emma thirty hours a week. We let my mother babysit often. We've become board members of the Northern Virginia SIDS Alliance chapter and have taken a course on peer counseling so that we may one day offer hope to a couple suddenly kicked into that parallel universe of loss. That hasn't happened yet. But enough babies still die of SIDS that we will probably need our training. The phrase "sacred duty" comes to mind when I think of helping a couple in free fall after a SIDS death.

We still light a tiny candle for Lily at family gatherings. We still have pictures of her up on the walls. We want Emma to know about her sister when the time is right. "I figure we'll just tell her the truth," Jane says. We recently attended the dedication of a small garden created in her honor at my parents' church in Glen Echo, Maryland. We have yet to decide what to do with her ashes, which are still in the blue urn on the mantel.

We'll never get over losing Lily. We don't want to. Her short life is forever part of ours. But we can remember her without automatically suffering now. We spend more time looking forward than back. Emma is learning to crawl and we are beginning to childproof the entire house. She turns her head when we call her name. And when she crawls fearlessly to the edge of our bed, sure that nothing can harm her, when we play with her in the mornings before getting up, we tug her gently back to safety and nuzzle the special spot on her neck and listen as she dissolves into low baby giggles. It is the sweetest sound on earth, a sound that binds us to this child forever, a sound that makes broken hearts whole again.

KILLING TIME

Hunker down, brother. These are the pale months, the time when Mother Nature looks over the evidence and sentences sportsmen to ninety days in the hoosegow for having had too much fun the rest of the year. So now we tough it out, waiting on April and the promise of decent fishing.

How bad is it? Put it this way: When the mail dives through the front-door slot at noon, the dog and I both bark. The day's haul includes a death threat from the Book-of-the-Month Club, three credit card offers that no reputable institution has any business extending to someone with my history, and an ad for one of those new drugs that turn you into a babe windsurfing over an endless wheat field. I feed the dog last night's tuna casserole, which she polishes off in three bites. For my own lunch, I nuke a small venison steak to defrost it, add butter, and slap it under the broiler. And I remember the coping mechanisms that can help get a man to spring: Tune up your fishing tackle. After years of working on today's ever-more-complex fishing reels, I have finally perfected this technique. Get an empty egg carton. Better yet, get two. Disassemble your favorite reel. Using an old toothbrush and a rag, clean each screw and gear, then put them in sequential order in the pockets of the carton. When you're through, carefully close the carton and put it in the trash. Order yourself a new reel.

Daydream. When winter blues render you incapable of even getting up from your chair, at least you can evoke the most memorable moments from last year's hunting and fishing. If you're honest with yourself, you'll find that these are generally not the hero moments of boating the bass that could swallow a cantaloupe or bagging the buck that everybody in camp hoped would be theirs. No, they will be moments of humiliation or grace or camaraderie that stick in your mind for other reasons, ones that you might not be able to explain. Here are my two.

In early October, I was on stand just at the end of legal shooting light. I'd heard a deer feeding just beyond some thick bushes, its feet shuffling slowly in the leaves. I froze, waiting for it to come. While I was waiting, a little yellow bird flitted up from the scrub beneath my stand and landed on my chest. It stayed there for about five seconds, fluffing its feathers and whispering something to itself before flying off. I could actually feel its tiny weight against my chest. The deer never came. But I felt the heartbeat of the woods that day.

One January morning before dawn I got nailed going 60 in a 45 mph zone in a rural town on my way to the last deer hunt of the year. "What's the hurry?" asked the cop. Since he had me dead to rights, I opted for the truth. "Just another overanxious deer hunter," I said. He handed back my license and registration and stood there a moment. "Well," he said at last. "You aren't the first one I've caught. Just slow down, okay?" I was stunned. It was the first ticket I'd ever beaten in my life. I shot my hand out the window and shook that cop's hand. Hard.

Oops. The smoke alarm has just gone off by the kitchen. Lunch is served. Hang in there, brother. Spring will be here before you know it.

BUBBLE BOY

Matthew, the seven-year-old son of close friends, was having trouble in school, his mother confided to me at his birthday cookout. Matthew, the kid whose IQ was pushing four digits? She saw the look on my face and rolled her eyes. "Not *that* kind of trouble. It's the social part."

He'd been different from the beginning—a grown-up intellect attached to a child's body. Matty had the self-defense instincts of a manatee. He was the kind of boy that schoolyard bullies sharpened their teeth on. The thought of it made me wince. She told me that at recess, while the other first graders played cops and robbers, Matty tried to organize the stragglers into his current obsession: a reenactment of Stonewall Jackson's valley campaign.

Only nobody else wanted to play. "He says the other kids tease him, ask him if he just beamed in from Jupiter. They call him Bubble Boy, 'cause he lives in his head so much." She was trying to smile as she told the story, but then she turned to wipe her eyes.

I took a pull on my beer as I tried to think of something helpful to say. What came out was "How 'bout I take him fishing?"

"Oh," she said, her face brightening, "he'd love that."

I'd always liked this kid, different as we were. And it wasn't just because we were the exact same age thirty-six years apart. When he was just a few weeks old, I'd come over to visit, then fallen asleep on the couch. I woke to find that my friends had placed the sleeping boy on my chest, and that there was baby drool collecting in the hollow of my collarbone. I lay still, feeling his body rise and fall against mine. I couldn't explain it if you made me listen to the complete works of

John Tesh; all I know is by the time he woke up fifteen minutes later, we were blood kin. And it was my job to protect him.

He worried about hurting the worms. "I don't want them to suffer," he fretted. We'd just dug a cupful from a compost pile near the farm where our two families were spending a weekend. We'd bagged a few of the jumpy, wiggly kind we call snake worms around here, a few skinny little ones, and from deeper down where the compost was heating up, half a dozen monster night crawlers.

Matty looked hot and uncomfortable in the July sun. I sliced open the shrink-wrap on the Li'l Fisherman outfit and put the thing together, marveling at how little first-fishing-rod kits have changed in thirty years: a push-button reel, three tiny red-and-white bobbers, six hooks, and a bunch of split-shot sinkers you wouldn't need fishing worms on a farm pond.

Suddenly I remembered I'd been worried about the worms my first time, too. A camp counselor had pinched my cheek with his rough fingers. "That's as bad as it hurts 'em," he'd told me. Now I did the same for Matty.

"That's not so terrible," he said.

I showed him how to cast, baited one of the crawlers, and turned him loose. The bobber landed all of eight feet away. The worm was probably resting on the bottom. Hey, I was happy he'd hit the water. "Perfect," I said. We waited. When the bobber went under, all Matty could say was "Gosh!" When the bluegill darted toward open water, he said, "Whoa, it's really pulling hard!" When he landed the five-inch fish, the two of us began shouting and high-fiving each other.

He dropped the rod on the grass, shouted, "Gotta show Mom!" over his shoulder, and left me holding the fish as he ran toward the house. It was the fastest and longest I'd ever seen him run. By the time the sun set, we'd pulled three more bluegills, a ten-inch largemouth, and a three-pound catfish out of that pond. His mother had shot two rolls of film of her son smiling brighter than any time in the past year. Bubble Boy had turned into Bobber Boy.

"This boy is a one-man fishing machine," I announced to the entire dinner table. "Tomorrow morning we'll do it again," I told Matty.

"Yeah," he said, knocking over his milk.

I was awakened the next morning at five thirty by a seven-year-old thumb gently pushing up my right eyelid to see if there was anyone alive inside. It was Matty. He was holding the rod and a Styrofoam cup. "Uncle Bill," he whispered urgently, "I already got the worms. You wanna go fishin'?" In that twilight moment between dreaming and waking, I found myself face-to-face with the boy I'd been three and a half decades back.

"Yeah, buddy, let's go get 'em."

A SPORTSMAN'S LIFE: DRUM ROLL

Every so often, it's worth remembering that life is a limited-time-only offer. Last December I found myself worrying about all the things I'd been putting off all deer season. There were the leaves on the lawn, now two inches thick and the consistency of Red Man Chewing Tobacco. Bills that had begun arriving in specially colored envelopes with notices reading, "Your lack of response to our repeated inquiries in this matter has left us no choice but to . . ." I was just about to give in to my guilty conscience when the phone rang. It was Link, my sometime fishing partner, a self-employed carpenter who, unlike most of mankind, has never let the necessity of making a living interfere with the luxury of living itself.

"Hey, man, less go down to Hatteras, see can we bang us a coupla red drum. Purtiest fish you ever seen, color like a hot penny with a black eyespot on the tail."

I explained why I couldn't go and reminded him that in any case Cape Hatteras was four hundred miles away. "Why we gotta leave now," he answered. "Have ya back by tomorrow night. Surf stick and chest waders. Pick you up in forty-five minutes."

Long story short, an hour later we had cleared town, heading south. Guilt was not along for the ride. There are few things in life that rival flying down the highway with a thermos of hot coffee toward the promise of big fish in the company of a friend you've known so long that neither of you feels compelled to muddy up the silence with conversation.

Red drum are vampires, extremely wary of the sun and best pursued in darkness. You never know if or when they'll show up, even during a so-called run. And they're uncommonly finicky as saltwater creatures go. While a bluefish will tear into anything that doesn't bite it first and flounder are so gullible they can be caught on bottom-fished hankies, red drum will delicately mouth only the freshest, juiciest baits.

By dark we are on the beach in four-wheel-drive. All ruts lead to the Point, an ever-shifting spit of sand that narrows into the Atlantic. Link and I get out, struggle into waders, rig up six-ounce pyramid sinkers and heavily baited hooks. There must be sixty of us crammed shoulder to shoulder on the last bit of sand. You stagger a few yards forward into the surf, heave your bait up into the night, and return to take your place. Then you stand there for hours, shifting your feet so the surf doesn't dig you into a hole.

After a couple of hours the cry of "Fish on!" comes a few yards away. A man moves forward into the surf, rod bent as the fish takes line on its first run. Five minutes later he has brought the copper-colored animal onto the sand. Tiny flashlight in mouth, he kneels in a circle of light, one hand on the fish's belly to keep it from injuring itself. Great fish out of water are fragile creatures, their organs suddenly vulnerable to gravity. He gently removes the hook and measures the fish. Then he lifts it carefully in his arms and moves into deeper water, resembling a groom carrying his bride over some strange threshold.

By 3 A.M. I'm out of bait. Link and I have agreed to meet back at the hotel if we get separated. As I'm walking out, I hear a truck engine sputter to life. I knock on the window and ask, "You guys mind if I ride in back?" The passenger looks up from a beer. "Hell, no. We can use the ballast." I roll over the side and wedge myself in tight, spread-eagle on my back, staring up into the night sky while the truck bucks over the sand. Suddenly I'm smiling, completely alive in this moment and more than a little amused that I could ever have been worried by leaves on my lawn or the silly pieces of paper in my mailbox.

SPRING CANOE TRICKS

Every year, in celebration of the return of spring and fishing, I try to have at least one colossally stupid experience involving a canoe. Some people might call it a jinx, but I prefer to think of it as an involuntary tradition. All it takes to have a near-death experience in a small boat is to put aside common sense for a few moments. After that, everything takes care of itself.

There was the year I took my then girlfriend straight into a Class III standing rapid, a white mare's tail shaking in the blue air at the bottom of nearly half a mile of small rapids. We had negotiated these with a skill and dexterity we did not, strictly speaking, possess and were feeling pretty good about ourselves.

Meanwhile, high spring water levels had turned the normally negotiable standing rapid into a monster, a fact I realized about the time we entered it. One second we were above the water and canoeing; the next we were four feet under and wondering why it was so hard to breathe, paddles bonking us on our heads, tackle disappearing into the depths. I lost three rods, two hundred dollars' worth of lures, and my knife. I came up sputtering in a PowerBait oil slick with a small gash in my forehead that bled colorfully. We were towed ashore by kayakers who made no effort to conceal their delight at our stupidity.

Another spring, river, and girlfriend. This time I decided to drag the anchor down a brisk stretch of water, so I could fish while the young lady read her paperback. A length of chain tied to the stern works well for this, and a couple of old window-sash weights are an acceptable alternative. What you do not want is a four-fluked folding grapnel anchor, even a smallish one. The first ninety seconds were vernal bliss. I even coaxed two acrobatic little smallmouths into the boat on a three-inch white grub. Then the anchor caught.

Since I'd tied it to the middle thwart (for easy access), the boat immediately swung broadside into the current. "What's happening?" the young lady asked, alarmed. The boat had begun to lean upstream, and the gunwale was now barely an inch from the rushing current. Once we started to take on water, the boat would go under in a flash. "You might want to lean downstream, uh, real hard," I said, trying to keep the panic from my voice as I searched for a blade to cut us free. Then I remembered that my knife was at the bottom of the first river. I finally sawed us loose with the tiny blade on my fishing-line clippers. Years later, I can no longer recall that girl's name. But I still miss that sweet little anchor.

My wife Jane has too much sense to get in a canoe with me, but I still manage to keep the tradition alive. This year I was out with a buddy on an unusually warm April day when storm clouds moved in from the north, at which time the crankbait bite picked up considerably. "Heck, I don't hear any thunder," I said. "I don't mind getting wet." My friend responded that in an aluminum Grumman packed with graphite rods, I'd better hope we didn't hear any thunder. He began paddling for shore immediately.

The sky turned black, and the first strike hit not a quarter mile away as we touched shore. The temperature dropped 20 degrees, the lightning turned to heavy artillery, and it began to hail. We abandoned the canoe and hunkered down in the woods, soaked, freezing, and listening to the occasional tree fall around us.

Eventually, the storm moved downriver, and we began to bail out the canoe. Then the storm decided to turn around, come back, and throw more lightning and hail at us. Half an hour later, the two of us shivering so hard that we could barely speak, my buddy turned to me. "You're a damn ji-jinx," he said. "You know th-that?"

I thought it over. "M-m-maybe," I said.

THE KID IN THE PHOTO

If you are holding this magazine, there was a moment in your life when you caught the fish. You remember the one. It was not necessarily your first fish, just the pivotal one, the one that rearranged the molecules in your brain and created a fishing fiend. If you are lucky, there also exists, somewhere, the photo. Usually but not always taken by a parent, the photo shows the fish (usually between three and seven inches) and you with a look of accomplishment on your face not unlike the one David had after bouncing a rock off Goliath's noggin.

If you still have the photo, keep it in a safe place. There will be times in your life when you'll need it to remember that somewhere hidden inside you there still lives a young boy capable of seeing the world in all its glory and wonder.

I got lucky the other day when my version of this priceless souvenir resurfaced after nearly four decades, and the memories came circling back around my head like a school of minnows. I was nine years old, immortal, with a full head of hair and the world as my tackle box. My parents, sister, dog, and I were on a two-week vacation to Canada that seemed to last a thousand years. Our chariot for the voyage was a new, white Oldsmobile station wagon the size of a river barge with windows that went up and down at the touch of a magic button and a rear seat that faced backward.

I had my very own wizard's wand, a spincasting rod made of that miracle material, fiberglass. It had three ferrules with a tasteful wrapping of red thread around each, a silver trigger to rest your forefinger on while casting, and a black Zebco 202 push-button reel on the cork handle. I thought it had descended from heaven by way of Sears, Roebuck. I remember only that my desire to fish was so overpowering that I burst into tears every time we passed a body of water without stopping. It made no difference whether the water was fresh or salt, six inches or a thousand feet deep, clear or muddy. Fish lived in water, and water was where I would fish for them.

Somewhere on a nameless lake in Canada, it happened. I slung my only lure, a red-and-white Dardevle Imp spoon, off the end of the dock. Something seized it and began pulling back. Hard. I turned the crank, but this merely produced a hoarse buzzing sound from the Zebco. Having no idea how to play a fish, I simply pointed the rod tip at the water and began trying to walk backward, discovering why so few experts recommend the tug-of-war as an effective method to bring a fish to hand.

Then a boy about my age ran down from the parking lot and began jabbering at me in French. I figured that witnessing my great battle had robbed him of normal speech and that he was speaking in tongues. But then he had a stroke of genius and began to pantomime the action of pumping and reeling the rod. Within minutes I had a huge, green, predatory-looking fish flopping on the grass. I laid it alongside the ruler on my tackle box and found that it was so big it wouldn't fit at one whack, being just over seventeen inches long. I immediately ran to my parents, who snapped the picture that now sits on their mantel, along with photos of my infancy and wedding.

The fish is a northern pike, less than an inch shy of legal length. Alexander the Great never had a prouder moment.

The photo was lost for many years. It turned up after my parents' house, the one I grew up in, burned down early one morning. They are alive because a passing newspaper carrier banged on their window to wake them up. Going through the rubble later, they discovered a forgotten box of snapshots, including one of a boy with a fish.

Nearly losing your parents gives you new appreciation for them. It taught me to hug my father when saying goodbye instead of merely shaking his hand. It felt funny the first time I did it, brushing his hand away awkwardly in the kitchen and snaking my arm around his shoulder and neck. But as I stood there for a moment with my father feeling strangely small in my arms, I saw the photograph on the mantel over the rebuilt fireplace. And for just a moment, it wasn't the fish that boy looked proud of: It was me.

NONE DARE CALL IT HAPPINESS

A fishing catalog from one of the major retailers just landed on my doorstep, and I'm lucky not to have been standing in the way. Weighing in at nearly one and a half pounds, this is the kind of incoming artillery that can hurt you. I quickly sneaked the catalog down to the basement, set aside the day's gainful employment, and abandoned myself to the pleasures of material acquisition. Or at least fantasizing about those pleasures.

At last count, I owned just thirteen spinning and casting outfits—not counting fly rods and saltwater gear. They, along with my wife Jane, stepdaughter Molly, and daughter Emma, live in a house in sore need of a new asphalt shingle roof, interior and exterior paint, and rather extensive masonry work on the front steps (probably from the impact of all those catalogs). Inevitably, the question arises: Can I really justify the purchase of another fishing rod and reel?

My answer is "yes" and, upon further consideration, "hell, yes." Like any other American, I have an unshakable belief that material goods, acquired in sufficient quantities, bestow happiness. (This is why I own the rods. This is also why I need more.)

The other day I heard some nonsense on the radio to the contrary. A so-called expert, a college professor who had done years of study, said he had arrived at a disturbing conclusion about the relationship of money to happiness. This know-it-all said that the average American, whether he earns $30,000 or $300,000 a year, believes he would be significantly happier if he could make just 20 percent more.

There are just two things wrong with this, he said. One is that as your income climbs, that 20 percent figure represents more and more money and is therefore harder to come by. The second is that you still won't be happy. People who get a 20 percent raise experience a bump in happiness, but it's only temporary. They acquire a bigger house or a 43-million-modulus graphite fishing rod with a Portuguese cork handle and titanium-plated Fuji SiC guides, but pretty soon they notice that they still don't have as much as some folks. And so their happiness suddenly evaporates, although they could get it back if they just had a little more money. The college professor had even coined a cute little phrase for this dilemma. He called it the "hedonic treadmill."

This man is clearly a fool and a danger to our way of life who should be given a one-way ticket to the developing country of his choice and made to work in a McDonald's there.

Upon opening the catalog, however, I realized that the people who put it out had bought into the treadmill idea big-time. Only they were aiming for folks who can make it go around a good deal faster than I can. Flipping through the pages, I quickly fell for a sweet little spinning reel: floating shaft, thirteen ball bearings, titanium-lipped spool, a tad over eight ounces. It cost $500. A few pages over, I eyed a nice, light-action spinning rod from one of the better makers that would match the reel. It was $300.

I shut the catalog and took a few deep breaths. If only I made nine times as much money as I do now, I could easily afford such equipment and the happiness they would bring. In the meantime, I ordered a Mitchell 300X, the latest version of the venerable 300: five ball bearings, oversize aluminum spool, durable as a tank, and just $39.99. I paired it with a five-foot, ten-inch Shakespeare Ugly Stik, a $27.99 rod that isn't much good for anything except catching fish.

Don't tell the professor, but a strange and not altogether disagreeable sense of anticipation came over me as I completed my order for this decidedly down-market equipment. It might have been called happiness.

SNOOP

Most nights when it's not too hot or cold, Snoop and I head up the old railroad-turned-bike-path behind the house for a short walk. As in all the best man-dog relations, both sides benefit. I get my butt off the sofa long enough to miss the parade of senseless cruelty that passes for the ten o'clock news, and Snoop gets one more chance to break her personal best of twenty-two scent markings in a mile-long walk (set the evening my wife Jane left an entire pot of chicken soup to cool in the mudroom).

One night about a month ago, Snoop winded an unfamiliar critter in the underbrush and veered off to investigate. There ensued a tremendous two-part caterwauling, and Snoop exploded from the bushes with a terrified *what-the-heck-was-THAT-thing* look on her face, snapping the frayed leash required by local law. "Dammit, Snoop, that's a raccoon," I told her as I trotted up the path to where she had stopped to collect her wits. "What'd you expect it to do, kiss you?" As I tied the leash ends, we looked back to see the raccoon, clearly illuminated by a full moon, calmly walking back up its tree.

Snoop, as you will have guessed, is not what we humans refer to as a working dog. She cannot, for example, point birds, herd sheep, or follow a scent trail that crosses other, more interesting trails. She will retrieve a thrown ball or Frisbee, but only to come back and taunt you as she perforates it. Her other favorite game is Escape, which involves tunneling or leaping the backyard fence and then trotting around to the front door to stand—for hours if necessary—until let in. She derives immense satisfaction from Escape. She is about one-half of a guard dog, threatening great violence upon meter readers and repairmen as long as she can't get at them. Once they are inside, she retreats silently to her command center beneath the sofa in the den. After they leave, she resumes barking. Snoop is, in short, a mess.

This is not entirely my fault, as the family adopted Snoop six years ago, when she was already grown. I remember the first time we saw her among the other dogs at the Humane Society—a slender animal, just over knee-high, a mixture of beagle, hound, and God only knows what else, with heavy mascara around her eyes that made her look particularly soulful. It was Saturday, the day of reckoning at animal shelters. On Saturday, the lucky dogs—the puppies, the purebreds, and the ones who've somehow picked up the art of charming humans—get a new home. Many of the remaining dogs, along about Wednesday or Thursday, get a short appointment with a long needle.

My stepdaughter Molly, guided by the infallible radar that children possess for a few years before the world drums it out of them, positioned herself before the dog sitting quietly and alone at the back of the cage. Molly's fingers tightened on the chain-link fence. "That one," she said quietly. I asked why. "Because," she said, "if we don't take her, nobody will." Molly was nine at the time, but nobody's fool. And so this descendant of the wolf came to share our cave.

Some people say otherwise, but I think Snoop knows exactly what we saved her from. Every so often, for no apparent reason, she will rise from her bed beneath the mantel, walk over to my chair, and press her forehead against my knee for a few long seconds. There is something about these moments that can move me to tears. It's Snoop's silent acknowledgment of how fragile life is, how mysterious the mechanism by which we intersect the beings we will love during our brief time on Earth. It is as eloquent as any words ever spoken by a poet. On the other hand, if it happens to be around ten o'clock, it's just her way of telling me that it's time we went for our walk.

PARADISE LOST

Every so often in a man's life, paradise comes calling with a bright red apple. Sometimes there's a worm in it. The knock came last week in the form of a phone call from a guy I'd hunted deer with a couple of years ago. "I've come across the most incredible piece of property on the Eastern Shore. And I've been hunting Maryland the better part of twenty years . . . oh, hell, I guess it's thirty years now." He described a pie-shaped tract of 750 acres between the Blackwater River and Raccoon Creek with a mile and a half of riverfront, incredible duck and goose hunting, loads of deer, turkeys, and about twenty coveys of quail.

There were deer stands and duck blinds already built. A decent cabin featured a woodstove, a main room, two more small rooms with bunks, and an outhouse. A working ATV was included to haul out deer, as was a storage shed containing, among other things, three dozen old goose decoys.

The geography of the place, along with a single gated road providing the only access, rendered it almost unpoachable. The caretaker, a local who'd been there for years, would be happy to stay on in exchange for nothing more than the right to hunt waterfowl. The place was so prime that my friend, Jeff, wasn't interested in leasing it. He was putting together a group of ten guys to buy the property outright. Eight shares had already been spoken for, mostly by fellows he'd hunted with over the years.

"Sounds out of my league," I said. "But tell me the price tag. Just for grins."

"Ten grand up front, then four grand a year for fifteen years. After that, it's paid for. And hunting land on the Eastern Shore will have doubled in value by then. Personally, I'm not in it to make money. I'm thinking I could hunt here for the rest of my life." He told me there was no pressure either way and gave me directions to the property.

I hung up thinking it might as well be $10 million. But I didn't sleep that night. Or the next. I kept thinking about those wide-racked Eastern Shore whitetails. About a place to hunt that was *mine*. And about straining my back lifting a ten-pointer onto the ATV as the twilight faded to black. Such thoughts quickly transform *What if?* into *Why not?*

I drove down forty-eight hours after talking to Jeff, so jazzed I couldn't keep the car anywhere near the speed limit. When I finally parked at the locked gate and double-timed it down the gravel road, I saw the place was everything he'd described. Except for one tiny detail: It was almost all salt marsh with just a few stands of pine. It looked like world-class waterfowl country, all right. But deer? I called Jeff half an hour later. "Tell me again about the whitetail hunting," I said.

"Oh, hell, there's not a whitetail on the place," he said. "It's all sika deer, tons of 'em." My heart sank. I knew about these little cousins of the elk. I'd hunted them myself. They were a perfectly fine game animal; they just weren't whitetails, the creatures that ran through my dreams all year round.

I got back in my car and started punching the SEEK button on my radio. I was surprised at how heavy the sadness was. *You can't lose what you never had*, I tried to tell myself. Then the radio stopped on a station, and through the static there came an unmistakably nasal and plaintive voice—Bob Dylan, singing "Knockin' on Heaven's Door." He was as close as you could get without being inside. And he wasn't going to get inside anytime soon. I started singing along.

ONLY SO MANY

We interrupt this column to bring you the following news bulletin: It's now officially November. God knows what you're doing at the moment. You may have picked up this magazine in the waiting room of the auto service center where three guys with ball-peen hammers are now joyfully working over your radiator. Maybe you're reading it at home, sunk in your La-Z-Boy, carefully rehearsing how you'll tell your mate that cleaning the gutters now is a bad idea in light of a new study showing that a wad of tightly packed leaves actually filters the downspout water, resulting in significantly healthier shrubs. Maybe you're channel surfing, wondering how it is possible to have 328 cable selections and not a single damn one of them worth watching.

Whatever you're doing, stop it. Open the window and listen. The universe is trying to tell you something. *Wake up*, it's whispering. *Get your butt out to the woods. Now, before it's too late.*

To a deer hunter, right now is Christmas, the Fourth of July, and a big, fat tax refund all rolled into one nifty package. It's the annual window when the stars momentarily align and otherwise unkillable old bucks decide to go courting at noon. There's no guarantee that you'll bag one, of course. The only guarantee is the one a carnival barker whispered in my ear one summer evening several decades ago and that I've been hearing ever since: "C'mon, bud. Can't win it if you ain't in it."

Which leads me to the $64,000 question. How many huntable Novembers do you figure you've got left? I'm serious. Forty? Twenty? Ten? Human vanity being what it is, most of us don't like to consider

127

the question too closely. We don't like to admit that a November is coming we won't be part of, and it's natural to push such thoughts away. But we all live on borrowed time. The only November you have for sure is the one passing through your hands right now.

I love everything about the month. I love the today's-gonna-be-the-day hopefulness that suffuses the darkness as I stumble on my way to my stand on the frost-slicked ground. I love the lonesome feeling of watching a leaf that has hung on tight for nine months suddenly decide that this particular gust of wind is the one it wants to straddle for its joyride to the ground. I love the way my heart speeds up when a doe walks nervously into the clearing, glancing back over her shoulder to see if she's still being pursued. I even love standing groggily in front of the convenience-store microwave at four thirty in the morning as I nuke the sausage-egg-cheese biscuits that my doctor has forbidden me to eat. (He recently told me to cut down on cigars, too. I liked that doctor. I'm going to miss him.)

I expect to spend a great deal of this November hunting hard somewhere between fourteen and twenty-five feet up. There's an oak flat about a mile from the nearest road that nobody else seems to be hunting, and I've got six trees picked out to handle varying winds. With a doe already in the freezer, I'm now hunting for glory and antlers. If I kill one, it's going to be a long drag out. I'm looking forward to that particular backache. A man only gets so many Novembers.

AS GOOD AS IT GETS

Just when it seems like everybody you know is sharpening their elbows in the great national Race to the Bottom of the Toilet, you run across a guy who didn't even fill out the entry form. Grayson Chesser lives in Virginia on the Eastern Shore, the narrow spit of land separating the Chesapeake Bay from the Atlantic Ocean. Near as he can tell, his people landed a few miles down the beach in the 1600s and never found a good reason to leave. He lives on land farmed by his great-grandfather and great-great-grandfather.

"You could make a good living here for quite a long time, you know," he says. "Chesapeake was good for fishing, crabbing, oystering. The soil was rich. And the waterfowl hunting was as good as anywhere on earth." Chesser went to Old Dominion University, got a degree in business, and was in the process of losing his shirt farming when he decided to go into decoy carving and guiding full-time.

The decision paid off. Chesser isn't trading in his twelve-year-old truck anytime soon, but he's not going back to farming, either. Of the two hundred or so decoys he makes each year, most are sold before he even gets around to carving them. Collectors snap up a lot, but about 20 percent are bought by guys who have the audacity to put them in the water and hunt over them, as does Chesser himself.

Chesser's decoys—which he carves in species from teal to Canadas—are made of pine, cedar, and other types of wood. (You may remember wood, that hard, fibrous stuff that was once used to make bows, boats, rifle stocks, fishing lures, and countless other needful things. It's now used primarily to frame town houses on what was recently hunting property.)

"It's nice to win ribbons," he says of the contemporary carving scene. "But it's nothing compared to watching some bird—that was maybe born up near the Arctic Circle and can go anywhere in the world it wants—cup its wings and come in to the decoys you made. That's all I ever really wanted out of life, to be able to carve and see that, and to hunt and guide."

It's healthy to do work you love. At fifty-six, Chesser's black hair is untouched by gray. The lower part of his face is permanently tanned. His forehead, usually shielded by his cap, is as white as milk. His mind is quick but his speech is slow, and his movements slower still. There is about him the aura of a historically misplaced person, someone who one day woke to find himself in the twenty-first century, cut his eyes left and right, and decided the best move was not to let it bother him too much.

Chesser killed his first duck at the age of twelve over three of his father's old decoys, including one made of papier-mâché that had a broken bill. "That was it for me," he remembers. "Hunting over decoys was addictive—like how people talk about their first hit of crack."

This was about 1960, just as plastic decoys were replacing wood. The boy began hanging around a number of old carvers, including Miles Hancock, born in 1888, a former market hunter, guide, and all-round waterman. Hancock made a deceptively crude, flat-bottomed decoy that was wonderful to hunt over. "A lot of decoys look good on a mantel but dead once you put them in the water," Chesser explains. "His didn't."

The old-time carvers like Hancock were more than teachers to the boy; they were his heroes. "It was like a kid today meeting sports celebrities. These guys didn't have much book learning, but they'd studied the bay their whole lives. And I thought they were wealthy as kings because they loved their work. One day in his shop, Miles leaned over and said, 'Grayson, don't ever do something for money that you wouldn't do for free.'

"I've never forgotten that."

130

CAMP RULES

Field & Stream, November 2003

1. If a camp member should get lost, the distress signal is three shots, with an interval of 10 seconds between shots. This is so members may distinguish between the truly lost and those who are merely poor marksmen.
2. Nobody over 300 pounds permitted in upper bunks for any reason. One member is still removing plywood splinters from his backside after last year's incident involving Tiny Binstock.
3. No lawyers allowed as guests. Ever. Even if he or she is a blood relation.
4. A dish is deemed clean if the user cannot identify the last foodstuff eaten off of it.
5. Any hunter observed missing a shot under 150 yards at a standing deer will have his shirttail cut off in the presence of all camp members that evening. However, the "Henderson exception" stipulates that no hunter shall have more than 3 shirts destroyed in said manner per day.
6. Polypropylene long johns may be worn for no more than 5 days, or until fumes can be seen emanating from them, whichever comes first.
7. The Saran Wrap over-the-outhouse-seat trick may not be perpetrated after the first week of hunting season.
8. A member shooting a buck under 100 pounds live weight (or doe under 70 pounds) must leave the animal where it drops. A

party including the shooter and a majority of members present will then be assembled to retrieve the deer. Members hauling the carcass will express incredulity at the immense size of the animal and voice the fear of injuring their backs. This is intended to promote camaraderie and group cohesion.

9. A deer taken by a member may gain no more than 2 antler points per hunting year, with a 4-point maximum. To wit, a 6-pointer may be referred to as an 8-pointer the following season, and a 10-pointer the season after, but will never become a 12-pointer no matter how long the hunter lives.

10. Peeing off the porch is prohibited during daylight hours. Peeing off the south end of the porch after dark is permitted provided no members are sleeping in impact zone.

11. Any boy shooting his first buck will, at that evening's dinner, be given the choice of eating either the right or left testicle of the buck. Cook will serve 2 hush puppies of not less than 3 inches diameter each to the boy. After a suitable silence, boy's father or guardian will say, "Hell, I'll make it easy for you, son," and consume one hush puppy whole. He will then smack his lips and declare, "Now that's a good testicle!"

12. All poker debts incurred after 9 P.M. are to be rolled one decimal point to the left. Thus, $100 becomes $10, $1,000 becomes $100, etc.

13. Cell phones will be confiscated and dropped down the most-used hole in the outhouse, to be retrieved at their owners' convenience.

ALL ALONE IN TARPON PARADISE

Before we head out into the steamy afternoon on Nicaragua's remote San Juan River, Philippe Tisseaux wants me to pay a visit to the hospital. Or rather, he wants the hospital to pay a visit to me. "Carlos! *L'hôpital!*" he calls in French to one of the barefoot boys who are always in evidence around the new two-story lodge on almond-wood piles he built here at the junction of the San Juan River and Lake Nicaragua.

Carlos returns with his "hospital"—a wooden box filled with the mangled bodies of large Rapalas. "My wounded," Tisseaux says tenderly. He is a cheerful expat French businessman and angler who fell in love with this place after discovering that he could catch tarpon up to 250 pounds all year round. A few of the lures are merely chipped or gouged, or have had their stainless steel intestines pulled partway out of their butts, but most have been totaled, the metal ripped from their flanks at crazy angles and twisted into corkscrews.

I climb into the boat with Elieser (El-ee-AY-sir), one of Tisseaux's top guides, and young Carlos (whom everyone refers to as Plomo, which, as near as I can tell, means "lard-ass"). We head downriver to a bend that has been productive lately. We pass dugouts with fishermen staking gill nets in the reedy shallows for *guapote*, a toothy, white-fleshed member of the perch family that makes wonderful eating when fried in garlic. Every so often, we pass a shack set on stilts by the water. But there is scarcely another motorized boat in sight—much less anybody fishing for tarpon.

This wasn't the case as late as the mid-1970s, when several tarpon camps operated along the San Juan. But the vicious civil war between strongman Anastasio Somoza and the rebel Sandinistas, then the Sandinistas and the Contras, put a serious damper on business. Thirty years of rest have done wonders for the fishing. There are a lot of big, unpressured tarpon here once again, and it's only a matter of time before the word gets out.

You wouldn't know it today, but this nearly deserted waterway was once one of the most important in the New World. After the Spanish relieved the Incas of their gold, they shipped it east across Lake Nicaragua and 125 miles down the San Juan to the Atlantic. Later, thousands of eager young men reversed the route to California during the Gold Rush. When the Panama Canal was built, the area returned to its former obscurity.

Nicaragua is a big, ruggedly beautiful place without a lot of people telling you what you can and can't do. The lack of infrastructure keeps the country well off the tourist circuit. What this means is if you like clockwork schedules and dependable electricity, stay the hell away.

Lake Nicaragua is the largest in Central America (3,300 square miles, most of it pristine) and contains islands with standing pre-Columbian statues, as well as the world's only freshwater sharks. The country is loaded with wildlife, short of guardrails, and subject to earthquakes, volcanic eruptions, hurricanes, and mudslides. You are pretty much guaranteed not to run into anybody who went to your high school.

Bowing to the King

At the bend in the river, Carlos idles the motor while Elieser and I rig four rods. When the water is low and clear, you can sight-cast to breaking tarpon with fly or conventional tackle. If it's running high and stained, as it is now, the sensible thing is to troll. We're fishing heavy rods and light lines: stout 7-footers with flexible tips, 12-pound test, and 8-foot leaders of 100-pound mono spooled on Catala baitcasting reels. The drags are set just tight enough so that we don't lose line as we ride slowly back up against the current.

You want the drag as loose as possible for the initial strike, then you tighten down slightly for the fight. We make runs of about half a mile up the river, returning each time to the same spot at the bend. Elieser speaks little English, and I less Spanish, but he is fluent in pantomime. He explains that you wait until the rod is well arced before you take it because a tarpon will often bruise a lure once or twice before biting.

Set the hook three times with long, smooth sweeps of the rod at water level, so you don't goad the fish into an early jump. Pull too hard and you'll draw it out of his mouth; too soft and he'll spit it out. Make your move too early or too late, and there will be nobody there. You can screw up in any number of ways, it seems, and have one chance to get it right. If you connect, just keep the pressure on—not hard but constant.

Tisseaux has already told me that a good average is one hookup for every three fish that hit the lure. You can't overpower something as strong as a tarpon on light line. That you can catch *Megalops atlanticus* at all, he says, is because the battle takes place as much in the fish's mind as anywhere else. There comes a moment in each fight, he believes, when the great fish begins to wonder whether its unseen opponent is stronger than it thought. If you're bearing down at this instant, you can break the fish psychologically. This is why two-hundred-plus-pound fish are sometimes boated in fifteen or twenty minutes. If you are not pressuring the fish at this juncture, however, the fish will fight on. And a defiant tarpon will fight longer than you can.

On our fourth pass, the rod with the 4³/₈-inch redhead Rapala bobbles once, twice, and goes down hard. Elieser shouts. I grab the rod and do the triple hookset while he and Carlos scramble to reel in the other lines. Strangely enough, the fish is swimming toward me, and I have to crank as fast as I can to stay connected. Stranger still, it stays hooked. Elieser watches the angle of my line closely, and when he sees it starting to flatten out, he yells what sounds like "Brita! Brita! Brita!" It's an unlikely time to endorse a brand of water filter, but then it occurs to me that the fish must be getting ready to jump.

Tisseaux has talked me through the procedure of "bowing to the king," of lowering the rod tip to accommodate a leaping tarpon. But when I see the silver missile launch itself fifty yards away—see the impossibly vivid fish, clad in bright chain mail, levitated and soaring sidewise over the water—I have a brief out-of-body experience. I stand there mesmerized, watching as if from a parallel universe. The tarpon, exempt from the laws of gravity, is, by many orders of magnitude, bigger, more beautiful, and more violent than anything I've ever hooked.

Suddenly I am aware that the line has gone slack, and that everybody on the boat is busily looking anywhere but at me. My mouth opens as I struggle to join up brain and tongue. At last, demonstrating my keen grasp of the obvious, I blurt out, "Big fish!" Elieser, who has busied himself with some task at the front of the boat, doesn't turn around. But he nods his head once as if he has just heard something encouraging. Perhaps this gringo is not a complete fool after all; he knows when he has lost a big fish. (In the debriefing that follows, I discover that what Elieser had been yelling was not *brita* but *brinca*—"he jumps.")

The One That Didn't Get Away

We head back down for a few more runs before dusk. Pushing my beginner's luck, I hook another tarpon almost immediately, this time on the shad-colored Rapala. Remarkably, again, it stays hooked. I've got nearly one hundred yards of line out, and at first the fish feels like deadweight. Then it starts taking line and swims downriver and toward the far shore. Elieser positions the boat ahead of the fish, motioning for me to keep pressuring. By urging the tarpon to go where he's already headed, we make him change his mind and turn back.

After a few minutes, I gain some line. I'm concentrating so hard on feeling what he's doing that I'm not really watching the water. But now when Elieser shouts "Brinca!" I'm smart enough to drop the rod tip. The fish is a little smaller than the other, but still a good one. My guide thinks he may go 130 pounds, an average tarpon on the San

Juan. When he jumps, I look to the side to avoid being mesmerized. I want this fish.

I am not aware of the moment of doubt in the tarpon's mind, but it must come because just twenty minutes later, Elieser has the leader in his hands. Then he mouth-gaffs the fish and disgorges the lure with pliers. The tarpon stays there briefly, riding in the current alongside the boat, surveying us with a wild, inscrutable eye. Elieser moves him to and fro in the current with a gloved hand. Then with a giant, indifferent shrug the fish disappears beneath the water. Elieser whoops and claps me on the back. It is only now as I finally smile and the adrenaline subsides that I realize I've been fighting the fish with every muscle in my body. But I've done it. I've caught a tarpon.

A Town in Darkness

It is nearly dark as we head back up toward the tiny port town of San Carlos, set where the river flows out of the lake. As we get closer to shore, Carlos and Elieser put on their sunglasses and motion for me to do the same. "Chayul," says Carlos. A moment later we are immersed in an endless cloud of tiny nonbiting insects. There are billions of them, so many that you cover your nose and mouth to avoid filling up on live protein before dinner. Light must increase their concentration, for the entire settlement is dark, a ghost town.

We stumble off the boat and directly under the roof of a cement-floored restaurant where a single red neon Carta Blanca beer sign provides the only illumination. Apparently the bugs can't see red light very well. Beer arrives at the table with a napkin over the mouth of the bottle and a straw poked through the napkin, the local version of bug armor. Meanwhile, night falls. Someone sets down a plate of what seems to be garlic-fried guapote, rice, and beans before me. It is delicious, even if I can't see it. Over-the-top Spanish pop ballads blare from the stereo. For dessert, someone hands me a stiff Flor de Caña rum and Coke with another napkin-and-straw bug guard. I down it and find that I can't stop grinning.

The Death of a Giant

The next day, we motor over into Lake Nicaragua to fish for *guapote*
and rainbow bass, its slightly larger cousin. Elieser outfishes me badly
using the exact same crawfish crankbait, smiling all the time. The
guapote run two or three pounds but hit like freight trains and are
far stronger than largemouths. The rainbow bass, which run four to
eight pounds, are reputed to fight even harder. I don't know, because I
don't get one. But Elieser hooks a six-pounder. When it heads for some
reeds, Carlos strips off his shirt, dives off the boat, and swims right
into the cover to flush the fish out. Elieser yells and dances a little jig
when he gets it aboard. It makes a very tasty dinner.

Back on the San Juan the next day, I pay for my earlier successful hookups by missing three fish, one per hour. Then, at about four
o'clock, the big one hits, once more on a shad Rapala. It takes about
fifty yards of line, then starts swimming back and forth downriver.
I move up to the bow, barefoot and crouched, feet spread wide for
stability. Carlos sneaks up and buckles the fighting belt around my
waist, and I jam the rod butt into it. Every time I feel the fish change
directions, I counter so that I'm always pulling back across the length
of his body.

The weight and strain on the rod signify a fish bigger than the one
I landed, and even bigger than the one I lost. He takes line at will, and
when Elieser shouts, "Brinca!" I see that the fish is so heavy he can't
get his whole body out of the water. He jumps, but only two-thirds of
him appears. Then he crashes back like a falling tree. Even so, I bow
to him, so far that I nearly lose my balance and go into the drink.

I try to calm down and force myself to concentrate. You don't "play"
a fish this big; you just attempt to keep from breaking off. When he
jumps again, only half his body emerges. After a while, I start to gain
on him. Twice he comes close to the boat, but when he sees us he
surges. On the third time, Elieser snatches the leader and gaffs him in
the mouth. The fish lies glistening alongside the boat just under the
water, wide and long enough to walk on.

My guide looks inside the tarpon's mouth and shakes his head rue-fully. He has taken the lure deep, down into his gills, and the fight has torn them up. If we release him he won't make it, but there are folks along the river who can use every ounce of the meat. It takes three of us on the long-handled gaff to haul him over the rail into the bow of the boat, whereupon we all hightail it to the stern. Elieser says he'll go about 185 pounds.

The great fish lies there, occasionally slamming his body around, sending scales spinning across the deck like big silver medallions. There is enough power in that body to break your leg and then some. I watch him die, watch him change colors as he goes, a veil of purple descending over his silver scales, the black of his back deepening. The colors are fleeting and beautiful, like something that burns too bright to last long in the ordinary world. The moon in his eye sinks away to nothing, and the eye goes cold. I am glad to have caught him but sadder than I ever would have expected to be the agent of his death. And I am afraid to go near him until I'm sure the last spark of life has left his body.

We stop at one of the shacks on the river, where a small boy and I wordlessly drag him up the path with a rope, like you would a deer, to where his father sits on his haunches sharpening a knife on a stone. His wife and four more children watch shyly from a distance. I shake the boy's hand, and his father thanks me. We walk back to the boat as the sky darkens. In my pocket is my trophy, a single round scale, thick and hard as a toenail, flecked with silver. We head back up the river. Five hundred yards from the unlit town of San Carlos, Elieser gives the signal and we all put on our sunglasses.

GOOD COP, BALD COP

Not long ago, curious to see firsthand how local government wastes my tax dollars, I hitched a ride with the only game warden in the District of Columbia. Actually, any police officer can enforce game laws, but over the years it's been Dennis Hance who has devoted himself to the task. If you call up the D.C. Police and ask to speak to a game warden, he's the guy who answers. If President Bush decided to fish the Potomac without a license, Hance would be the guy to write him up.

The department public information officer had told me that due to liability issues, members of the press were prohibited from riding in the patrol boat. So when Hance invited me aboard, I slapped myself in the head, inducing a bout of temporary amnesia, and jumped in. Almost immediately, Hance, who bears a passing resemblance to Harrison Ford, pulled up to a guy fishing from shore. "See your fishing license, please?" he asked pleasantly.

The angler in question, like most inner-city residents, had the ability to detect hostility or condescension from a cop in parts-per-billion concentrations. He glared at Hance. "I know who you are," he muttered. "You gave me a hard time 'bout not having one last week." I stood there and tried to look like Hance's tough but taciturn backup. The guy's eyes swept over me, and I could sense him thinking, *At least I don't have to worry about the bald guy.*

"Then it ought to be easy for you to show it to me now," Hance said.

The angler's radar kept pinging away. But the strangest thing was happening. It was coming up blank. "All right," he said. "I bought one after last time, but I ain't got it on me."

Hance ran a sniff test. He believed the guy. "Look. You know it's a fifty-dollar fine. This is number two. I'm gonna cut you a break, okay? I'm gonna be back here and so are you, so let's not make trouble for each other."

And then the guy actually smiled. It wasn't so much the words—it was the vibe. Hance has something they don't teach in the police academy: It's called the common touch. And if you could bottle it, you could name your own price. "You're all right, man," the guy said.

This encounter, lasting all of one minute, blew me away. If it had been me, I'd have tried the soft approach, too. Only the moment it started to go south, I'd have turned Clint Eastwood on the guy: reached for my Glock, cuffed him, and demonstrated why nobody messes with Officer Heavey.

"Easiest thing in the world to be a hard-ass," Hance told me. "The trick is to leave 'em smiling. That guy'll remember me. And I bet he'll have his license the next time I see him."

Lest you think Hance is someone who takes the easy way out of a situation, you should know that he has been cited three times for risking his life while trying to save people who were drowning.

What I like about the guy is that if he thinks you made an honest mistake, he'd rather help you than punish you. But if you're deliberately breaking the law, don't come crying for mercy. Once, he found two men in possession of 138 out-of-season rockfish. He wrote them up for the maximum, a total of $27,600.

Later that day, we came across a man and his daughter pushing bicycles. His was loaded down with rods and a five-gallon bucket full of herring and perch. These fish were legal, and the man had a license. "Do you have any more fish, sir?" Hance asked. The fellow shook his head. Hance walked past him and pulled a stringer of carp and channel cats from beneath some bushes. "Sir, I saw you put these there not two minutes ago." The limit on channel cats is three a day, and the guy had six. Hance wrote the man up for three $100 violations. The little girl's face was a stone mask the whole time. Hance finally leaned down and said, "If you don't smile, I'm gonna have to ride your bike." The vehicle under discussion: a pink Barbie model. That brought a grin.

Hance reflected on the encounter. "Was it tough to give that guy a three-hundred-dollar fine? Yeah. Was it fair? Yeah. He wouldn't have hidden those fish if he didn't know it was illegal. Now the word will get out to everyone he knows that you can't take too many fish. And when his little girl grows up, there'll still be fish here."

Hance's days on the water may be numbered. Because he's good at what he does, he's up for a promotion. So a guy with consummate people skills and knowledge of the river may end up driving a squad car or, worse, a desk. The good news is that D.C.'s police department, like most bureaucracies, can be counted on to screw up a good part of the time. For the sake of the fish, let's hope it malfunctions correctly. It would be a gross miscarriage of justice to elevate such a deserving public servant.

III

NOT ENTIRELY UNTRUE
STORIES, 2005–2009

THE 2005 ELMER AWARDS

"Be vewy, vewy quiet." With these words, Elmer Fudd invariably seals his doom. He can't stand playing the fool, but he is fit for no other role. The universe delights in taunting him. Truth is, there's a little bit of Elmer in all of us. And a whole lot of him in a few of us. We here at *F&S* salute those brave souls. They make the rest of us look far more competent than we really are.

The Opportunity Knocks Award

Bryan Parker picked the wrong place to spotlight his first deer. The Hartselle, Alabama, man, twenty, was driving home with a Smith & Wesson pistol he'd bought for his father when he saw a deer frozen in his headlights and shot at it. He happened to be right in front of the Morgan County sheriff's house at the time. Sheriff Greg Bartlett, who at first thought someone was shooting at his home, chased but lost Parker's truck. Parker was arrested thirty minutes later at his home after the sheriff identified the vehicle. He was charged with hunting after dark, hunting on a public road, hunting from a vehicle, and hunting without a permit. "I've never toted a gun," he said. "When I saw the deer, I said, 'Oh, I've got a pistol.' I must have been out of my mind."

The Price of Marriage Award

Edwin Nichols was a little too focused on the flying carp for his own good. At least that's what his wife, Vivian, would say. The two were on the Missouri River with a friend last summer when a silver carp leapt from the water and whacked her in the face, breaking her nose. While her husband and the other man were whooping it up, trying to grab the thrashing windfall, Vivian fell back across the center console, blood streaming from her nostrils. "They didn't realize I had been hurt," she said. "They were saying, 'I can't believe this fish jumped into the boat!' I'm going, 'Hey, guys!'" No word as to which couch Edwin slept on that night.

The Let Me Show You How It's Done Award

Stalking wary whitetails requires three things: patience, stealth, and a sibling who agrees with you. Gregory Moss, forty, and his brother, Charles, thirty-five, were hunting private land near Zanesville, Ohio, when they found themselves in less than total agreement about how to proceed. The discussion turned into an argument; the argument became a wrestling match over who got to carry the shotgun; and the wrestling match caused the gun to discharge. Gregory was treated for a head wound at a local hospital. He declined to press charges, saying the shooting was accidental. There was no word on whether their mother had grounded them.

The We're Gonna Need a Bigger Boat Award

Intrepid Floridian Sherridan Bouges, forty-seven, was fishing with live shrimp on Lake Harris last February when he hooked an unfamiliar critter that caused him great trepidation. It had sharp, spiny fins, a menacing mouthful of teeth, and what looked like heavy body armor. Who knew what a fish like that could do to a man? "It scared me," he later admitted. Fortunately for Sherridan, his mother was in the boat. "He was afraid to bring it in," crowed the elderly Esther Bouges. "I told him to pull it in with a net." The fish, all twelve inches of it, was identified as a Plecostomus, a sucker-mouthed scavenger that feeds primarily on algae and is therefore common in aquariums. Nancy Tucker, manager of the nearby Animal World Pet Center, said somebody had probably dumped this one into the lake from a fish tank.

The Everything I Need to Know I Learned from the Terminator Award

As president of the Tift County, Georgia, school board, Richard Golden knows that it's not enough to say the right things; you have to follow through with deeds. Otherwise kids will see that you are not sincere. That's why when he discovered Derek Pettiford, twenty-two, fishing on his property, he not only threatened to kill him—he also shot up his car. Pettiford said he saw no posted signs along the pond off U.S. 319 but admits that he should have realized the land belonged to someone. "But I didn't feel like I was causing any dangerous harm," he said. Golden, ever mindful of his position as an educator and role model, begged to differ. He used a shotgun to discipline the car in the radiator, windshield, hood, and trunk. He pled guilty to pointing a firearm at another person.

The You Can Arrest Any Citizen if You Try Hard Enough Award

The owner and the manager of Bellar's Place, Indiana's largest private deer-hunting preserve, were just trying to make hunting less troublesome for their clients. But try telling that to overzealous federal officials. Russell Bellar, forty-nine, and Hinds Jones, thirty-six, are facing more than thirty felony charges just because they let hunters measure a buck's rack before the selected deer was tranquilized, led into a pen, and "hunted" for as much as twenty thousand dollars. According to the U.S. Fish and Wildlife Service, since 2001 the two men have conducted more than fifty of these deer . . . hunts. Authorities said their investigation also found illegal weapons, unlicensed hunters, and the use of bait. Bellar, a developer, denies that he charged hunters huge sums to kill particular deer, saying they had merely paid bed-and-breakfast fees.

He dismissed the case—each of the thirty felonies carries a potential five years in prison or a $250,000 fine—as a political vendetta by the state department of natural resources. "This is all political stuff; that's all it is," said Bellar on the day of the raid. "They are against anyone that raises whitetail deer."

The Shouldn't Be Allowed Outdoors Award

Golfer Roy Williamson, sixty, hit a tee shot on a Georgia course that ended up in a wetland area. "I saw my ball pretty much in plain view," he said. "Unfortunately, it was being tended to by a rattlesnake that I didn't see." Williamson said that as he retrieved the ball he felt what he thought was a brier scratch his right temple. Then he saw blood and a rattlesnake he insists was six and a half to seven feet long. His brother, son, and brother-in-law (apparently golfers go out in groups because it's safer that way) came running to his screams. He remembers their bringing him to the clubhouse, but when he was next aware of anything at all, three days had passed. Although the snake bit him twice, he will live to chase the little white ball again. Doctors' greatest concern was the bite on the forehead, alarming because of its proximity to the brain, even in golfers.

ON TRACK

I woke the day before Easter to find an inch of fresh snow outside and the house echoing with the kind of silence that means your child is playing with matches, putting epoxy on the dog's feet, or seeing how far she can stick her tongue into an electrical outlet. Picking up the trail of powdered cocoa on the living room rug, I followed it around the dining room table and into the kitchen. Emma was humming happily and using a crescent wrench to blend equal parts cocoa, skim milk, and maple syrup in a mahogany salad bowl. Busted in midstroke, brown smudges covering the CHOOSE A CAREER IN LAWN ENFORCEMENT T-shirt that she has adopted as a nightgown, she stared up at me with the pinprick pupils of a girl high on sugar and caffeine. I surveyed the map of maple syrup drippings and cocoa on the floor. The dog chose this moment to rouse itself and shake, filling the kitchen with a fine brown fog. Like a chicken that continues to dance even though its head has been cut off, my daughter reflexively offered an excuse. "I was hungry," she explained.

Parenting books say that disciplining a child in an altered state of consciousness is counterproductive. They also say that direct contact with the natural world is the only way to convince a kid that the best places to play are not necessarily the ones with the most pixels per square inch. With this in mind, I handed Emma a roll of paper towels and said, "Look at me. Clean this up. Every last bit of it. Then we're gonna go track deer before this snow melts."

It took a moment for the fact of her escape to sink in. Then I heard a shout of "Yay!" followed by the slap of wet paper towels on linoleum as I went upstairs. An hour later, we were tramping through a stand of thirty-foot-high bamboo in a pocket park between million-dollar homes in a nearby suburb. Bamboo is not native to North America, but bucks rub it just the same, leaving what look like hastily scrawled notes to one another on this nearly barkless grass. Emma quickly got stuck in the undergrowth of briers.

"You need a stick to beat those things down," I told her. I cut one of the rubbed stalks with the saw on my Leatherman, then cut a length for each of us. Emerging from the bamboo, we jumped seven bedded deer not twenty-five yards away. They rose and hightailed it across the road.

"Whoa!" Emma shouted. "I saw a buck!" There are, of course, no antlered deer in the woods in April. Somehow I stifled my automatic impulse to correct her. The goal, after all, was to whet Emma's interest in the outdoors.

"Cool!" I exclaimed. "How many points?"

"Seven," she said matter-of-factly. "I mean eleven."

We knelt to examine the beds, dry ovals of compressed leaves. We picked up white belly hairs and released them into the wind. We looked at the exploded dirt and snow granules behind the tracks of their initial leaps. Then Emma took over, finding and showing her student each new print. "Look, another one!" she cried over and over. "Whoa, this one's huge! That's the buck!" I was beside myself with happiness. My child was getting hooked on the primal energy of the nondigital world, on deer, and on tracking, the world's first and best game of connect-the-dots. And she was already showing the exceptional imaginative powers, also known as lying, necessary to hunters.

These moments of blissful father-daughter communion, I've learned, are as rare as free beer at birthing classes. Sure enough, the drugs wore off minutes later and Emma crashed. I gave her a juice box and cheese sticks, but they didn't pack the same jolt. She started to cry and said that this whole endeavor was stupid. She demanded to go home. Now. I hoisted her onto my shoulders, removed her pink rain boots to rub her feet, and discovered she had decided to go sockless. Her toes were as cold as ice, so I stuck my gloves on her feet. I looked as if I were carrying an angry little puppet through the woods on my back. She grimly hung on to her stick, which banged me in the ribs every third step as we looped back toward the car.

"And I'm never going tracking with you ever again!" she blurted out, as if making me angry might somehow lessen her own suffering. By now my own euphoria had worn off. I strapped my child into her car seat. As I stamped the snow off my boots in preparation for the long and whining road home, I was primed to deny television time if she so much as whimpered again. It was at this moment that Emma suddenly whispered, "Daddy! Buck! Big one. Over there!" I instinctively turned my head. "Aw, you just missed him," she lied. My heart, almost against its will, softened at the speed with which she could morph from irritant to huntress, and at how easily she could pull me with her. I asked how many points he had. "Sixteen," she said solemnly. "I'm serious, Daddy. He really did. We have to come back here."

"We will, monk," I told her. "I want to see him, too."

LOST IN THE WOODS

The crossbeams of my world have been buckling lately, and as is my custom in such situations, I've been spending a lot of time in the woods. It's too early for fishing and too late for hunting, so I've been after sheds. This has given me time to think about a persistent problem in my life—the great number of people and things that don't live up to my expectations. At any given moment, I could name dozens of examples. Here are three: 1) the person who tells me that setting up a digital trail camera is "intuitive," 2) anyone who brings cranberry-flavored beer to my house expecting me to drink it, and 3) people who get divorced.

I know that divorce, like fruit-flavored beer, is a fact of life and that many otherwise honorable people get divorced. Still, I've always believed it was the quitter's path. The way I see it, if you stand in church before God and somebody's fat aunt with a video camera and declare, "Till death do us part," you don't get out of it before one of you is pushing up BioLogic Full Draw (a proven blend of cultivars that contains an astonishing 38 percent crude protein). And so the fact that I myself am in the midst of a divorce poses a dilemma: I must either admit to being a hypocrite or add my own name to the list of people who, in my personal opinion, fail to measure up.

The details of my marital breakdown are not particularly juicy. Nobody lied, cheated, or tried to become an Amway distributor. If there was anything out of the ordinary, it was the event that finally set the split in motion, which just shows that no one ever completely understands his own heart. In my case, the trigger was the death of my best friend's father, Lou, whom I'd known and loved since I was a boy. He was ninety-five. He'd lived about as full a life as a man can. His death should have come as no shock. And yet that's exactly what it was. It turned over something deep inside me as surely as tumblers align in a lock when the right key is inserted. I suddenly recognized what had been staring me in the face for quite some time. The marriage wasn't working, and despite counseling, I didn't know how to make it work. I asked for a divorce.

Rattling around at night in a nearly empty rental house, replaying the words I'd slung and those slung back, I felt like a ghost, like a man so lightly tethered to this earth that a good breeze might come along and blow him into the next world as easily as it would a column of smoke. More mornings than not, I'd sit down to a stack of work and find myself unable to focus, unwilling to try, and not particularly heedful about any consequences I might be courting. Then I'd drive until I found some likely-looking woods and walk south-facing ridges and fence lines and deer trails until it was too dark to see. I got cut up pretty badly the first few times.

After a while I also started noticing footprints headed to the same places I went. Hey, I thought, somebody else is getting a divorce, too. The only strategy I could come up with was to look in places others weren't willing to go. I up-armored myself in Filson Tin Cloth chaps and jacket, long, leather-palmed work gloves, and a heavy stick to beat down the briers. For the really thick brush, I took a machete I'd filed very sharp. I wasn't finding many sheds, but the few I did were good ones, enough to keep me coming back. More important, the woods were the only place where I understood the rules anymore, the only place my body seemed to regain its weight and substance. Sometimes, after a few hours there, I would remember that millions had been through the same horror and survived. Occasionally I could even imagine being happy, feeling whole again. And every so often, when I stumbled upon an antler and thought of an old, wild buck standing there a week or a month earlier, when I touched that smooth, hard shed, I would feel blessed for a moment. It was like I'd found all the wildness and ancient knowledge of the woods distilled and compressed into a tangible thing. At that instant, the fact that I was alive, that I was able to have a life full of sorrow and loss, joy and experience, was itself a miracle.

This happened to me just last week. It was my turn to have my daughter Emma the next Friday, which was forecast to be balmy. We had already planned our first cookout at my new place. When I got home from the woods, I called Jane and asked if she would like to join us.

She seemed taken aback for a minute, but we talked for a bit and at last she accepted. "Bill?" she said as we prepared to hang up. "Thank you. Really."

I put the shed, a five-pointer, on the table with the others. And felt good about myself for the first time in a long while.

STALKING THE HIGHLANDS

I'm no stranger to unusual stalking situations, but this is definitely the first time I've had whortleberries in my pants. I am crawling down a 50-degree slope right behind my guide, Niall Rowantree. Right on my heels is gillie Steven Grant, eighteen, dragging the padded rifle case behind him. We are low-crawling through the heather or gorse or whatever the hell you call the wet, tundralike stuff covering the Scottish Highlands, trying to keep from getting busted by the dozens of red deer scattered across this mountainside. I don't know about the others, but I'm doing more sliding than crawling. To stop, I have to stiffen my arms and shove them into the ground before me while flexing my toes to vertical and dragging them like anchors.

Meanwhile, the farther we travel in this manner, the more vegetation finds its way into my clothes. Every time Niall (pronounced "Neal") stops to assess our progress and the disposition of the surrounding deer, we rear-end one another with all the precision of the Three Stooges trying to burgle a house. I use these occasions to retrieve handfuls of herbage from my pants.

We are sneaking on a big red stag, an eight-pointer, lying on a bench several hundred yards below us. At least I think he's still below us. The weather was glorious this morning, when we were glassing the hills from the road below. Since then, curtains of mist and pattering rain have begun moving through from the southwest, reducing visibility to eighty yards.

A Land of Myth and Legends

I have come to Scotland on the advice of my dentist. He told me that for the price of an outfitted elk hunt, you could fly here, sleep in a clean bed each night, eat like a king, hunt the legendary Highlands, and almost be guaranteed success on red stag. These deer, the largest land mammal native to the United Kingdom, are smaller cousins of the American elk.

For a long time, the beasts were reserved for royalty and landed gentry. Today, they attract English, German, and Scandinavian hunters, as well as an increasing number of Americans who, like my dentist, have discovered that red stag offer a challenging and satisfying hunt. I searched on Google, asked around, and eventually found Corrour (Ka-RAH-wer).

My first impression as I leave Glasgow and drive north into the Highlands is one of disbelief. Given that the whole of the United Kingdom is a little smaller than Oregon, I figured the Highlands would have the character of a good-size American theme park—you know, a few castles and golf courses, deep-fried Snickers bars (a national specialty, I've been told), and tacky little shops selling plaid T-shirts. Wrong. The "road" from the highway to the lodge and cottage where I'm staying, for instance, is twelve miles long and takes forty-five minutes to navigate. One false move and you'd end up four hundred feet below in a stream gushing along like a loose fire hose.

The estate itself is fifty-two thousand acres and more isolated than you'd imagine was possible in Europe. Before the access road was finished in 1972, the only way to get here was by train via the tiny Corrour rail station, the highest and most remote in Britain.

It's not hard to see why. Big, stark, and strangely compelling, the countryside is nearly deserted, with a population density rivaling that of Papua New Guinea. This place zeroes in on your psyche and grabs hold. What I'm experiencing is not déjà vu, the sense of having been here before, so much as the feeling you get when you meet another person and intuitively sense that you already know each other's stories. Maybe it's ancestral.

This is, after all, the WASP Mesopotamia, the place from which my forebears and those of millions of other Americans were cast out or fled when the Highland clans, the last vestiges of the feudal system in Europe, collapsed in the eighteenth century. Niall says that nobody lived here year-round in the old times. The winters are too brutal. It was only in 1899, when the wealthy classes created by the Industrial Revolution took up the gentlemanly sport of stag hunting, that a grand estate house was built, complete with four stalkers' cottages.

"The clans would send their cattle up here to graze each summer, tended by the women, children, and old men. Younger men farmed the glens below. The Road to the Isles, the route people from the Western Isles used for centuries to drive their cattle to market at Falkirk, runs right through the property. Almost every hill here has a legend or myth associated with it. It's all stinking with history."

A Terrible, Yet Oddly Appealing, Scent

In the morning, through Niall's ridiculous-looking collapsible telescope, we see at least three groups of deer from the road, including a nice buck feeding alone and into the wind below a rocky bowl. The telescope is just window dressing, I'm sure, something to complement the stereotypical image of the rustic Highland guide. I say so. Niall shakes his head.

"Pure practicality. I loathe high-power spotting scopes. It's always windy here and you can't hold them still. And they weigh a ton. Twenty-power is all you really need in this country. Plus it fits in my pocket." He shows me how to steady it—right hand resting on the bones of my eye socket and cradling the eyepiece, left hand holding the objective lens, a car door or shooting stick as a brace. Suddenly I can count the tines on an animal half a mile away. I hand it back, impressed.

"Right," he says, collapsing the thing and tucking it in a pocket. "Feel like stalking him?" He doesn't have to ask twice.

To get in position, the three of us drive on down the road well past the deer, get the Argo eight-wheeler off the trailer, and ride it bucking and kicking up the mountain to get altitude and the wind in our favor. It takes several hours—and some rough walking. The ground is so uneven that I have to play the age card and commandeer Niall's ram-horn-handled walking stick or risk a fall.

"Hell, you do this every day," I growl, doing my best David E. Pet-zal. "Besides, you're barely forty." While I'm appropriately dressed in a Cabela's Dry Plus rain suit that performs admirably when vertical, we're not spending much time upright. When the mist lifts momentarily, we see stags and hinds not 150 yards distant. Red deer can spot a man a mile away, Niall says, and they know it's hunting season. Every move we make is careful and slow. When Niall freezes, Steven and I do, too.

All this crawling gets to be warm work after a while, and when a slight updraft hits, it wafts a mixture of my own familiar BO and the aromatic scents of the crushed flowers and plants inside my duds. I smell not unlike a wet mule sprayed with herbal bathroom freshener. It's a scent that might appeal to a certain kind of woman. But she would probably look like Petzal.

Why the Kilt Was Invented

Niall has stressed from the outset that this kind of stalking requires close, careful travel. "The only animal that walks abreast is man. An alarmed red deer runs a long way. If we go single file, one that just gets a glimpse may take us for another deer." He should know. The Rowantrees have been in this part of the Highlands for centuries, since the days of the warrior-clan subsistence farmers. A nearby crag even bears the Gaelic version of the family name.

He motions behind his back with two fingers for me to slide up even with him, then hands me the binocs. "He's facing us," he whispers. "About a hundred and sixty meters. Get ready." It takes me a while to pick out the stag, but he's there, alone and bedded, the wind at his back. Steven uncases the Sako .308 with an 8x scope and a Reflex T8 suppressor at the muzzle. (The sound-reducing device is the law here, required to protect the eardrums of working guides. Niall says it also improves accuracy and reduces recoil without affecting range.)

I set up the rifle on its bipod at my feet and twist around to get the stag in the scope. "Don't shoot until he stands," Niall whispers. "You've got a so-so kill shot, and you'd chew up too much meat. Standing will give you a better angle on both counts. We'll wait. When you do this right, they never know what hit them." I can't help but respect the man. It's obvious that he loves to hunt. He could easily end his day's work now by allowing me to take a killing shot, but ethical shortcuts, however slight, don't appear to be part of the deal.

Downhill and feet-first is an awkward position to shoot from, not to mention a good way to put a hole in your foot. Also, my pants are steadily sliding up as the minutes pass, creating a massive whortleberry-scented wedgie. It strikes me that it could have been precisely this situation that led to the invention of the kilt, which suddenly sounds eminently practical.

The stag, it seems, has very few appointments today, for he stays bedded. While we wait, Niall breaks out sandwiches, and we pass around his thermos of hot tea. Somehow, he and Steven both manage the trick of wearing tweed knickers and matching Sherlock Holmes–style deer-stalker hats without looking as if they've wandered off the set of *Queer Eye for the Straight Guy*. The fact that Niall is built like an oak might be part of it. Frankly, I don't know how Steven pulls it off. He's a quiet boy; it's his boss who tells me Steven was raised on a farm and is an expert sheep shearer and champion Highland dancer. He passed up a good-paying job on an Australian sheep farm to come here. One day he hopes to be a full-fledged stalker like Niall, and to count one of the four stalking areas—or "beats"—on Corrour as his personal kingdom.

How Scotland Nearly Died

The weather clears a bit, though the wind remains. To take my mind off how wet my butt is, I ask about the land's history. The Scottish Highlands, my guide explains, are, for all their beauty, a collapsed ecosystem. As late as six hundred years ago, they were covered in Scots pine, aspen, juniper, and oak. Not so long ago, European brown bears, wolves, and lynx kept the deer populations in check. There were also beaver, hares, wild boar, and polecats. Over the years the forests were cut down and the predators disappeared.

After the English troops came and the clan system collapsed, the destruction escalated. The feudal commons became private land. Local small farmers were forcibly evicted and their homes burned down in the infamous "clearances" to make room for profitable sheep farms. The livestock quickly overgrazed what was left. The decayed vegetation became acidic peat, which supports only a narrow range of plant life.

The heyday of gentlemen's sporting lodges didn't arrive until the 1890s and was nearly over by the 1930s. During those glory days, wealthy European sportsmen arrived by private railcar, then boarded a steamboat and motored three miles down Loch Ossian to the lodge. Currently the estate is owned by a publicity-shy Swedish couple who did rather well designing and marketing cartons for milk and orange juice. They are interested in trying to balance continued hunting with restoring the biodiversity of the Highlands.

Taking the welfare of the land itself into consideration is a relatively new concept here, a break with the long tradition of exploiting nature for immediate benefit and damn whoever comes next. It means not only harvesting larger numbers of deer but also reinvigorating the herds by taking animals other than the largest and healthiest, another break with the traditional trophy mentality. That idea has led the owners to build a state-of-the-art processing facility on the premises to market its own Taste of the Wild brand of gourmet venison. The idea is to capture more of the profits and jobs for the local economy.

Hunters Make Good Soldiers

Looking over this country, you can't help but wish them well. For all the indignities it has suffered, this remains a magnificent hunk of the earth. Wild brown trout, native pike up to thirty pounds, and otters swim in the lakes. The moors still hide red and black grouse, ptarmigan, kestrels, and golden eagles. There are still foxes and pine martens. Distilleries that produce some of the world's most sought after whiskies, Oban and Talisker, are nearby. I'm already hooked, wondering how I can come up with a way to stay longer than I planned.

"This country has always been good at raising three things: bards, poets, and warriors," Niall tells me. Both his father and grandfather were stalkers. His grandfather also served as a sniper in World War II in the famed Lovat Scouts, a force composed of Highlanders. Circa 1900, the British Army thought it was taking a chance on accepting the rough Scotsmen into its sophisticated ranks. It soon discovered, however, that with generations of experience in fighting, stalking, and thriving in rough country, the men made superb soldiers. They gained a reputation as legendary warriors, scouts, spies, guides, and horsemen.

The Lovat Scouts were the forerunner of the elite British SAS. Niall's own father was sent into the Royal Navy to learn a trade, "but he didn't like it, so he came back to the Highlands to be a stalker." I ask what he did in the navy. "Well, actually, he got a PhD in nuclear physics." When I look at him skeptically, he shrugs. "We're not a dumb people," he explains. "We just never had a lot of money." Niall works seven-day weeks for months on end as head guide and manager of the estate, and suffers more than the occasional fool client in the process. It's the only way he can stay on the land he grew from.

"It's not always easy, being a rich man's plaything," he'll confide over several wee drams of the Cragganmore single malt that I found out he likes—by asking the office manager—before coming. (Always a good idea to keep your guide happy.) "But we Highlanders have long been dispossessed in our own country."

The Winter of '89

My scope is still on the deer, but he's on stag time, happy to lie there and chew his cud. Niall doesn't want to try anything tricky like throwing a stone to get him to stand for the shot. He's a pro, and a pro knows how to wait when the situation calls for it. To pass the time, I ask when he knew he wanted to go into the family line of work.

"I've been obsessed with deer," he says, "since I can remember," ever since he saw his father bringing stags down out of the mountains after dark on specially bred hill ponies. Deer have been his life. He took whatever work he could find to stay around them, working as a forestry ranger and then as a contractor controlling deer populations for both private landowners and the state.

He tells me about the winter of 1989, when hundreds of deer died from starvation and exposure, the result of overgrazing, destruction of the forests where they sheltered, and populations spiraling ever upward. Ironically, to save the animal he loved, he killed an average of one thousand of them a year for the next six years.

"It was sad, but it had to be done." His gun of choice was a .308 Mannlicher SSG, and he speaks admiringly of cartridges like the .300 WSM and .338 Lapua for long-range work.

"It was a bloody way to learn, but learn I did: how to tell what they're going to do next by what they're doing now and how they're doing it, how to identify the dominant stag or hind in a group at first glance, which way and in which order they'll run when alarmed, the best way to use the ground to your advantage, tricks about the wind . . ." His voice trails off, as if he's revisiting things he'd rather not see again.

Ninety minutes later, after my limbs have gone to sleep and come back several times, the stag finally stands, shakes itself dry, and then, as if offering himself, turns broadside. I squeeze the trigger, and when I recover my sight picture he's down. "Good shot," says Niall. I remove the magazine, clear the chamber, and hand the rifle back to Steven, who cases it and hustles off for the Argo.

Niall and I make our way down. We gut the animal, leaving the heart and liver in the carcass, which will be logged in and individually tagged at Corrour's processing plant. I admire the lyre-shaped antlers, smaller than an elk's, bigger than a whitetail's. He's handsome and hardy, with a belly round from fattening up for the coming rut. A stiff red fur ruff encircles the throat as if to protect that vulnerable area from the stag's primordial enemy, the wolf. Niall estimates he weighed about 220 pounds on the hoof.

Stroking the stag's side, I murmur my thanks and my apology for having stolen his life, and again admire the graceful antlers. My guide says this one is between seven and nine years old, a bit past his prime, a good candidate for the hunt.

Basin of the Bones

As we wait for Steven to bring the Argo, I notice a tree trunk half buried in the peat and gesture at it. "That's a Scots pine, probably a thousand years old, from the forest that was once here," Niall says. "The peat preserves things." He shows me a knob on the blackened trunk where stags, which were originally woodland animals but have adapted to the loss of the forests, have rubbed their antlers, revealing the reddish wood beneath. He looks up at the rim of the mountains above us and says something in Gaelic.

"It means Basin of the Bones," he says. "The story is that a fellow stole some cattle belonging to one of the clan chieftains. When he heard the chieftain was after him, he claimed he hadn't stolen them but knew who had, and would see they were punished and the cattle returned. He gave the cattle back, then murdered some people here and scattered their bones so it would look as if they'd been eaten by wolves. Hence the name." It's a grisly tale, and faithful enough to human nature to make you believe there's at least a germ of truth to it.

Steven shows up with the Argo, and we swing the stag aboard. Driving back toward the lodge, Niall makes a slight detour to show me Loch Treig, a nine-mile-long lake bordering Corrour. "The water level is up, or you could see part of a crannog, a fortified island made from piling up stones, where people built their houses to be safe from attack. This one dates from the Bronze Age." He points across the lake to a somewhat sinister-looking saddle with nearly sheer walls rising on both sides.

"This road we're on is one of the old cattle droves, and it goes right through there. Place named Black Mouth in Gaelic." It fits. It's a dark, creepy little passage. Niall asks if I've ever heard the term blackmail. Of course, I say. "Well, you're looking at the place it comes from. There was a band of cutthroats who controlled this place. You paid a toll to go through or suffered the consequences."

One Stag? Coming Right Up

We're bumping our way back to the lodge in the Land Rover to check in the stag when the sun, absent nearly all day, focuses a shaft of light atop a far mountain. Some kinds of beauty pierce your heart like a pain, and this moment is one. These ancient, stark hills may be the ruins of great forests, but they're lovely all the same.

The next morning, I'm around when Niall meets a just-arrived client, a wealthy man from the Netherlands and his son, who doesn't hunt but wants to accompany his father. The man is upset because the airline lost his rifle. It's his favorite, a double in some elephant-killing caliber, very old and expensive. Also, his son needs to return by 4 P.M. to take an important conference call. Niall tells him he'll do his best, and when the fellow leaves, he offers up a silent prayer that the rifle is not found anytime soon. It may be hard fitting it with the suppressor, and the rifle will likely either be unscoped or knocked off zero by now. Much better to use the lodge's .270.

By lunch they are back with a large-racked ten-pointer, one that was apparently just over the hill as breeding stock, riding in the back of the Argo. The man is beaming and very excited, clapping Niall on the shoulder.

"Mein Gott!" he exclaims. "He is a devil, this one! We approached downwind. Downwind! And when I shot, they ran toward us before mine fell."

Niall takes me aside and draws me a quick diagram. The stags were indeed upwind, but grazing in a high saddle about a kilometer away. But he noticed that they were grazing slowly toward one side of the saddle.

"So they were moving into the area where the peaks of the saddle cause the wind to swirl. And they don't like swirling wind, don't feel safe there. I was betting they'd keep on going in that direction until they got to a steadier breeze. And in any saddle, there's a place where the eddies create a current of air flowing against the prevailing wind direction. That's what I was banking on.

"But we had to move fast, because you could tell by the clouds that a front was coming in as we got closer to noon. And so we only had a half hour or so before everything changed. I wasn't sure he could move fast enough, but the adrenaline kicked in when he saw the stags.

"It was a bit of gamble, but not much, really. I knew the carry—the Scottish name for what the wind is doing in relation to you and the game. It was just a question of getting there quick enough, before noon. In Genesis, they refer to that as 'the windy part of the day.' "

He sees the slightly incredulous look on my face and says, "Oh, yeah. Dad was always a big Bible thumper."

Actually, it's a toss-up as to what I'm more amazed by: the Bible as hunting reference book or the fact that he is playing the stalking game at a level I can only hope to reach. I find myself blurting out that he has to come to the States. He has to try hunting whitetails. He has to try bowhunting.

"Can't," he says simply. "I'm afraid I might not come back." I look at him and suddenly get it. He's as crazy for hunting as I am, maybe more. And lives in a place where, by law, neither bow nor black-powder firearms are used. If he got hooked on, say, ground-stalking whitetails with a bow, he might very well leave the whole package—family, job, and country—to chase his addiction. Ah, well. I tell him I'll smuggle a bow over next time and at least let him feel what it's like shooting a hunting compound.

"Officially, I couldn't allow it," he says loudly, then lowers his voice. "Unofficially, how about next year?"

DAYCARE FISHING

I killed my computer the other day, an action I can't recommend highly enough. The cause of death was coffee, the original smart weapon. Pour some into a human and he becomes alert and productive. Spill even a few drops on a laptop and that sucker checks right into the digital version of the Long Pine Condo. In memoriam, I decided to go fishing. The perch were running, so I called my friend Paula, who not only keeps tabs on the annual run but also curses better than anybody I know.

She was waiting at the dock when I showed up. Selecting her favorite rowboat, one of the seventy-year-olds that know the river the best, she steered us down to an ancient sycamore leaning out over the water. "Drop the rock and let out enough line so we're clear of them," she said, nodding her chin upward. A dozen cormorants perched above us, ready for any shad venturing near the surface. "You do not want a [expletive] cormorant to crap on you," she said. "Trust me, honey. That [expletive] stuff is like battery acid." As if on cue, something white and semisolid splatted into the water not ten feet away.

Five hours later, my hands numb from filleting a couple dozen iced-down fish ("It's [expletive] hell on your hands, but it keeps the fish from going mushy," Paula explained), I realized I was going to be late to pick up my daughter. I drove home, dumped the rods, threw the fish in the fridge, and raced to school. Emma came over at a gallop. "Retta's mom is taking some kids to her grandma's house at Lake Barcroft," she announced breathlessly. "Can we go? Can we?" Ten minutes later, we were caravanning to a tiny private lake in a community so upscale you can probably be fined if caught doing your own yard work. We were six kids, two moms, and one fishy-smelling dad. The kids ran for the beach, screaming and kicking sand at one another.

"We wanna go fishing!" they declared. Retta's mom said sorry, the fishing rods were locked up at Grandma's. I had no rods, but I had hooks and mono in my tackle bag and a knife in my pocket. And I'd noticed a grove of bamboo by the parking lot.

"Who wants to go fishing?" I called. A tide of screaming children charged straight toward me. Just in time, I yelled, "Who thinks they can find some worms?" The tide split around me as kids began turning over rocks and logs. I cut six lengths of bamboo and began stripping the branches off. (The trick, I found, is to snap them off briskly rather than peel them.)

Measuring lengths of mono two feet longer than the rods, I attached line to pole and hook to line. I baited each with a worm, and whenever a child dared express a preference for a pole other than the one I was handing him, I recited the one phrase no parent can do without: "You get what you get and you don't get upset." One by one, they ran down to the water. The lone holdout was an older boy, Jonah, a fourth grader.

"Don't you want to fish?" I asked.

"No, that's okay, I'm good," he said, playing it cool, as a fourth grader will when faced with the unknown and its looming potential for failure and embarrassment.

"Oh, man!" I said. "Try it. When I was your age, fishing was all I wanted to do." I pushed the rod into his hands and told him I'd come check on him in a minute.

A first grader, Ian, went through five worms in short order. He would return and wordlessly hold up the bare hook for rebaiting, as patient and determined as a cop awaiting the world's last donut. Shrieks of triumph began to erupt here and there along the shore, followed by the hoisting of a bluegill in the 2–3 inch class. At last Ian connected, racing up and down the sand. "I did it!" he kept crooning. "A fish!" Ten minutes later, Jonah, still fishless, was facing the special humiliation of being the oldest kid and the only one to fail.

"Fish like places they can hide and ambush other fish," I said gently. "Sticks and stuff." He moved his line over to a visible stump end. A minute later he had a live one flopping in the grass and a two-hundred-watt glint in his eye. "Yes!" I said, high-fiving him. One of the smaller first graders, John, wandered over to examine Jonah's fish.

"Black crappie," he said. "Everybody else caught little pumpkin-seeds." John's father is an angler, his mom told me, and the boy is a maniac for field guides of all sorts.

"Wow," I said. "Sounds to me like you know nearly everything there is to know about fish."

"Well, yeah, pretty much," he said, then explained, "I've been to Florida."

"It shows," I said.

When it was time to go, we stashed the poles in a bush, ready for the next time we came back. As we headed to the cars, I felt as if I were walking six inches off the ground, like I was the catcher in the rye. I'd hooked six kids and a bunch of perch. It was as good a day's work as I can remember doing in my life.

ALWAYS ON CALL

If you close your eyes, you can almost imagine the sound is a distant mountain stream picking its way down through rocks and riffles. Open them and your trout fishing fantasy snags on the inescapable reality of a windowless and fluorescently lit room the size of half a football field. The carpeting, walls, and 144 cubicles here are beige. Throughout, women and men babble endlessly into headsets, their voices merging into a low hum, the sound of the well-oiled machine that is Cabela's, the "World's Foremost Outfitter."

This is the Customer Service Center in Kearney, Nebraska, one of five in the state. On a day like this in early May, the company is almost coasting: 120 operators on the phones at any particular moment handling about 15,000 calls a day. During peak season, October through January, there will be 500 people handling 100 calls each per day. That's 50,000 interactions, the vast majority of which result in orders. All around me, the operators—Cabela's calls them customer relations associates, or CRAs—are fielding inquiries about Cross-Lok snapswivels and logo T-shirts, ATV harrow drags and women's wildlife boxer shorts, Hevi-Shot Dead Coyote shotshells and the kid's video chair in Seclusion 3D camo (so that your child can partake of the outdoor lifestyle while playing Feeding Frenzy on his Xbox).

CRAs are highly trained and talented people who are adept at working with the public, a skill I'll later test in myself. After all, what's the point of coming all the way out here and not damaging the company's reputation in the eyes of at least one loyal customer?

Channeling the Outdoors

Standing on the other end of the telephone line like this, I'm intrigued by what a complex dance it is, Cabela's and you. The company's strategy has never been to be the cheapest. Wal-Mart has pretty much cornered that market. What Cabela's is selling is something different altogether: a brand that associates you with the outdoor lifestyle. Cabela's wants you to think of its wares whether your dream trip is car camping at the local lake for catfish, or hopping a private jet to Tierra del Fuego for sea-run brown trout. It knows you won't place your next order unless you're satisfied with your last one, so if you aren't happy with what shows up, you're welcome to send it back for a full refund or exchange. Above all else, Cabela's is betting that superior customer service will keep Americans responding to the more than 120 million catalogs it sends out annually under seventy titles, from *Tackle Craft* to *Home & Cabin*. Cabela's is a juggernaut (publicly traded on the New York Stock Exchange since 2004) that last year broke the $2 billion mark in revenues for the first time in its history. It owns about 5½ percent of the outdoor market, roughly twice that of Bass Pro Shops. When I visited, managers were still celebrating Cabela's ranking as No. 15 in *Business Week*'s top-25 list of major American companies for customer service excellence.

Like any for-profit company, Cabela's wants your money. It also wants to keep you coming back. To do so, it has evolved from its roots as a catalog-only operation into a "multichannel" (the new industry buzzword) retailer, with catalog, Internet, and bricks-and-mortar components. As of summer 2014 there are fifty-seven stores operating in the United States and Canada, with plans to open another seventeen soon. These are big "destination" stores, averaging 150,000 square feet, built to have what the company calls a "contagious, electric atmosphere" with museum-quality wildlife dioramas, natural wood and stone materials, aquariums, waterfalls, live fish, laser shooting arcades, and candy shops. Cabela's likes to say it "brings the outdoors indoors" in its stores, converging design, atmosphere, and merchandise to create this sensation. The average length of a customer's visit is three and a half hours. Some families stay much longer, planning their vacations around visits during which they shop, eat, play, and look. What this means is that for some of us who supposedly enjoy the outdoors, a vacation means driving a long distance to park and then spend the time indoors.

A Smooth Operator

Many a wife wishes her husband would remember a birthday or anniversary half as easily as he does that famous toll-free number: 800-237-4444. Dial those digits and here's what you *don't* get: a recording instructing you to listen closely because the menu options have changed, directives to push 1 for English or 2 *para español*, or a guy in Bangalore trying to make you believe he knows all about ice fishing. Instead, you get something that is rapidly becoming as rare as fried panda on a stick: a live American asking how she or he can help you today.

You get somebody like Nancy Sayles, fifty-eight, who taught primary school until the apathy of her students' parents drove her crazy. She also worked in a factory that made air filters and assisted a manager at Nutrisystem before signing on part-time and discovering that she is a natural at telephone sales. Right now, she's talking to a guy who's interested in a Humminbird 565 fish finder with dual-beam sonar and a 60-degree area of coverage. He wants the deluxe model, the one that gives your speed and the water temperature. It runs $229.95. It's Thursday and he needs it by Monday. Can they do that?

"We sure can," Sayles chirps and repeats back his shipping address. But she makes a mistake, saying "street" rather than "avenue," an error the customer impatiently corrects. "So it is," she says, unflappable. "The old bifocals, don't you know." His only reply is "Yep." But suddenly the whole tenor of the call has changed. Sayles's throwaway explanation of the mistake, "the old bifocals," and her lack of defensiveness have somehow bridged the gap across the wires. She has, in effect, let the customer know that he is speaking to another human being, one who knows her business, and likes her customers. What could have been an annoyance has instead become an endearing asset. It's a quiet victory for the company, an experience that may not even break into the customer's conscious awareness, but which registers nonetheless. "That comes to $267.89 with the three-day shipping," she says. It's his move now. He stalls, makes the universal tongue-clicking sound of somebody mulling over his options. "Would you like to place that order?" she asks sweetly after ten seconds of dead air. "I guess so," he says. Sold.

They Know What You Did Last Summer

The array of information available to the person answering your call is now so sophisticated and extensive that more than one customer has been convinced that Cabela's telephone operators are psychic. The No. 1 customer complaint is not getting an order by the promised date, so detailed tracking information is available for each shipment. Nancy Sayles recalls an irate man calling to complain that his order hadn't arrived. She brought it up and saw that the delivery driver had put the box in the customer's vehicle, something commonly done when bad weather prevents access to the front door. Her notes specified a red pickup in the driveway. "I asked if they'd been getting snow recently. 'Yes,' he answered. I asked if he had a red pickup. 'How'd you know that?' he said. I asked if he'd looked in the truck. He put the phone down, went outside, and came back in with his package. 'Wow!' he kept saying. 'How'd you do that?'"

Every caller's name, address, and order history is displayed automatically when the phone is answered by a CRA: your past business with the company, every item you've ever purchased, dollar amounts, and how much merchandise was returned. "So when you get some guy who says he's ordered dozens of times, you know if that's true." The software is also useful for crank calls from kids. "You just ask to speak to their parents using a first name and they hang up pretty quick."

Software can't do everything, however, and the human element leads to interesting stories. Sayles remembers one time when a special offer changed in the middle of an order. "It came up so fast, I flubbed the words. It changed to a lure kit. I was trying to say, 'These lures swim erratically,' but I said, 'These lures swim erotically,' and I got so embarrassed! I apologized, but the gentleman on the phone just said, 'I believe I'll take two just in case you were right the first time.'"

Every customer relations associate has war stories:

- A customer called asking about a mesh vest. "That mesh, now, does that have holes in it?"
- Somebody returned a toilet seat after a year because his wife got tired of looking at the fishing lures embedded in the clear acrylic. Even though Cabela's does not resell used toilet seats, he received a credit. He was a good customer. You want to keep a guy like that happy. And if it takes accepting a used toilet seat, well, okay.
- A guy wanted a refund for a broken fishing rod, explaining that it had failed while he was fighting a big alligator. It wasn't an accidental hookup. He'd been targeting gators. He did not get a refund.
- A customer from New York City kept ordering and returning cuckoo clocks. After the third return, he was asked the reason. "Everybody knows that if you pack cuckoo clocks in cardboard, it makes the cuckoo louder. But you guys keep doing it anyway!" Orders for cuckoo clocks from that individual are no longer accepted.
- One man asked how loud a Gamo pellet gun was. About like a .22, he was told. The next sounds were the cocking of a rifle and a shot. "Damn! That is loud!"
- A bailiff was whispering his order into his phone as court was about to convene. He paused to announce, "All rise!" then resumed ordering.

The Gear Gurus

CRAs are well versed in both the habits of callers and the gear they're selling to them. A lot of orders are placed from America's bathrooms, they know, and they are unfazed by the sound of toilets flushing in the middle of a call. Likewise a line that suddenly goes dead when a boss walks into the office. Or a parent who breaks off to separate a child who has taken a hammer to the head of a sibling. You will never hear a Cabela's employee say, "I don't know." Instead, they'll say, "That's a really good question," and try to run the answer down. They can display any of the seventy-six camo patterns currently offered side by side and explain how they differ. On their computers, using what's known as the Alpha System, they can call up product guides and information that are many times more detailed than what is on the website. If the CRA can't answer the question, the caller is referred to the company's product information specialists. These people are Cabela's gurus, knowledgeable about big chunks of the 250,000 items offered at any time.

One of them is JayDee Flohr, who works out of the Grand Island call center, about fifty miles from Kearney. He's a big guy whose cubicle is adorned with a photo of the turkey he took last year with an Osage longbow. "I was walking into my ground blind when I heard him," he says. "Never made it there." Like all Cabela's product specialists, he is a generalist, but counts himself particularly adept with trail cameras and other electronics, muzzleloading, and other traditional hunting gear. A customer wants to know if a spare-tire cover's dimensions relate to the rim size or the tire size. Rim, Flohr tells him. Another needs to make sure the short-sleeved version of a shirt has the same two front patch pockets as the long-sleeved. It does. Somebody asking if a certain women's New Balance athletic shoe has a removable insole prompts him to place the person on hold to consult with the specialist behind him, Mike Beltzer. "Mike is the shoe god," says Flohr. Beltzer says the insole is removable. Flohr relays the information and takes an order. I notice Beltzer is wearing an unusual pair of basketball shoes and ask about them. "Vintage Air Jordans," he tells me proudly. "Cherry condition. Probably worth a bundle on eBay." Beltzer sold shoes for five years in Kansas and managed restaurants but didn't need the aggravation. This is a job he doesn't have to take home with him. His wife's an accountant with the company. He does a lot of upland bird and turkey hunting.

I listen in on a call Flohr gets about a Garmin 60CSx. The customer had bought the MetroGuide software and wants the more comprehensive City Navigator instead, plus he wants to replace the standard 64-megabyte chip with a 2-gig chip that Garmin customer service said he needs in order to download the whole program. Flohr checks and says that Cabela's stocks the software but not the chip. The guy says he'll check around and hangs up. Flohr shakes his head. "You could tell he was wanting to get off the phone. Otherwise I'd have told him those processors in his unit can't really handle that huge card. Those units aren't designed for that much load. It'll work, but it'll be real slow. He'd be better off if he would just download parts of it, but a lot of guys want to download the whole thing. It's a judgment call, whether you tell them all that." He shrugs. "And he seemed like he wanted what he wanted."

My Customer Disservice

Flohr's screen lights up with a call. A guy who just got a wood lathe is looking for a lure kit recommendation so he can start making his own. Barring that, he'd at least like the screws and eyelets to attach treble hooks to the bodies. "Guy can't get a lathe without wanting to justify the expense," the fellow jokes. "I'm not going into it in a big way, just like to be able to display some at craft shows and stuff." Flohr looks in three specialty catalogs but can't find the kit. "A lot of times, guys see it in Bass Pro Shops and call us instead," he tells me while searching with the customer on hold. He tells the customer he can't find it but knows what the fellow means. "I used to do the same thing," Flohr says to the caller. "Give them away at Christmas and whatnot. I just bought screws at the hardware store." The customer

175

insists that his buddy bought little screws and plates to anchor the trebles to at Cabela's. Flohr finally locates the items on page 41 of the *Tackle Craft* catalog. "I just flat-out missed them the first time," Flohr admits. "Hook hangers, that's what you want. And belly screws, round bibs, cup washers. We got 'em all."

"Cool," says the customer. "I want to get into waterfowl calls next. 'Course, anybody with a lathe wants to turn out waterfowl calls. Do you all teach a class on that or anything?"

Flohr says he doesn't know of one. Then he reads from a script that has evidently been distributed in advance of my coming to Grand Island. "We have a special guest on the line today, a writer from *Field & Stream* magazine, Mr. Bill Heavey. He'd like to talk to you if you don't mind." Suddenly, I'm on the line. And on the spot. I make the mistake of saying what I'm thinking. "Uh, sir, I could be wrong about this, but it sounds to me like you don't have enough to do." Flohr looks away, claps a hand over his head, and shakes his head. I am, evidently, not CRA material.

"I got plenty to do," the customer says, bristling. "What are you doing at Cabela's?"

"Just hanging out," I tell him. I change directions, asking if he finds the people who answer the phones here helpful. "Most of the time, yeah. Every once in a while you get somebody who's not that good, but usually they're pretty helpful."

Flohr comes to my rescue, interrupting the heavy silence that has fallen on both ends by thanking the customer and telling him that for talking to me today, he is being offered his choice of a free year's subscription to this magazine or a twenty-dollar Cabela's gift certificate. "I already get *Field & Stream*," he says. "I believe I'll take the certificate."

"Heck, get two copies," I blurt out. "One for upstairs, one for downstairs."

"We're already stocked with Charmin," the guy says, "all we need."

Flohr reaches over and unhooks my headset from the jack. It is evidently time for me to leave the call center. Outdoors, the Nebraska sun is blindingly bright and hot. It feels great to be outside again.

THE WILD CARD

When I phoned Richard Stucky with the news that I'd drawn a Kansas archery tag and would be showing up at his house for another deer season, he was in his truck outside the Krispy Kreme on West Central Avenue near Wichita. "Ham on uh meck, Buh," he said. I heard chewing, gargled coffee, and a deep sigh. "Oh, man. Just out the fryer." Richard and Connie live in Pretty Prairie, thirty-two miles from the Krispy Kreme. But sometimes Richard will be out on an errand and the next thing he knows his truck has driven itself there.

By the time I showed up in mid-October, Stucky had already staked out several bucks. One was the same eight-pointer I had seen and could have killed three times the previous year with a gun. I'd gotten a good look at him through my 8x50s. He was a honker.

The patterns had changed this year, Stucky said, because of what had been planted and where, but he'd seen "my" buck, now a wide, tall ten, as well as a couple of new guys. I'd learned the hard way that bucks in flat farm country are not the slam dunk many big-woods hunters imagine. Sure, crop fields are deer magnets. But the endless seas of shoulder-high grass that spring up on uncultivated Conservation Reserve Program (CRP) land are as good as the thickest swamp for sanctuary. And food everywhere means a pressured buck has no reason to budge before it's thick dark. I keep showing up, however, on the theory that there's got to be a big Kansas buck dumber than I am.

The first morning, I watched the sun come up from a ladder stand tucked into a thirty-foot-wide shelterbelt. To the east lay 140 acres of CRP land. To the west, an irrigation circle of picked corn and sprouting turnips where the deer fed heavily at night. It was bright and blustery, each gust sending stand, tree, and hunter on a shaky little polka. A 360-degree field of view and the knowledge that deer seldom show from the predicted direction soon had my head doing laps around my neck. By 10 A.M. I had seen exactly one deer: a small doe sneaking into the CRP field four hundred yards to the south. I was about to climb down so that I could check out what kind of sign was around, when I caught a flicker of movement in the shelterbelt just to the north. It was an ear. The ear was attached to a head. The head belonged to a bedded buck with the biggest rack I'd ever seen. I sat back down. I didn't know if he'd sneaked in or been there all along. It didn't matter. He was certainly there now, just over thirty yards away. Observing the unwritten laws of deer hunting, he lay in my one obstructed quadrant. No lanes.

I watched him for ninety minutes. I figured trying to rouse him by grunting or rattling this close would cause him to bolt, and that the smart move was to wait him out. He'd eventually stand, and if he moved five yards to either side I'd have a shot. All the while, my brain kept telling me to calm down. And my adrenal glands kept advising my brain to go to hell. He was just too damn big and too damn close. Worse, he seemed to be making full use of that psychically disruptive force field that surrounds exceptional beasts. I was a wreck.

At 11 A.M., Richard rolled up in his truck to get me, passing within feet of my quarry. You would not have wanted to play poker with this deer. With his sworn enemy just steps away, the deer studied his cards, motionless. Though frantic, I dared not gesture broadly. Richard squinted while I put on a little puppet show with my fingers, finally took the hint, and motored slowly away.

Half an hour later, the buck lumbered to his feet, peed, and scratched his ear with his hind hoof. He looked around and moved to the right and away a few steps. He was quartering away more severely than I would have liked. He looked as if he were going to head up the thicket edge. It was now or never. I drew, aimed just to the rear of his rib cage, and released.

The buck took off, his gait showing no telltale hitch or wobble. I felt like a placekicker who puts one wide with no time left and his team down by two. Richard rumbled up five minutes later. "Staked out the road where I figured he'd cross if you didn't kill him outright," he said. "He was carrying the mail when I saw him. Flying. That's the one you were on last year. He was a big 'un all right."

I put my bow behind the seat and got in the cab. Understanding the healing properties of coffee and a couple of glazed chocolate donuts, Richard gave the truck its head, and it went straight to the Krispy Kreme. I had a sneaking feeling that a) the deer in Kansas hadn't gotten appreciably dumber over the course of one year, and b) I hadn't gotten appreciably smarter. On the other hand, I discovered that three or four Krispy Kremes washed down with a bucket of coffee is the strongest pain reliever you can get short of a doctor's prescription.

GOOD GRIEF

The guy who usually draws me looking like an idiot on this page every month had lost the dog he was counting on having at his side as he pushes the odometer on his own hunting legs. Jack Unruh comes from good stock; his mom is ninety-six and still "feisty," as they say down South. But no man's days afield are endless. The sudden and unexplained death of Annie, a young shorthaired pointer, on a quail hunt in West Texas had hit him hard.

The email from Jack's wife, Judy, said he'd been hunting with a friend of many years. The day before, they had found a rusty pickax atop a small rise in the middle of nowhere. They'd joked about it being a sign that their days were numbered. Now they hunted it up to dig Annie's grave. Judy had hinted that Jack wasn't sure he'd still have his hunting legs by the time he got another dog made—let alone the inclination to risk that kind of heartbreak again.

Jack lives 1,500 miles away, and we rarely get together. But a guy who sees right through you and likes you anyway is a guy you hang on to. (The one time I grumbled to Jack about depicting me as an idiot, he cut me off, saying, "Heavey, you do the idiot part yourself. I'm just trying to keep up.") So I called to offer up the empty words one says in these situations. Since Jack wasn't home, I waited for the beep. And then I encountered the passing strangeness of the human heart: Six seconds into my semi-rehearsed lines, I found myself choking up, warm tears taking toboggan rides into my mouth. This was not in the plan. I wasn't speaking to Jack. Hell, it wasn't even my dog. It was all I could do to choke out a few words of apology before hanging up.

Ten years ago, I'd have been embarrassed by my tears. I'd have felt like a wimp. But among the many things the years change are your ideas about manhood. I've come to accept my impulse to tears as just another act of fate, not much different from tornadoes, tomatoes, or ingrown toenails. Like these things, tears themselves decide when to visit. They aren't particularly worried about whether the timing is convenient.

Every man totes around his own invisible boatload of heartbreak— that steady accretion of loss (the deaths of parents and friends), regret (failed relationships, things done and left undone), and self-assessment (those long nights when you try to square who you are with who you hoped you'd be). This ship of grief that we usually keep under such tight wraps never stops loading cargo. Every so often it slips its moorings and goes where it pleases, reminding you that sometimes you're more cabin boy than captain.

I've always liked Norman Schwarzkopf's statement: "A man who doesn't cry scares me a little." I like it because there are times I cry like a damn baby. I think it's genetic hardwiring. I cried recently at a kids' movie, *The Water Horse*. I was once overcome in the car of a friend by nothing more than hearing Guy Clark's "Desperados Waiting for a Train," a song about the friendship between a boy and an old man.

But nothing infiltrates a man's defenses like the untimely death of a dog. All of us, men and women, carry the imprint of—and the craving for—the unconditional love we received as children. As a child, you may puke on your parents at the start of a long airplane trip, knowing they'll cheerfully receive your vomit in their cupped hands. Then they'll clean you up, feed you the same food all over again, let you repeat the performance, and still love you as much as ever when you finally land.

Our protestations to the contrary, adult love is never unconditional, never absolute. Screw up bad enough or long enough, and love folds its tent. That's why we need dogs. You could axe-murder everybody in your office, carjack your own mother, and plow into a crosswalk full of schoolkids while fleeing the police. But when you pull into the driveway two days later, your dog would still shiver and whine with uncontrollable joy, in effect saying, *Boy, did I miss you!*

If the loss of that kind of love doesn't make you cry, then I agree with Stormin' Norman: You scare me, too. So if, like me, you find yourself ambushed, find yourself crying at things you don't understand, you may not be completely normal. On the other hand, I'd like you to know you've got company.

A SINKING FEELING

It's hotter than two mice in a wool sock right now, and the heat makes a man do strange things. After years of eyeing a cattail pond—really more of a marsh—two miles from my house, I've decided it's time to fish it. A forgotten little triangle of urban wetland, it's hemmed in by an interstate highway, the parking lot of a six-story office-condo complex, and an asphalt bike path. The county refers to it as a "park," but you never see anyone inside.

Although the area is 90 percent swamp, there's an arm of open water forty feet long. I've seen mallards putting about here, turtles sunning themselves, and ripples from what are almost certainly rising bluegills. Bluegills, of course, are reason enough for a fisherman. And where there are bluegills, there may be bluegill-eating bass.

Waiting until dusk to avoid the worst of the heat, I biked over carrying my pack stuffed with chest waders and a four-piece five-weight. Even at six thirty, it was still in the mid-90s, and I showed up dripping sweat. It was the strangest suburban park I'd ever seen: no trails, no trash, no evidence of anybody ever having been inside. I might as easily have walked into a coat closet and emerged in Narnia. I wouldn't have been surprised to look up and find a talking centaur advising me that an Orvis Enrico's Turbo Frog Popper was his go-to lure this time of year. The untended greenery was as thick as any jungle. It took me twenty minutes to crawl, slash, and bull my way to the water's edge.

Once there, I saw that getting into position to make a cast required wading out about thirty feet through cattails, spatterdock, hydrilla, and God knows what else. With my first step, I sank up to my waist and got a good whiff of the gym-bag-from-hell odor that any marsh emits in summertime when disturbed. At least that's what I told myself. *Surely*, I thought, *they'd have had to put up signs if this was the local Superfund site.* With my next step came the realization that I had yet to touch bottom; I'd been walking on matted vegetation. The good news was that it appeared to be holding my weight.

In this case, the distance from "so far, so good" to "so what the hell did you *think* was going to happen?" was exactly two steps. It was at that point that the vegetation decided it had supported me long enough. My feet punched through and I sank right down to my clavicle. I remember thinking of the word *clavicle* at the time because I had the odd feeling that the water level had sought out the slender, horizontal bones at the top of my chest to draw attention to the fact that I was now within six or eight inches of having my nose and mouth submerged, at which point it would become challenging to continue the breathing process that had become habitual with me.

Meanwhile, my waders were shipping water just below my armpits. This was not an unpleasant sensation, as it cooled me off and restored some brain function, at which point my interest in fishing decreased dramatically. My revised goal for the evening was to avoid drowning. I attempted to turn around but found that my feet, sunk firmly in the muck, were uncooperative. I suddenly recalled reading an obituary of a well-known flyfishing writer some years ago who had perished in the spring flow of his favorite trout stream. His death had been a great loss, the fishing community agreed, but many had found consolation in the fact that he had passed away doing what he loved. This rationale irritated me even then. He didn't die fishing; he died drowning: choking and flailing against the overpowering force of water.

Now highly motivated, I heaved my body shoreward, attempting to spread my weight out evenly over the matted weeds, like a man negotiating thin ice. This worked briefly, allowing me at last to free my feet and establish a higher center of gravity in relation to the water. But then the mat gave way and I began to sink again, the difference being that I was now arranged horizontally, like a swimmer too heavy to stay afloat. It occurred to me that my death would be rationalized in a different vein than the flyfisherman's. I could see people shaking their heads and thinking, *That idiot drowned in downtown Arlington, Virginia, at rush hour, people within a hundred yards of him in all directions, in a grubby little hole nobody in their right mind would have fished.* They would sigh, shrug, and say, "Tell you the truth, I'm surprised he lasted as long as he did."

I grabbed at the plants ahead, pulling carefully so as not to break any of them. Inch by inch, I hauled myself into the shallows. I'd never even assembled my rod.

Wet but alive, I rode home, enjoying the cooling effect of water evaporating from my clothing. As I coasted into my driveway, a neighbor saw my rod tube and asked, "How'd you do?" I smiled at him and said, "Pretty good, actually." And for once, a fisherman was telling the absolute truth.

I'VE BEEN CAUGHT

Online dating being pretty much the freak show you would imagine, I didn't rush to join. And when I finally did decide to put together a profile, my first move was to see how other guys chose to misrepresent themselves. Reading just the first two—YOUR MOM WILL LOVE ME! and PARTNER SOUGHT FOR DANCE OF LIFE—convinced me that against this kind of fake sincerity, my only hope was to take the low road. REDUCE YOUR EXPECTATIONS AND WE'LL GET ALONG JUST FINE was what I ran with. I figured it would weed out any woman who expected me to wear a tie.

I had lots of encounters in which, five minutes into a lunch date, my soul got up and left, leaving me behind to explain what I'd meant in my profile when I wrote, "Would rather pound nails into my head than shop." Then, quite recently, I found a live one. Which is why I am standing by a river with my canoe hauled halfway up the shore so that the woman in question may enter without getting her feet wet. She seems to have bought new Italian backpacking boots for the occasion—Zamberlan Tundra GTs, if I'm not mistaken. It's a gesture I know I should appreciate. She is a city girl, after all, but game. Curmudgeon that I am, the thought that crosses my mind is that short of steel-toed logging boots, you could hardly pick worse canoe shoes.

I initiated contact with this woman by sending a note saying that I liked her smile and was grateful to find one person whose favorite things to do had not included long walks on the beach. "You strike me as either an unusually honest man or a total whack job," she wrote back. After our first date—coffee in a well-lit café with multiple exits

186

and a uniformed security guard—I asked if she'd reached a decision. "Jury's still out," she said. But then she gave me a smile I haven't been able to shake. That was two dates and five phone calls ago. And I now find that she occupies more of my mental hard-disk space than I care to admit.

Keep your damn mouth shut about the shoes, I tell myself.

On our last date I had confessed a predilection for moving water and smallmouth bass. I told her that fishing had helped me get through some of the rougher patches in my life, that it was the one thing I could count on for temporary relief from the guy between my ears, the guy whose job is to observe and criticize every single thing I do. She'd listened. She'd nodded.

And then she asked that I take her fishing.

I paddle us out to the head of a long island in the center of the river and run the boat up on a flat rock, kneeling and steadying it with both hands as she steps out. By prearrangement, she will sit, read her book, and watch. If this were solely about fish, I'd be spinning. But for her first time on a river, fish are not my primary goal. And it is hard to romance a woman while using a six-foot, medium-heavy Ugly Stik and root beer–black fleck Yamamoto Hula Grubs. So I'm toting a nine-foot five-weight and a handful of streamers. Take that, Brad Pitt. I saw the movie.

I start casting a Black Woolly Bugger. I'm just beginning to feel as if I'm regaining the hang of flycasting when I drive the streamer into the back of my head. "Are you okay?" calls a voice. She has put her book down and is shielding her eyes from the sun, her face a mask of concern and fear. "It's nothing," I say, facing her to hide the hook, yanking it out too quickly, and pressing the spot hard with my thumb before she sees any blood. "I just like to do that sometimes to keep from getting cocky." Her face changes back. She rolls her eyes. She's showing concern, and I'm being a jerk. "Right," she says evenly. "Don't wanna get cocky." She returns to her book.

Seeing no way out of my jerkdom, I go back to casting. I miss a strike, then catch and release two bluegills and a seven-inch smallie.

When I next look up, I realize I have lost track of time. During which I failed to check on her, to ask whether she's enjoying herself.

I smile a hangdog apology her way. "Sorry," I call. "I sort of got distracted there." She holds up a hand, indicating that I should cease talking. The gesture scares me at first, but then I see that she's smiling. "Not distracted," she says. "More like really focused. I got to see something I'd never seen before." Her tone, and that smile, have me completely bamboozled.

"You mean you've never seen flyfishing before?"

"No," she says. "I'd never seen you before. I'd never seen you not doing whatever act it is you do. I liked it."

I stand there on my rock, fly line tangled about my feet, and look at her. She looks right back. Her words hover strangely in the air. Suddenly I feel disarmed, transparent. Don't let anybody tell you city girls can't fish. This one already has me hooked and knows it. "What now?" I ask. She stretches and smiles. "I want to watch you fish some more. Then you can take me to dinner." She goes back to reading.

I'm headed for a world of trouble. Which could be exactly what I need.

UNSINKABLE

Now that gas prices exceed four dollars a gallon in some places, my canoe is looking better to me every day. I recently took it out on the river again for the first time in a few months and marveled at its design, a perfect marriage of form and function. Anything you could add to it would be superfluous. Anything you took away would be disastrous. In this way, the canoe, the archetype of the aboriginal boat, closely resembles the archetypical aboriginal drink, beer. Some brewers add cherries or peaches to beer. Others remove alcohol or calories. But then the end product is something other than beer. If you want to drink it, that's your business. Just don't do it in my canoe.

One of the great things about a canoe is that you can leave it upside down on sawhorses for years at a time with no decline in performance. It will still attain a top speed of 2.5 mph and burn about two hundred calories per mile. This is also one of the terrible things about a canoe. Anglers, particularly those who chase bass, are lustful creatures, and virtually all of us yearn for something young, sleek, and ridiculously expensive. In short, we want bass boats. The object of my current fascination is the Allison XB-21 BasSport with a 200 Optimax Mercury. It comes with everything you ever wanted on a boat, including remotely adjustable headlights with Lexan covers that fit into molded cavities so they are flush with the bow. Never again will you be late getting back to the dock and lose a tournament because of headlight drag. A specially designed windshield allows you to wear your hat with the brim forward at top speed, which is 82 mph. You need that kind of speed, mostly to get from one gas dock to the next and still have time to fish.

In my heart, I lust after the XB-21. In my wallet, I find that I'm about $68,000 short. So, I'm sticking with the canoe. Mine is a seventeen-foot Mad River Explorer, about twenty years old and made of Royalex, the miracle fiber of its day. I know little about Royalex, but I will say this: In all the time I've owned my canoe, it has never once needed ironing.

In fact, in the decades I've had it, the canoe has needed only two repairs. One came after the first three years, when both cane seats gave out within days of each other. I am not a big-butted man, and I had expected greater durability from the seats. Then it occurred to me that a bony-butted man might be harder on seats due to a concentration of weight on the ischial tuberosities, or "sit bones." I have rather angular tuberosities. And these had been applied regularly to both seats. Some canoe owners insist on sitting in the stern as an assertion of dominance, since the stern man decides on the directional heading. I'm just as happy in the bow. You get first shot at the fish and are spared the mental labor of deciding where to go next. I tried to repair the seats with clothesline wrapped tightly around the frames, but that resulted in a numb butt and spaghetti-like indentations that remained for hours after canoeing. I ordered new webbed seats.

The other repair was about ten years ago, when I saw that repeated encounters with boulders, gravel bars, docks, and garage doors had combined to damage the "skin" at either end of the keel. I dropped about a hundred dollars on a skid-plate kit, which came with Kevlar felt pads and a two-part polyurethane resin that you mix up, inhale, and then apply to your eyeballs because you are hallucinating that the devil is about to materialize out of the ground and turn you to stone if you meet his gaze. Somehow, I had the presence of mind not to glue my eyelids shut, though it was tempting at the time.

Actually, the only effect of the fumes was to exaggerate my inherent cheapness. Having spent a hundred bucks for the kit, I thought it wasteful to leave any portion unused. I skipped the "trim to fit" phase, so that the Kevlar felt pads nearly met on the keel of the boat and extended six inches above the waterline at each end. I performed this operation at night, using my car's headlights for general illumination and a mouth-held flashlight for detail work. The next morning, I discovered that my boat looked as if it were wearing a helmet.

A fishing buddy razzed me about my canoe's ugliness and said I'd been stupid to add weight. I said that the modifications were deliberate and meant to discourage potential thieves. Further, I claimed to have reinforced the keel of my boat "the same way that the Vikings did theirs." This was total bull, yet it leapt from my lips so decisively that by day's end I halfway believed it myself. Self-deception can be a positive thing. My fishing buddy is generally a better angler than I, but that day I outfished him, catching five bass to his two. My biggest was about three pounds—just the right size for a Viking canoe.

HAVE GUN, WILL TRAVEL?

Because I want to do my part to keep the country safe from terrorists, I'm speeding toward Reagan National Airport carrying a rifle and no plane ticket. I'm doing this to register my gun with U.S. Customs before heading to Canada for whitetails next week. This step is mandatory, I've been told, if you want to bring your gun home. Late for my appointment, I worry about being pulled over for speeding. ("In a hurry today?" the officer will ask. Yes, I'll answer. "What's in that case?" A rifle. "Where you headed?" Airport. "Sir, I need you to step out of the car and place your hands on your head.")

Once inside the airport loop, I find FULL signs up at both the daily and hourly parking lots. This leaves a) economy parking, an asphalt wasteland two time zones away or b) valet parking, just forty dollars per day or fraction thereof. The attendant at hourly is unmoved by my plight, but I manage to sweet-talk my way into the daily lot.

The airport is designed so that the only way to cover the two hundred yards to the terminal is by shuttle bus. I decide to bushwhack instead. Using dead reckoning, I cut through the rental-car terminal. My Doskocil case, tan with fake-alligator texturing, is the choice of budget-minded gun owners everywhere. It thumps against my leg at every step and fairly screams *Gun!* The desk attendants call out "May I help you, sir?" in concerned voices, but I keep going. Outside, I lumber over a chain-link fence and find myself facing a wall of ornamental grass taller than my head. I could be following up a wounded lion on the African savanna for all I can see. Parting the grass, I sidestep

192

down an embankment to where four lanes of traffic are zipping past at NASCAR speeds.

By now registering my firearm has become a quest, so I wait for an opening, scoot, and find myself playing dodgeball with the traffic. Reaching the far side, I crash through more savanna grass, climb over another fence, and jog through a landscaped parking lot reserved for the exclusive use of Supreme Court justices and members of Congress.

At last I attain the main terminal. I am directed upstairs to the administrative offices, a parallel universe of tranquillity. The linoleum floors here are buffed to a high sheen, the universal sign of a powerful bureaucracy where no purposeful activity takes place. I finally relax. It feels safe here. I want to stay.

The customs lady in Room 245 sees my gun case and passes me U.S. Customs and Border Protection Form 4457, Certificate of Registration for Personal Effects Taken Abroad. Form 4457 is a small slip of paper with boxes for name, address, and "description of articles." I write that I have a Winchester .270 bolt action. "I have to see the gun, hon," she says. I try to hand it over. "Oh, I can't make out those little numbers on the barrel," she says. "Just read 'em to me." She signs and stamps the document. "There ya go," she says. "It's good for life."

I sit there turning Form 4457 over and over in my hands, trying to make sense of what just happened. I now have a piece of paper certifying that my rifle is "registered." On the other hand, the word *registered* has just been rendered meaningless. No one has confirmed my name, address, or citizenship. No one has verified anything about my rifle: make, model, caliber, or serial number. The customs lady has kept no copy of the form, logged no information in her database. There is, in fact, no record of my ever having been here. I search the fine print on the back of the form for an explanation. It says that the Paperwork Reduction Act requires that I be told that Form 4457 has been "provided for your use, strictly at your option, in lieu of or in addition to bills of sale, appraisals, and/or repair receipts to show the

CBP officer proof of prior possession of the article(s) in the U.S. The completion of this form by you is strictly voluntary."

Apparently I have risked life and limb bushwhacking my way across the airport grounds all so that I may prove that I owned my American-made firearm prior to visiting the anything-goes discount arms bazaar that is modern Canada. I am so confused that I make the mistake of asking a direct question. "Ma'am, what's the real purpose of this form?" The customs lady stops in mid-keystroke, alarmed. "Why, it's to prove that you owned the rifle before you left."

"Yes, ma'am. But if it's strictly voluntary and you don't even keep a copy, why was I told I had to have it?" I am immediately sorry I have said this, because now she looks at me as if I probably shouldn't be allowed to own a firearm. "Well, because if you don't have the form they could confiscate your gun or make you pay duty fees on it."

It's clear to me now that I will be locked up if I continue this line of questioning. I nod, smile, and make a quick exit. Outside, the sun is shining brightly. I can see the parking garage, just two hundred yards distant. I decide to wait for the shuttle bus.

WHAT I BELIEVE

At a dinner party recently I was confronted by a woman who said, "I believe that hunting is indefensible and ought to be outlawed. What do *you* believe?" I believed she looked like a red-haired cream puff left out in a hot car and then stuffed into a green dress. But I didn't say this, of course. And since I can't remember what I did say, I intend to be better prepared next time. Here, then, is a list of what I believe:

I believe that God does not deduct from a man's life the hours spent fishing. On the other hand, He is really strict about overdue library books.

I believe that hunting and fishing are too important to be left to the experts and that enthusiasm trumps skill. Sure, I've been so delaminated by the sight of a big buck that I tried to kill it with a rangefinder instead of a rifle. I've swamped full canoes on mirror-calm waters. So what? If you're having fun, you're doing it right.

I believe that after the nuclear holocaust that destroys all other life, whitetail deer will shake the fallout debris from their backs and head for the blast sites to feast on radioactive browse. When that's gone, they will thrive on vinyl siding, construction rubble, and auto parts.

I believe that people who eat meat but condemn hunting have that right. But the next time they hit the drive-through window they ought to be magically sucked into the speaker and taken on a brief journey where they would see, hear, and smell all the steps by which a living, breathing creature ends up on a bun inside a paper bag.

I believe God sees us watching hunting or fishing TV shows and thinks, Don't they know that's all there is to do in Hell?

I believe that every bit of "breakthrough technology" that will be introduced for the next twenty-five years in hunting and fishing gear has already been designed and manufactured. When some suit decides the moment is ripe, it gets released and we millions of outdoorsmen wet our pants with excitement.

I believe that you should never pass the muzzle of any firearm over anything you aren't willing to destroy. In other words, should I ever meet the guy who recorded the "Your call is very important to us" message you get just before your call is dropped, I hope for both our sakes that I am not armed.

I believe that any man who initiates a boy or girl to the eternal mystery of the woods—even if by nothing more than having the child stand in a forest and hear the hand of the wind through the trees—deserves the honorific "father." Especially if the child in question is not his.

I believe that the Remington 870 is all any man truly requires in a shotgun and that anything beyond that is purely discretionary. Having said that, there is a $100,000 20-gauge side-by-side at the Holland & Holland store in New York that I would not mind having the next time I go sit on my bucket in a dove field.

I believe that every man encounters in his life both a David E. Petzal and a T. Edward Nickens, and that both must be opposed. Petzal, because anyone who so openly harbors an affection for cats is clearly in the service of Satan. Nickens, because he's one of those men who are so honorable and devoid of guile that I almost regret putting that CROSS-DRESSERS FOR PETA bumper sticker on his truck.

I believe that camouflage makes you more easily detected by deer, mostly because all camo fabric sold in the United States is used as bedding for the workers' dogs for ninety days before it leaves the mill.

I believe that with more than twenty years of hunting experience, I could now walk into any deer woods in the country, locate and read deer sign, set up in a tree stand, and be asleep within half an hour.

I believe that if a guy like me can have a successful column in a magazine like this, it means very few people are paying attention.

What I Believe

I believe that truly dedicated flyfishermen represent the highest expression of a fine and noble art. Just kidding.

I believe that if your bass jig hits bottom without any sign of a strike, and you notice after giving it a tiny "test pop" that the lure feels "mushy," "tight," or "sticky," it's a sign that you have an enlarged prostate.

I believe that the versatility and potential of the drop-shot rig is so great that it will stay in the bottom of my tackle box until the estate sale following my death.

I believe that if you thought I was kidding about the cable hunting and fishing shows, you should read William Faulkner's "The Bear." It describes hunting as "the ancient and unremitting contest according to the ancient and immitigable rules which voided all regrets and brooked no quarter." I believe these words are true.

YOU CAN'T TOUCH THIS

Two things happened last week that I'm still trying to reconcile: I picked up a roadkill deer, and *National Geographic Kids* magazine showed up at our house.

First, the magazine, which I subscribed to hoping it would arouse Emma's curiosity in the natural world. Instead, she just rifles through the pages for photos of cheetahs—her current favorite animal, one she is convinced would make an ideal ninth-birthday present—and tosses it immediately if there are none. The interesting thing was that it came wrapped in a four-page ad for Purell Instant Hand Sanitizer, whose slogan is "Imagine a Touchable World." You need to imagine a touchable world because the one we live in is seething with highly motivated germs the size of Clinton Portis that will infect your children with horrible diseases. All that stands between your child and certain death is Purell, which they should use about every eight minutes. The Purell website lists ninety-nine common places where these germs lurk, including school bus seats, crayons and, of course, library books.

The deer I encountered one morning just after dropping Emma off at school. Traffic slowed to a crawl as it passed an antlerless deer lying in the road. Judging by the police cruiser behind it, the animal was very recently deceased. I was seized by what would be a logical thought to any hunter who lives in a touchable world: *Backstrap!* I parked and approached on foot. I couldn't see through the cruiser's tinted glass, so I stood there, waited for the officer to lower his window, and asked, "You mind if I take that deer?" He was a nice-looking young man, slightly lumpy in the way that anyone wearing a bulletproof vest while seated would be, and he looked startled at my request. He looked me over long enough to decide I didn't match any recent wanted lists, shrugged, and said, "Sure."

I pulled in front of him, opened the trunk—and found that the still-limp deer (which had almost no external injuries and was a young buck that had recently shed its antlers) was more than I could lift by myself. After a moment, the officer got out to help but looked hesitant.

"You, ah, got any gloves?" he finally asked. I fished out the green army-surplus liners I'd just stuck in my own pockets rather than get them dirty moving the deer and handed them over. He looked at them and I found I could read his mind: *These are wool, which is porous. Latex would provide a better barrier against whatever diseases a wild animal carries, but they're better than nothing.*

After I thanked the officer for his help and got my gloves back, I asked for his card in case anybody questioned the untagged deer in my vehicle. As I drove off, I was trying to square the fact that a road full of commuters, all on their way to the jobs they needed to put food on the table, had passed up free-range, organic meat that would go for more money per pound than USDA prime beef—if there were a place you could buy it.

Wanting to swap venison for assistance with butchering, I drove the buck to the house of my friend Paula, a fellow scrounger. "Hell, yeah, I'll help," she said. "I'm a sucker for a dead deer." We promptly set to field dressing it on a tarp in the backyard. It was messed up pretty bad on the inside, but she figured that most of the meat, backstraps included, could be salvaged. At a certain point, she asked me to hold the trash bag while she used a shovel to load the guts in. Problem was, they were so slippery that they slid off every time she lifted the shovel. "Well," she sighed, "guess I'll have to do it the old-fashioned way." She rolled up her sleeves and scooped the innards into the bag with her hands. Then, carrying her knife, she went around to the front of the house to the outside faucet to wash off while I tied the bag, put it inside a second one, and placed it all in the garbage. When she came back, she was laughing so hard she had to stop every few feet to catch her breath.

"You shoulda seen it!" she gasped. "The bike path is just up the street, y'know, so we get these yuppies on their thousand-dollar bikes bopping down the sidewalk all the time. Usually they damn near run you over." One had been bearing down on her when he saw the knife and her bloody hands. "Man, this guy steers onto the lawn of the house next door, goes through the hedge, and nearly wipes out! Oh, man, the poor guy! He musta thought I'd just killed somebody!" She was squeezing out tears of mirth now, acutely aware of how impossible it would be for the average modern suburban commuter, even one who traveled to work under his own power, to make sense of someone actually butchering her own meat.

"Hey, Paula," I said, wanting her take on the modern germ phobia. "Can you imagine a touchable world?"

"What the hell are you talking about, Heavey? You got some strange notions sometimes, you know that?"

CURRENT CRAZY

It's been raining so much that I've revised "go" fishing conditions to "river levels rising, but at a slower rate than last week." And I'm thinking of raising tilapia in my basement. Every morning, I don Crocs and descend for the ritual sucking up of the previous night's seepage, wearing my shooting muffs against the roar of the wet-vac. In the midst of this reverse-baptism one day, I felt my cell phone vibrate. It was the tobacco-cured growl of Paula Smith. "River's rising like a $%&#@. Last chance for perch, baby. You in?" Paula's desire to fish, like mine, had overridden her judgment. Fishing in current conditions was like investing your retirement in Hummer futures. "I'm in. Meet you at Fletcher's," I said.

I left with water lapping at the cardboard box holding my tax records. You made up the numbers once, I reasoned, you can do it again. Paula was waiting and irritated—her normal state—at the dock. Nearby, police launches rumbled past, searching for two anglers who had misjudged the river and paid accordingly. Paula shook her head at the spectacle. "If a body doesn't pop up immediately, it's *wedged*, okay? Takes four, five days to get bloated and pop free. Till then, they're just burning gas and eating donuts." The rain had resumed. I rowed while Paula tapped the side on which she wanted power. Slipping into the main current, I pulled hard for the next eddy. Paula was unable to keep even a shielded cigarette lit, which made her even crankier. She suddenly said, "This is #(*)@% crazy, you know that?" I didn't have breath to answer. But Paula's threshold for crazy is legendarily high, so being out here with her didn't reflect well on my own mental fitness.

201

I had meant to propose a retreat upon reaching the eddy. What I actually said, however, was "Think that anchor'll hold?" Paula pondered at length. "Might."

The anchor turned out to be the only thing that did hold. Our jigs, despite two ounces of lead, couldn't, which indicated more current than the perch would fight to stay here, much less stack up. As crazy people will, however, we fished for another half hour. Finally, facts had to be faced. Crazy is not the same as stupid.

Back at the dock we found Dickie Tehaan, maker of the very jigs we'd been using. Upon hearing that we'd blanked, he said, "Hey, that's better than I did with Paula the other day." I asked how that could be. "We were out perching—nothing biting—when Paula sees this dead beaver floating our way. She grabs a leg and swings it aboard. Big sucker. And ripe. So I decide I've got other things to do. Soon as we get in, Paula pulls her knife, starts cutting off the head right on the dock—"

"Hell, yeah, I cut off the head!" Paula interrupted. "The #@%$& yuppies love a beaver skull. Don't ask me why. Must remind them of the summer camp they never went to. You let the beetles clean it up, glue the teeth back in, you're looking at fifty bucks, baby!" As she worked, a D.C. cop had approached. "He says, 'What're you doing?'" Paula continued. "And I say, 'I'm cuttin' off this beaver head!' So he thinks this over and asks me why. 'Because I want it!' Cops can be sorta slow sometimes."

Meantime, Gordon Leisch, in whose basement Paula lives, had anchored nearby to fish with a beloved old Shad Pappy dart. "She's got the head," Dickie said, "so she rows back out and chucks the carcass. Except she doesn't look. So the carcass snags Gordon's lure, washes downstream, and breaks him off. Gordon, understandably, loses it. 'You got the whole damn river to throw that thing in, and you throw it at me?'" Dickie said, imitating Gordon.

"Aw, jeez, I felt terrible," Paula said. "I thought I was gonna have to take the bus home. Well, I learned my lesson. From now on, I'm gonna look *before* I throw a carcass in the river." I let this hang in the air for a moment, then observed solemnly, "A wise woman learns from her mistakes." Paula started to laugh, shaking her head. Then Dickie started giggling, and pretty soon the three of us—soaked and fishless and suckers for the river in all its stages—were hooting it up at the divine madness that had driven us to this.

Looking back, it was one of the highlights of the season. And the #@%$& yuppie who ultimately bought the beaver skull was yours truly. "Why?" Paula asked, incredulous. I said it reminded me of the summer camp I'd never been to.

CLAY-BIRD BRAIN

In the 1920s, a group of grouse hunters seeking to hone their skills invented a shotgunning game called "clock shooting." After destroying every clock within fifty miles, they decided to try moving targets. They called the new version "skeet," an Old Norse word meaning "close, but no horn of mead." Modern skeet, enjoyed by literally dozens nationwide, is designed to ruin your shooting confidence. I know because I recently took a lesson. One of the pleasures of skeet is finding someone who shoots even worse than you do. At the thirteen-field range I visited, that someone was me. My goal had been to minimize the humiliation caused by my performance at the dove opener. But the crowd I drew here made the dove field seem like my own private island.

Standing with feet aligned on the point where the target is to be broken, eyes "soft" to pick it up faster, I call for the bird, which zings out and rises to fifteen feet, where it hovers briefly. I shoot at this moment and watch it fly on untouched, breaking silently as it hits ground. This—the going-away bird from the low house at Station 7—is the easiest shot, the one designed to make novices say, "By golly, I can do this!" I miss it three times in a row.

I miss because skeet—like sex and beer pong—is largely a mental game. In that it makes you mental. Schizoid, in my case. Part of me accepts my inability to hit a bird as logical. I often can't hit the tollbooth basket with a quarter from a stationary vehicle. Meanwhile, another part of me is astonished, enraged, and wants to break into the low house and bludgeon every bird there to dust with the butt of my gun. Which is the one part I can use effectively.

Chill, I tell myself, each shot is a whole new beginning. "You hold the gun so tightly," says Alonso Abugattas, my gentlemanly master instructor, who has shot skeet since his boyhood in Peru. "Think of holding a bird in your hand. Too tight, you break her bones. Too loose, she flies away. Softly, but with control." I nod. And then, softly but with control, I miss. My eyes roll back into my skull, as if I am possessed by demons. "Let's have a Coke," says Alonso.

At the beginning of each round, each of your shooting errors takes a number and awaits its turn. Remember to swing the gun through the shot and you will forget to lead the target. Get the hang of shooting slightly below falling birds and you will lift your cheek off the stock. Take a break to use the men's room and, once in position, you'll remember to call "Pull" but forget to unzip your fly.

Refreshed by nerve-steadying caffeine, I'm ready for more agony. Out of nowhere, I crush one. I stand amazed, entranced by the tiny orange cloud I have wrought. "Good for you!" shouts Alonso. "Quick, another one, without thinking." But between his injunction and the next shot, there is just enough time to ponder not thinking. Which makes me miss.

I want to burst into flame, scream bad words, or become an anesthesiologist. My arms feel like cement. For this I blame T. Edward Nickens. Back in 1993, needing a shotgun and not wanting more money tied up in my gun safe than in my house, I sought his advice and bought an economical and perfectly good but heavy gun. In my hands it has conserved more wildlife than the federal duck-stamp program.

Alonso, who showed up with three shotguns, puts one in my hands. I don't know the make, but it's a featherweight over/under that shoulders nicely. When you break it open, two smoking hulls jump right up into your face. Somehow I make the sky rain orange bird soot. "Bravo, Bill!" shouts Alonso. "Again." I dust another one.

Finally, it is time to go. Alonso puts a finger to my chest—a gesture that only certain foreign-born men can do in a way that makes you feel befriended rather than confronted—and says, "You shot very well there, my friend. I'm serious." I want to kiss this man in gratitude and take off running with his gun. Instead, I ask what it costs. "About five thousand dollars," he says, shrugging apologetically. "But I am obsessed."

I am awake all night, likewise obsessed. The next day, I discover that nearly 2 percent of the 5.6 million Avon sales reps worldwide are men. So if you answer the door and see a bald guy hawking Avon Anew Ultimate Age Repair Day Cream, you should definitely buy some. It is reputed to give you younger-looking skin in just minutes. And I can absolutely guarantee that it will improve my shooting.

HOW TO BE THE MAN

As I watch the endurance leg, the final event of *Field & Stream*'s four-day Total Outdoorsman Challenge, outside Branson, Missouri, I come to the following conclusion: God did not intend for middle-aged men to do anything at high speed. This realization occurs while I'm watching John Sappington, a forty-six-year-old fishing guide and one of sixteen finalists. In this part of the contest, you start flat on your back in a laydown blind. Jump up, fire two blanks, and retrieve your "birds." Run to a tree and attach a climbing stand. Run some more and drag an eighty-pound sled twenty yards. Run some more and shoot two arrows at 3-D targets with a wobbly bow while sucking air. Run again and start a matchless fire. This, incidentally, is the spot I'm watching from, along with John Davis, the fiend who designed the course—the ringmaster of this circus. Davis cups his hands and hollers, "C'mon, John! Almost home, buddy!"

Sappington has entered a parallel universe of suffering. He's a big boy to start with (40-inch waist, XXL shirts, and size 13 boots), and forty-six is not one's athletic prime. And now his face goes splotchy. His eyes take on the wild desperation of a man lost in the deep woods. But Sappington didn't come this far to surrender. Somebody will ride out of here $25,000 richer. Somebody will claim the aura that comes from being the Man: the guy with the chops, the poise, and the grit to overcome.

It may be this desire to win that has Sappington unconsciously windmilling his arms as he runs, as if he might gain a step by pulling himself through the humid air. He lumbers toward the last station, sit-on-top kayaks at the edge of a stream. The goal here is to don a life vest, launch, and paddle twenty yards upstream. "Do it, John!" calls Davis. The finalists already regard Davis, who works for Blue 3 Productions, the firm coordinating the contest, as the Man, the one noncompetitor they respect. He's the guy they seek out when they have a problem with their gear, another competitor, or the scoring. When a hotheaded contestant gets out of line (you don't get here by being meek, after all), Davis backs him down. When that same guy blows an event he had counted on winning, Davis helps him find his confidence again. When the TV crew needs to set up a shot, they go to him.

Outwardly, he is a bearded, burly badass, an Arkansas hillbilly and flyfishing guide. Talk with him and you discover a hybrid redneck: a guy with woods smarts (his crew says he could hold his own with any competitor here) and plenty of gray matter. Among other tasks, he writes the blog about the contest, in which he has taken a couple of gratuitous but well-aimed pokes at me. He has a pretty wife, JaNan, and three young daughters (Elizabeth, Emme, and Ella Fu, the youngest, whom the couple traveled to China to adopt). He brags on how the girls are already outfishing their daddy.

He also has an aggressive form of lymphoma, a rare cancer in a forty-one-year-old. The doctors just found it two months ago. That he's here at all is surprising. The chemo has left him with circles under his eyes, pallid skin, and hair in clumps on his pillow each morning. When you're the son of a World War II marine, a countersniper in the Pacific, you grit it out. "Cancer's a good way to get clarity about your life," he tells me. Everybody working the event wears a green rubber lymphoma-awareness bracelet in John's honor. We're all aware of something else, too: The guy in the biggest contest here didn't even sign up. The fight found him.

When the event is finished, the overall winner is the smallest competitor. He's a rookie: Tom Boatwright, thirty-nine, of Perdido, Alabama (29-inch waist, medium shirts, size 7 boots). Davis had said of him: "He won't be distracted, because he doesn't care about anything in the world but hunting and fishing." John Sappington places third.

That night, at a dinner honoring the contestants, those who ran the event are asked to stand and be recognized. At Davis's name, the room hits its feet. The hillbilly smiles and waves, enduring this uncomfortably. What he cannot know is that our applause is as much for ourselves as it is for him. We beat our hands, secretly hoping that in his shoes we'd muster half his courage, grit, and grace.

IV

I WOULDN'T TRY THAT
IF I WERE ME, 2010–2014

THE LAST MOUNTAIN MAN

The good news, I tell myself after verifying no broken bones in the fall, is this will make a really good story if you survive. I'm trying to stay calm, trying to push down the bulge of dread rising in my stomach. I'm sitting in the snow, having bailed off a snow machine just after it lost traction and just before it left the trail, coming to rest on its side in a drift a good five feet below grade. It's my second fall in ten minutes, which confirms my suspicion that I missed a turn. Marty would never have put me on anything this steep and with this much sidehill.

It's 30 below zero, and I'm lost in the bush of eastern Alaska—a place that is pretty much all bush all the time. I've come here to spend some time with Marty Meierotto, a trapper who runs lines on about nine hundred square miles of public land, the location of which he would prefer I not identify too specifically. Not divulging our location isn't a problem because all I really know is that it took us two hours to fly here from Fairbanks in a Super Cub, that we're somewhere north of the Yukon River and south of the Porcupine River, and that the nearest other human is a trapper running lines some forty miles distant. Actually, Marty doesn't know if he's around. The last time he saw him was eight years ago.

I pick myself up slowly and brush off the snow. Stepping off the trail, I posthole up to my knees and hike down to the machine in its drift. After the first fall, I used a stick to dig the machine out, shoved some spruce boughs under its track, and finally got it back on the trail again. I've stuck it good this time. Marty told me he likes these old single-cylinder Ski-Doo Tundra IIs because they are the only snow machines small enough to fit disassembled in the back of his plane. Even so, I bet one weighs four hundred pounds. I tug on the handlebars. It doesn't move.

You're not going anywhere for a while. I simultaneously accept this fact, and deny it. My mind, like my body, feels sluggish and foreign, as if it's not mine at all but on loan from somebody else. I know this is a bad situation, but the sharp edge that the knowledge should carry simply isn't there. This fact worries me, and yet I feel curiously detached from it. I decide to make a list of what I know:

It's about 1 p.m. on January 30, not far below the Arctic Circle. The sun doesn't really rise and set at this latitude and time of year. It just sort of rouses itself, wanders about the edges of the sky for a few hours, then goes away. But when night comes, as it will in about four hours, it will stay dark for fourteen hours. That's a long time to be outside.

I'm really tired. Being outside in this kind of cold, no matter how well dressed you are, strains your metabolism. Your thermostat isn't wired for this. Even Marty, who has been trapping for twenty years, says he loses weight every time he goes to the bush. There's something about the cold that makes you breathe through your mouth, and the air is so dry that even if you're not sweating, you lose water fast. Thing is, despite the cold, I am sweating. I've been riding for four hours now. As a novice, I had no idea how physically demanding it is. In this kind of country, you ride standing up, the better to react to hidden bumps and holes. And you don't really steer a snow machine anyway. As I'm finding out, the handlebars are just a purchase you push against while horsing the beast in the direction you want to go.

I'm alone. Which is stupid. But I have a good reason for being stupid. Which is that I can't keep up with Marty, who I'm starting to believe is an unusually hardy member of the species. This is our third day here. Yesterday, we rode out from his main cabin and followed a trapline about thirty miles up to one of four smaller cabins he has built at intervals along his lines. Marty rode twice that, checking traps on loops off the main trail. We came upon a lynx, an exotic, elegant cat—black ear tufts, snowshoe feet, long buff coat—sitting motionless with one paw in a No. 4 trap. It hardly reacted as Marty approached, dropped the choke wire over its head, and suddenly jerked it tight. The cat's legs and claws scrabbled furiously for thirty or forty seconds, and then it lay still. It was hard to watch, and Marty didn't meet my eyes as he reset the trap—its bait of raw caribou hide still good for another set—and tossed the animal in the sled behind his snow machine. "Everything out here lives by killing something else," he said, still not meeting my eyes, as he pulled the starter cord. We rode on.

Today we were returning by a different route so that Marty could check other lines and do other loops. Again, I couldn't keep up. Already tired from yesterday, I suggested I make my way back to the main cabin ahead of him. He agreed, drew a simple map on a sheet of my notebook, made sure I had my expedition-weight gear strapped to the seat behind me, and told me to take it slow. Which is how I went off the trail. Slowly.

I have some survival supplies. I'm carrying a few chemical warmers, a couple of KitKat bars, two butane lighters, three paper towels for starting a fire, and a small pocketknife. Riding is such work that I'm only wearing a Cabela's anorak and lightly insulated bibs over wool long johns. Thank God I also have the heavier duds, a Northern Outfitters parka and bibs. I'm sweating at the moment from the brief hike down to the machine. Sweat isn't merely inconvenient here. It kills, freezing you fast once you stop and turning you into a Popsicle. I read somewhere how early polar explorers thought the Eskimos lazy, when in fact they simply understood the dangers of sweat. Even thinking feels strangely tiring. I stop for a moment, take a rest. But that doesn't help, either. So I force myself to resume, to add to the list of things I know.

I'll get a lot colder before I get warm. There are two reasons for this. Night is one. But more immediately troubling is the fact that in order to put on my expedition gear, I first have to take this stuff off. That means stripping to my long johns, removing my enormous mittens and even my boots. The discomfort is bad enough. The increased risk of frostbite is worse.

I need to get a fire going. It will help Marty locate me, and it'll beat back the darkness, which I'm starting to fear as much as the cold. I'm on a hillside studded with dwarf spruce trees, many of which look dead or at least pretty dry. That's good, but I'd give anything for a multitool with a saw blade instead of a blade more suited to peeling grapes. Serves him right, I hear someone saying. Heading out no better prepared than a child. The bigger concern is that I need to get the fire going the first time. I've already learned that lighters don't light in subzero cold. The butane doesn't atomize or something. I've taken to carrying one of the two that are always with me in the pocket closest to the heat of my crotch. But I'll have to take off my mitts for the moment of truth—turning the striker wheel. I learned the first day here that you have about fifteen seconds—and that's with liner gloves, not bare skin—before your fingers cease carrying out orders from your brain. What was it Marty said? Something about how if part of you gets cold and then feels warm not to trust it. You're not really warm, he said. It means your body, in its wisdom, has decided not to continue wasting warm blood on an extremity that has shown itself incapable of using the resource effectively.

Your body says, in effect, "Okay, we're not sending any more blood to Mr. Nose."

It's at this moment that the raven flies over. I am standing there dumbly, trying to remember my own list, wondering what key things I might have forgotten or overlooked, when I hear it. There is the unmistakable *wheshk, wheshk, wheshk* of down-stroking wings. It's louder than feathers beating empty air ought to be, and the only sound I've heard besides the wind since my machine stalled. I look up and see it, bigger than a normal raven, vectoring in on me. It is at once both full of intention and in no particular hurry. The entire world shrinks to the approaching black bird and me. As it pulls even with me, it dips briefly, then climbs back to its former altitude. And it lets fall a world-weary *croonnnk*.

The raven's shadow slides over the snow at my feet and on down the hill, a semaphore from the next world. The appearance of the bird, the dip, the cry—all of these fall within acceptable parameters of bird behavior. But the sliding shadow unleashes a jolt of pure terror. With the sudden clarity that descends at threshold moments, I understand its call. The raven's mind is not that different from yours or mine. The call is an oral reminder, a raven's Post-it note: Check back here in the morning to see if this man has become carrion yet.

You're going to be okay, I tell myself. You're in no immediate danger. It would be stupid to try to walk anywhere because you're already exhausted, not to mention lost. You don't need to get more lost. Marty will come looking for you when he gets back to the cabin. I try to avoid the fact that my survival is totally dependent on Marty. It's not that I lack confidence in him. He is almost ridiculously competent. But even Marty is subject to mishaps, and if anything should happen to him, I'll die here. And what I really try to avoid is my own growing awareness of what friendly terms life and death are on here, how easily things slide from the one state to the other. Except it's a one-way slide. Best not to think too hard on that at the moment.

No Country for Cold Men

My first impression of Marty when we meet at the Fairbanks airport is that he doesn't make a good first impression. He's forty-seven years old, maybe five nine, and medium-stocky. He has an unruly full beard and a head of shaggy red hair running to gray. His eyes, magnified by glasses, make him look a little goofy. Wearing a battered Carhartt jacket and beat-up boots, he is leaning against a counter and shooting the breeze with a friend who is also meeting someone from "the outside," as Alaskans refer to the Lower 48. At first glance, I'm thinking he could be the guy who fixes the vending machines in a bowling alley in Dubuque. We shake hands, pile into his truck, and drive through the night on a snow-slick highway to his home in Two Rivers, a town twenty-five miles outside Fairbanks. When I ask how he came to live in Two Rivers, he shrugs.

"Fairbanks"—a town of thirty-five thousand—"is just too crowded," he says.

The next morning we are standing in the snow-covered field behind his two-story cabin readying his little Super Cub. Marty checks the engine block heater he plugged in a couple of hours ago and kicks the ice from the plane's skis. I notice he's working over a wad of chewing tobacco, which he hadn't done last night at the airport, or on the drive back here. He does something to the propeller, tugs at guy wires to various parts of the wings, and unhooks the engine block heater. I ask if he chews often. "Only when I'm excited," he says. "And I'm always excited when I'm headed to the bush."

Giving a test tug to a bungee securing the front half of a plastic rifle scabbard to a wing strut, he seems satisfied that it will hold. In the scabbard rests a battered .358 Norma Mag, the go-to rifle that he calls the Bonecrusher. He only uses half of the scabbard because that's sufficient to protect the rifle in flight. The other half would be just an extra pound of plastic. In a land without roads to its most interesting places, the small plane fills the role the SUV occupies elsewhere. In a land without runways, a pilot lives and dies by the power-to-weight ratio of his aircraft. That's why Marty loves his 1937 Super Cub, of which only a rivet or two of the original aircraft remains. He says the Super Cub is unrivaled for its ability to take off and land "on a bug fart." Being somewhat obsessive, he has further modified his by stripping the extra stuff: the radio, the electrical system, the heater, and the original windows. He had his brother, Stitch, who works on planes professionally and lives next door, install the thinnest Plexiglas windows that would pass inspection. He uses a handheld, battery-powered radio in the plane, and the only heat on board is the windshield defroster. You get the feeling that Marty would yank off the landing gear and flaps if he thought he could steer and land without them.

I scrunch my toes inside my boots. They are already numb despite two charcoal heating pads in each.

I recall the famous line about how there are old pilots and bold pilots, but there are no old, bold pilots. I'd be worried flying with Marty if he were younger. But he's been at it for almost twenty years, and he'd have screwed up terminally long ago if he were reckless. Nevertheless, there's a glint of wildness in his eyes that his glasses can't hide. On a hunch I ask what kind of car he drove growing up in Wisconsin. "Just an old 1970 Torino," he says. "But I dropped a 429 Ford Cobra Jet in it." He says the speedometer only went up to 120, but one night on the highway he passed a buddy in a 454 Chevelle. The Chevelle's speedometer went up to 140. Marty smiles at the memory. "He told me he'd had the needle buried when I passed him." He spits tobacco juice into the snow. "You about ready?"

Just to verify that they are in fact without feeling, I scrunch my toes again. "Yep," I lie.

Now that Marty shares his cabin with his wife, Dominique, and their beautiful toddler, Noah Jane, he commutes to the bush. But he still spends more time there than not. From November through March, he traps. From April through October he works as a smokejumper, one of an elite group that parachutes into remote areas all over the United States to fight fires, sometimes for weeks at a time. His specialty is rigging cargo, much of it on pallets that get dropped in. It's demanding, dangerous work. It's also good money, which is handy, because nobody strikes it rich these days trapping.

With his breath pluming in the minus-30 air, Marty does a final walk around the tiny airplane. Then we shuffle into the heated garage to say goodbye to Dominique. She gives Marty a kiss, then puts her face close to mine. "Remember what I'm saying to you right now," she says. "Never leave the cabin without a lighter and some paper in your pocket. You got that?"

I nod, feeling like a third grader. In time, I will wonder if Dominique saw something in my demeanor that Marty didn't. And I will thank her for having spoken to me this way.

Marty and I are airborne almost as soon as he applies power. The skis lift off the snow, the engine buzzes like an angry mosquito, and then we're at 1,500 feet, basking in some toasty minus-25-degree air. I'm bundled up: parka, bibs, moon boots, and mittens the size of boxing gloves. The cockpit is so cramped I can barely turn my head, and the engine noise precludes conversation beyond a shouted word or two. The

219

defroster clears the windshield, but the side windows are iced over. It's like sitting inside a loud refrigerator being transported cross-country on a hand truck. When Marty makes a downward stabbing motion and shouts, "Moose!" I gently scrape at the window with the back of a mitten, trying to clear the Plexiglas, but he waves me off. "Easy, Bill!" he shouts. "You blow out a pane, gonna be real cold in here!"

I decide to pass on the moose viewing for now.

Welcome to the Bush

Marty's path in life took a sharp left turn when he was seven years old and his father took him outside their house in northern Wisconsin to check the trapline he ran. "It was all just so cool, is what I remember," Marty says. "Being on snowshoes in the woods on a snowshoe trail. Coming up to a trap and the anticipation that you might have caught something. And, of course, the animals themselves. I already knew how cool they were—wild and out there in the woods and somehow surviving. And the idea that you could get to understand them, that you could learn their habits and tracks, where they liked to go, and that you could catch them—that completely got me. I knew right then what I wanted to be when I grew up."

He would have become a trapper in Wisconsin, except there were too many people and too few animals. He came to Alaska as countless young men do each year: a few years out of high school with no money and less knowledge of what he was getting into. He slept in by-the-week motels or on the floors of friends' houses. He worked as a logger, construction laborer, and janitor so he could buy traps and a tent and hire bush transports to drop him off for his first forays into the bush. Marty says he's gone over the same trails thousands of times now but still finds each day different.

After two hours pass in the cockpit, the plane's skis slap snow in a small clearing along a frozen river. I have an urgent need to pee, so while Marty unloads and cranks up the snow machine he keeps under a tarp at the edge of the strip, I take off my mitts to begin undoing the relevant three zippers. Within fifteen seconds, however—by which time I'm halfway through undoing the second glove—my fingers dissociate themselves from me. They're attached to my hands but they aren't mine. Then comes the pain, as if they're being crushed in a vise. This kind of cold is outside my frame of reference. It's not about discomfort. It's about what's physically possible. I can wait to pee. I can wait until we get back to Fairbanks if I have to.

I stand on the back of the sled and hang on to its posts, legs braced against my duffel, as we take the short, cold ride to the cabin, which sits in a grove of alders. Surrounding it are outbuildings housing snowmobiles, gas, tools, extra food, and other supplies. A dozen or so marten—like mink but a little bigger, brown, and with paler heads and underparts—hang from a beam between two trees. It's Marty's catch from three days ago, and each animal is frozen in the twisted posture it assumed when thrown into the sled he tows. Larger predators don't eat his catch when it hangs outside the cabin because of the lingering human scent. "They won't risk taking one unless they're starving," he says. Lynx, he adds, are "bunny specialists," their numbers rising and falling with rabbit populations. They have huge feet that allow them to stay atop even lightly crusted snow. Marten eat squirrels and smaller rodents, especially voles, as well as carrion. The two species don't compete directly, Marty says, and yet they're never abundant at the same time. This year, for example, has been much better than average for lynx, but only so-so for marten.

Moose antlers are strewn around the campsite. A large cardboard box by the door contains raw lynx skulls. It's a startling sight: maybe seventy heads, all teeth and eye sockets and strips of red tissue still clinging to the cheekbones. "I get two or three bucks each from a guy in town," he says. "I think they end up on a website called Skulls Unlimited."

A large thermometer on the cabin wall reads minus 37. He pushes the door open, and as my eyes adjust to the dimness the first thing I see is a revolver hanging upside down on a nail by its trigger guard over Marty's bunk. It's situated so the barrel points toward the other bunk, where I'll be sleeping.

"That thing loaded?"

"Oh, yeah," he says. "That's my trouble gun—a .454 Casull."

Up here, when trouble comes calling, an unloaded gun is the more dangerous thing to have in the cabin. Marty tells me not to worry: Bears are almost all hibernating in January. This time of year, trouble is more likely to come in the form of a moose on the trail. Moose use the trails for the same reason Marty does, ease of movement. But they get ornery in late January, he says, because they're tired of the winter and running out of browse. A lot of times they don't want to cede the trail to a snow machine, and even when they do they'll sometimes get mad all over again afterward and chase after you. "You never want to break down on a machine," he says. "But you really don't want to with a moose on your ass."

At this moment, I find myself experiencing the strange nature of modern travel, whereby it's possible to arrive so quickly in a place that operates by such different rules that you can't quite make sense of it. I'm trying to wrap my head around the fact that this is not just an out-of-the-way place. This is a different kind of reality, a place where death slips in through the narrowest of openings—a lost glove, a minor mechanical problem, a wrong turn.

While the stove slowly drives the cold from the cabin, Marty talks as he pulls out caribou steaks for dinner. He says that frozen creeks are a good way to get around, but that one constant danger associated with them is overflow—the insidious layer of water pushed up by the pressure of the ever-increasing weight of the ice above. The water lies unseen beneath snow ... until you walk or drive into it. If it's more than a few inches deep and you're any distance from home, you can freeze to death in a hurry.

Then Marty gives me the lowdown on Alaskan cold:

At 20 below: It's business as usual for a trapper. Wiggle your toes in your bunny boots, and make sure you have your hood up when running on the snow machine to prevent frostbite.

At 30 below: Pretty much the same deal. Marty will still fly if he believes he can find warmer air up top, which is usually doable. "Nothing fun happens above five hundred feet," he says. "I like to see critters and tracks. And I prefer gloves when flying. Better feel for the plane. But at minus thirty, I'm wearing mitts."

At 40 below: He reconsiders whether he really needs to leave the cabin. "You might be fine. But the thing is, once you even start getting cold, it's hard to get any warmth back at minus forty." And things start to change. Gas doesn't flow the same. Marty carries a .22 Mag rifle to dispatch troublesome trapped animals because a regular .22 bullet "just sorta falls out the end of the barrel." For the same reason, he doesn't like semiauto anything.

At 50 below: You're looking at an entirely different beast now. "If anything goes wrong, it's bad. Period. I don't go much farther than the woodpile those days." Snow machines, even if you can get them started, tend to flood or stall. There is absolutely no mercy at minus 50. Your urine rattles when it hits the ground.

Marty seems happy and at home here, bustling about the cabin, cranking up the propane that powers a light. After we clean the dishes, I prepare myself for a dreaded but necessary visit to the outhouse. Once I'm there, I arrange myself to expose the absolute minimum amount of skin. But when I finally sit down, I am amazed to find that the seat is instantly warm. This just happens to be one of the miracle properties of the extruded polystyrene foam we know as Styrofoam. The outhouse seat is two full inches of the stuff carefully whittled to the appropriate shape. It is ingenious.

"Man, that Styrofoam is awesome!" I tell Marty upon my return. "Who knew?"

Then, as I fall into sleep in my bag, I nevertheless remind myself of the need to be careful. Don't be blinded by the false miracle of the toilet seat, I tell myself. There is precious little luck in this place. And less forgiveness.

A Self-Taught Loner

The next day Marty and I go for a short ride to get me used to the snow machine. He instructs me in the rudiments of riding—how to lean, how to absorb bumps with your knees. Even in this cold, I'm soon shedding layers.

It strikes me that what separates Marty from an uncountable number of other dreamers who pour into Alaska every summer is simply this: He refused to give up. Each time he encountered another obstacle, he set about overcoming it and never doubted that he could. When he realized that life out here depended on snow machines and chain saws, he taught himself enough mechanical skill to fix both. He learned carpentry so he could build cabins. He learned welding and electrical skills. He picked up a working knowledge of wildlife biology, of predicting where an animal will or won't go, by studying the critters and their tracks. When he realized he'd eventually go broke paying for air charters, he set to work learning to fly. By his own admission, he is not a particularly good shot, doesn't seem to be able to sharpen a knife without grinding it halfway to nothing, and is a lousy businessman. But he's good at being alone, and he doesn't give up easily.

The hardest part of being out here, though, is readjusting to society. "You get 'bushy' is what it is," Marty says. "You get so you can't have people around you." In the bush, for example, if something moves, you focus on it instantly. In society, everything seems to move all the time. He tells me about once going straight from a few months in the bush to a grocery store, having a guy walk behind him down an aisle, and "just freaking out." He left the store without buying anything. Another time, waiting at a counter at the post office, he saw a female clerk approaching and could not stop his feet from backing up to expand the distance between them. "It was just something I felt I needed to do at the time."

The Moment of Truth

You really need to get that fire going. I need it primarily to keep my mind occupied, to stop fixating on just how alone and helpless I am, on how quickly my body, with the help of the raven and all kinds of other creatures, would be reabsorbed into the ecosystem. I need it to stave off that shadow sliding over the snow.

The chemical warmers in my mittens are stiff. I can't tell if my hands are cold or not, but a stiff hand warmer is a spent hand warmer. To use my lighter, I'll need to remove the mittens—huge things that reach nearly to my elbows and are snapped to a keeper cord running behind my neck. I try digging down to bare ground with a stick to clear a base, but it doesn't work. Snow remains in the matted mosses and grasses beneath. Instead I lay a thick base of green boughs and begin gathering three times as much tinder, kindling, and fuel wood as I think I'll need. Lower branches of most trees are fine for tinder and kindling—dry and easily broken off. But fuel requires whole trees, none of which are much thicker than my wrist. These I break by grabbing the trunk as high up as possible and then swinging on them, using my weight to bend and, hopefully, break them. It's exhausting work. I kneel, fish out my paper towels, and tear off two sheets, reserving the third in case of failure. I build my tepee of tinder and kindling, place broken lengths of bigger wood beside it. It's time.

I transfer the lighter from its pocket to the inside of my right mitten and finger the striker, rehearsing the movement. You don't want to waste time, but you don't want to rush it, either. It works on the first try. The paper catches, the tinder crackles. The problem is that the spruce burns like gunpowder, done almost as soon as it's lit. I pile bigger pieces on and go looking for more. Within twenty minutes, it becomes clear that if I'm to stay warm tonight, it will be the physical activity of keeping the fire going that does it, not the fire itself. And I know I don't have the juice to do that all night.

It's about 3 p.m. now. I'm two hours in, with two hours until dark. I've eaten a KitKat. I'm very thirsty and wishing I had a metal cup to melt snow for water. I'm not especially cold, but it's better to bite the bullet now and put on my heavier duds. The stripping down and exposure to the cold in socks and a single layer of long johns are as bad as I'd feared, and it takes a while before my body is capable of generating enough heat to derive any benefit from the insulated clothing I've just put on. I find myself thinking of my daughter, Emma. I want to see her again. I want to hear her laugh again.

I wouldn't mind stretching out by the fire, just for a bit. I've been doing nothing but gather wood since I built it. It probably wouldn't go out entirely, and then I could stoke it again. But even in my reduced consciousness I know that this is not the smart choice. And now I'm nearly crying at how badly I want to see Emma grow up. My fear of the dark flares up again. You're being stupid. Worrying about what hasn't even happened yet. But the darkness, I know, will drive home the reality of how alone, remote, and helpless I am in ways I can keep at bay during daylight. Darkness is when the sentries of the mind drop their guard. Fire or no fire.

How will Marty find me? I note with a sinking feeling how the smoke from the fire doesn't rise. It heads directly downhill, as if an invisible hand were pushing it down and herding it along the ground into irrelevance. And even if I could build up a big flame, it wouldn't be visible for any distance with all the trees blocking the view. I'm on autopilot now, trudging ever farther along the path to break and carry back trees and parts of trees. The light is dimming now. I have fears of a moose stumbling across me and getting pissed that I didn't ask permission before trespassing. I'm scared that a bear may smell the fire and come to investigate. Bears, I remember reading somewhere, aren't true hibernators. Their temperature only drops a few degrees and since their sleep is not particularly deep, they may be fairly easily roused. By wood smoke, for example, or the smell of a man. Could a bear tell by the way I smell that I'm unarmed and vulnerable? I doubt a bear would consent to giving me time to drop my mitts and open my pocketknife just to make things more interesting. A hungry bear probably doesn't stand on ceremony. As the dimness grows, these thoughts and other distortions elbow their way to the front of the line outside the box office of the mind.

The Long, Painful Journey Back

A little after dark, as I'm resolving to take the night one load of wood at a time, I hear a fly buzzing. I'm standing by the fire, pondering how I have to walk a bit farther each time I seek wood. Then the sound dies. I lumber back into the darkness, which is not yet full. I'm saving my headlamp for emergencies. The batteries won't last long in this cold anyway. The buzzing returns. I'm afraid to hope. If it's not a snow machine, the disappointment will be too much to bear. But now the buzzing grows. It is a snow machine. I see its headlight crest a rise below me in the distance. I'm saved.

Marty is all up-tempo and good humor. "Well, I see you got a fire going, Bill!" He claps me on the shoulder. "You okay, buddy?"

I tell him yes. He is speaking to me in the casual tones experienced EMTs use when talking to traumatized people.

Marty will later tell me that he knew I was lost when he saw my tracks going straight when I should have turned. At that point, he was at least two hours behind me, long enough for me to have covered a good bit of ground. While he suspected that I wouldn't be able to hold to the trail going up into the high country, there was a slim chance that I could. The danger in that case was that I could end up even farther from camp and be that much harder to find. Having limited fuel and a sled full of fur, he'd decided to race to the cabin, gas up, unload the animals, and carry spare gas in the sled in case I needed it. The prudent thing was to plan for the worst, which meant heading to where I would have come out in the event I'd been able to stay on the trail. Only after having raced there and seen no tracks did he circle back to where I'd made my wrong turn and follow the tracks I'd made.

Marty's headlamp is blinding me. He has his face right in mine as he continues his upbeat banter.

Later he will tell me he was checking for frostbite. I like hearing his voice. It does what he intends it to do: It makes me feel like everything will be all right. It makes me want to keep it together when in reality I'm so exhausted and so relieved that I want to sob. He says the fastest way home is to keep going up rather than backtrack, but that the trail has a few steep spots before it levels out again. I nod. I'm an infant now. I'll do as I'm told.

He plods down to my machine, rights it, and starts the engine. He stands to one side, gunning it and pushing at the same time. He grunts and the snow machine rises up and returns to the path like a dog obeying its master. Later I will learn that Marty can bench 350 pounds and that to qualify for the annual physical for the smokejumpers, he has to run either 1.5 miles in 9 minutes, 30 seconds, or 3 miles in 22 minutes. I get back on my machine, but Marty remembers that its headlight doesn't work. He has to move both machines around so he can switch the sled to the one I was riding. He has a good headlamp, he says. All I have to do is follow him home.

The trail gets much steeper. I fall off within thirty yards and stick the machine in a drift. Up ahead, I see Marty's headlamp stop moving, then start coming my way. He walks down, again picks up my machine, and sets it back on the path. I fall off fifty yards later. He does it all over again. We come to a part of the trail that is even steeper. I tell Marty I can't ride this, that it's easier if he rides it up and I walk up. And it is. I would much rather walk than ride the damn machine another inch. I am exhausted. Every part of my body hurts. Marty rides my machine past his to the top of the hill. Walking back down to his as I'm walking up, he shines his lamp in my face again.

"Camp's not far, Bill," he says cheerily. "You okay? Warm enough?"

I nod and keep going. He steps off the trail into the snow to let me pass. The steep part is so steep that even he can't get up it pulling the empty sled. He unhitches the sled and rides the machine up, then hikes back down to push the sled up. I hear him grunting with each step. I turn my head and see the bobbing white dot of his headlamp below me. That poor bugger. What a trouper. Somebody ought to go down and help that man. I am no longer in the running as an asset, as a somebody. I'm cargo now—no more use than a dead lynx.

We still have to run almost an hour to get back to camp, but Marty wisely lies to me each time I ask how far it is: "Oh, about twenty minutes or so." Even though the trail is almost flat, I keep falling off at the slightest bump. I am a sack of potatoes. Marty keeps pushing or pulling my machine back onto the trail. Along one straight part, I lose my hat. When he next stops to check me over, he asks where it is. "Back there," I mumble. "It came off." I don't want him to go back. I don't care about the hat. I've got a hood that will protect me. I could be dropping hundred-dollar bills every five feet and I would not want to stop and have him go back to retrieve them. All I want is the cabin, warmth, a place to lie down. He goes back for my hat.

Finally, about the time I am imagining that I hear bagpipe music, the cabin comes into view. Inside, Marty lights a propane lamp, stokes the stove, and rustles up some stew, hot tea, and a slug of Scotch. It's all I can do to crawl the five feet from the table to my sleeping bag. "I was starting to get a little worried about you out there, Bill," he says brightly, as if he himself is surprised at the notion, and as if the idea of my actually being in danger was an outlandishly remote possibility that nearly came to pass. Which is probably how you want to tell a man in my condition that you were worried about him. To acknowledge that something has just happened, without saying it could have turned out any way other than happily.

I murmur, "Thank you, Marty," mean it, and fall into an endless drift of sleep.

HANDY MAN

2.6 million–2.5 million years ago: Our distant ancestors have long forsaken the trees and moved to where the meat is—the savannas of central Africa. Hairy little bipeds indistinguishable from hundreds of previous generations, they nevertheless produce the oldest knives known. Struck from larger stones and surprisingly sharp, they revolutionize butchering. Before, everybody just grabbed a hoof and tugged, a practice still seen in some western Pennsylvania deer camps. Archaeologists see evidence of extensive resharpening and conclude that the blades were—this will blow your mind—*prized possessions*. But science cannot verify what a knife guy already knows, which is that knives were the springboards to our most human traits: pride of ownership, jealousy, covetousness, and the way in which a man with four knives always loses his favorite one first.

9000 B.C.: On a ridge just below the Continental Divide in Idaho's Beaverhead Mountains, a hunter parts company with a spear point of obsidian, a kind of volcanic glass. Discovered by an archaeologist in 2004, it predates such human inventions as the wheel, SSRI antidepressants, and the cable TV industry that makes such drugs necessary. Obsidian surgical scalpels are still used today to reduce tissue damage or if a patient is allergic to metal. This material can be worked to an edge much sharper than any steel because it lacks the crystal structure of all steels. How are such precision scalpels forged? The same way the first ones were: by skilled knappers striking one rock against another.

June 16, 1965: I am ten and need a knife for my first sleepaway camp. At a surplus store, my dad buys me a large sheath knife. Eleven inches overall, it sports a six-inch blade, stacked leather washer handle, and metal pommel. On my belt, it reaches nearly to my knees. I have to tighten my belt to keep it from pulling my pants down. But I am in love with it, with its weighty sense of purpose and resolve.

October 20, 2006: I rediscover it in my parents' attic. Research reveals it to be a Pal RH-36, a fighting knife issued in World War II. I keep this artifact, this totem, atop my desk. It's still the biggest knife I own. Sometimes I hold it in my hand, remember my dead father, and resolve once again to be a better son.

1975–Present: For inexplicable reasons, I have trouble leaving the house without a pocketknife. Where I live, most people think this is an eccentricity, like wearing sock garters—until they need a blade. There was the mom rushing toward the soccer game, trying to bite her way into the plastic clamshell holding the required shin guards. There were the hosts of the ice-skating birthday party whose cake showed up forty-five minutes late, and who realized, as a dozen kids came down from their initial sugar high—they'd already started on the ice cream—that the only blade in sight was attached to the bottom of a figure skate.

June 11, 2009: Desperate to win the affections of a woman who loves to cook, I buy her the costliest knife of my life: an eight-inch chef's knife by Master Bladesmith Bob Kramer. The designation is earned by forging a knife that can 1) slice an inch-thick, free-hanging rope in one cut; 2) chop through a construction-grade two-by-four—twice; 3) dry-shave hair from the applicant's forearm; and finally 4) be clamped in a vise and bent 90 degrees without breaking. Kramer averages five knives per week, no longer accepts new orders, and bumps me to the front of the line only after I pester him daily for weeks. The knife is terrifyingly sharp and comes alive in the hand. It proves more durable than the relationship, which, subjected to pressure, breaks along the spine.

June 25, 2009: Off on a fishing trip, I arrive at the airport packing a Leatherman Wave, a Spyderco Dragonfly on my key ring, and a Benchmade Mini-Griptilian. Two of these I discover in a reflexive pat-down before locking the car. The Spyderco I discover as I'm about to enter security. *Think fast or you'll give the TSA another one,* I tell myself. Then I notice a horizontal beam running the length of the glass wall facing the airfield. I approach. In one of the most heavily monitored locations in the country, I palm the knife and pantomime a weary stretch. Yawning and extending both arms, I can just reach it. The beam has the hoped-for edge, and a layer of dust indicating infrequent cleaning. I stash the blade and mark the spot opposite the register in the Verizon kiosk.

June 30, 2009: At 11 P.M., I am back in the terminal, performing the same pantomime in the same spot. As my fingers close around my little knife, I feel a surge of satisfaction only a fellow knife guy could understand. Or maybe an extinct little hominid banging rocks together on the African savanna.

SALUTE TO TURKEYS

In spring a sportsman's heart quickens to the gobbling of *Meleagris gallopavo* and the primeval pull of the hunt. Okay, in my case *hunt* may be the wrong word. It's more like an ancient spring ritual in which I am drum major for the Bad Luck Parade. First, I head into the greening woods with a high heart and a tightly choked but largely ceremonial shotgun. Second, just when it looks as if I'm about to rewrite the old story with a load of No. 5 Xtended Range HD shot, I get bamboozled once again by a feathered dinosaur with a brain the size of a walnut. Third, the ensuing frustration sends me into a state of altered consciousness. From high above Earth, I see all of creation, of which my living, breathing failure is one small but essential part. At that moment, I no longer desire to hunt turkeys. What I want is to make a pilgrimage to the nearest hardware store and have an employee guide me to the special kind of hammer you'd use to nail your own forehead to a tree.

To date, I have had the good fortune to hunt turkeys in Virginia, West Virginia, New York, Georgia, Alabama, Mississippi, Missouri, and Oregon. Those are just the states I remember. Repeated disgrace can hamper the mind to the point where you misremember things of a highly unpleasant nature. I have hunted alone and in the company of experts. In all that time and travel, I have killed a total of . . . let me see here . . . one turkey. And my role on that bird was to stick my gun barrel out of the blind and apply pressure to the trigger. If you could train a three-legged squirrel to do something, it doesn't really count. What I'm saying is that a person could walk

233

blindfolded into the woods, fire three shots skyward, and expect to kill more turkeys.

Pop quiz: Wild turkeys exist in 49 of the 50 states. Which state has none?

Answer: I bet you said "Alaska." The correct answer is "Whichever state I'm hunting in now."

Extraneous side note: One bit of trivia that gets trotted out each spring is Benjamin Franklin's opinion—disclosed in a letter to his daughter in 1784—that the wild turkey would have made a better national bird than the bald eagle. I disagree. For one thing, there is no historical evidence that Franklin ever attempted to hunt wild turkeys. For another, we're talking about the same guy who gave the world the flexible urinary catheter. I rest my case.

Last May, I went hunting with a friend, Gordon Leisch, in the Blue Ridge Mountains. Gordon is a lifelong outdoorsman and a gentleman of the old school. He remembers when you could sight in a deer rifle on an open tract of land *inside* the Capital Beltway. Judging by the turkey fans scattered about his home, he knows how to close the deal. Within moments of setting up, once Gordon had made his first calls, we had two gobblers hammering back. Meanwhile, the ants from the hill I'd had the foresight to sit on had established a base camp inside my collar and were preparing an assault on Mount Nose. I allowed them their little expedition. Unable to contribute to our success, I had vowed to avoid detracting from it. Soon, one of the gobblers was wearing out his voice just over a slight fold in the hill. He couldn't have been forty yards away. For the better part of an hour, he and Gordon each tried to talk the other into moving. Eventually, he gobbled his way back up the mountain. "I don't understand it," Gordon said. "Two steps our way and I'd have nailed him."

That afternoon, we hunted for three hours and heard nothing. "I've never seen these woods so dead," he said as we headed back to his vehicle. "Not a songbird stirring." Ten miles later, warning lights for both the engine and transmission came on. Within minutes, the drivetrain and transmission had finalized their divorce. We were now two guys standing on the shoulder of the road in full camo with a dead truck and eighty miles to go. I noticed Gordon looking at me hard. "If I were the kind of fella who believed in such things," he said, "I'd say you were bad luck."

I told him that was nonsense. Then I asked whether he thought there was a hardware store within walking distance.

NONE FOR ALL

Every so often, I take stock of the jerks, losers, and whack jobs who are my friends and resolve to associate with a higher caliber of people. There are just two things that get in the way: that I *chose* them as friends, and that they're undoubtedly thinking the same thing about me.

I recently spent a couple of days quail hunting with two such men. One is the distinguished illustrator of this page, Jack Unruh—my mother calls him "that awful man" for his caricatures of me. The other is the distinguished Kansas farmer Richard Stucky, who has been going broke for so long that it's almost a career in itself and who—this is the really unforgivable part—nonetheless seems happier than I am. When they invited me on a quail hunt on Jack's lease in Texas, I accepted immediately.

Looking at a quail hunt on a cost-per-bird basis is a sucker's game. It leads to gnashing of teeth and misses the real point, which is to undergo financial and physical hardships so that, by walking around with a shotgun in the company of other men after dogs and birds, you may affirm your continued presence among the living. The hardships incurred this time for Mr. Bob included the following:

- round-trip airfare from Washington, D.C., to Dallas for yours truly, including airport cabs, meals, and—since I was on the company's dime—most of my Christmas shopping;
- a thousand-mile round-trip drive for Richard through record snowstorms both ways;
- three nights' lodging at the Cinder Block Inn, proudly offering in-room cold-water service from both taps; and

- three meals a day at which everything—check included—came chicken-fried.

Actually, now that I run the numbers, our per-bird cost was surprisingly low. Here's the scorecard: two full days of hunting, three guns, four dogs, zero birds. That's right, none. But since any number divided by zero is zero, we now come up against a mathematical paradox known as Unruh's Conundrum: Even though money flew from our pockets at every turn, our per-bird cost remained at zero.

In fairness to Jack (more than he gives me on this page), there have never been many quail on the place. He had a decent first year in 1995 and has been holding on ever since in hope of another. Jack has many flaws, but learning from his mistakes is not among them. This may be why we are friends.

Quail hunting is a bracing and tradition-rich affair. First, you load your shotgun. Next, the dogs bound from their boxes, trembling with excitement, and pee on the nearest vertical object, quite often your leg. Then they rocket away and out of sight, prompting lusty shouts of encouragement from their owners: "Back, Daisy! *Back*, dammit! *Back*, you *dumbass!*" You blow a whistle and punch buttons on the shock-collar transmitter, neither of which affects the dogs.

Hark! One of the dogs has locked up on a bush in the distance. Quickening your step, you plow through thorns designed by Nature solely to puncture your new $170 upland boots. By the time you arrive, limping, the quail have hotfooted it into the next county. The dog remains on point, completing the timeless tableau of the quail hunt: three armed men executing a citizen's arrest on a dangerous shrub.

The surprising thing about a disastrous hunt is how much fun it is. The three of us have knocked around together long enough that it's a pleasure just to be walking unbulldozed country with guns, dogs, and the possibility of birds.

Back at the Cinder Block after another birdless day, we sipped whiskey and reflected on our lives. Jack confessed amazement that people pay him to draw pictures, something he'd do whether it paid or not. I said that my luck in the writing dodge—both getting paid and having yet to be exposed as a fake—was equally wondrous. But Richard, who has lately gone into scouting and managing hunting land for wealthy clients, had the most telling perspective. He said that many of the people he worked for "have got money, but some can't enjoy it. They're always worried that somebody else has more land or better land. Whereas me, hell, I'm happy with what I got."

Lest the moment get too weighty, I said, "Oh, I don't know that I'd go that far."

"Heavey, you really are an idiot," Jack said. "So we gonna do this again next year?"

We were quiet for a moment. "Oh yeah," I said. "Hell, yeah."

LIZARD LUST

A lot has to happen before every long-awaited issue of this magazine rattles through your mail slot and gets shredded by the dog. This October column, for example, is actually being written in July. Of 2007. That's right, it takes three years—including story planning, fieldwork, and literally thousands of hours of online Sudoku—to produce a single issue. I anticipate great things in the next three years. By 2010, the following will have come to pass:

- Our troops will have finally come home from Iraq and Afghanistan.
- Gas prices will plummet to $1.50 a gallon, thanks to a bonanza in offshore oil production from deep wells in the Gulf of Mexico.
- The shaky American economy will resume roaring along like a Hummer H1 (whose ingenious front and rear helicopter airlift hooks will by then come standard on all cars).
- In sporting news, 2010 will be the year bowhunters finally say "Whoa!" to archery manufacturers and their product cycle. Currently, a new compound goes from "state-of-the-art" to "junk-it-for-parts" in less time than it takes to hang a scent wick. No more will guys like me be suckered out of a thousand dollars for a bow with a cable roller guard made of the same carbon fiber as astronaut toothbrushes and new string silencers that harness the sound-absorbing power of Gummi Bears.

Update: Sadly, this last prediction was no more accurate than the others. Many of us bowhunters would rather be caught wearing our girlfriend's Snuggie and watching *When Harry Met Sally* than be seen with last year's bow. This is understandable. I, personally, would love a new bow annually. Maybe a bow's life ought to be measured in dog years. That would make my five-year-old Hoyt thirty-five. Thing is, it still shoots better than I do. In the bow-human interface, the human—me—is almost always the weakest link.

But I still want a new bow. Maybe psychologists are right about discretionary purchases being governed by the reptilian brain rather than the rational one. Fine. Then the lizard in me wants a new bow.

Money aside, one other thing gives me pause: Somewhere up there, Holless Wilbur Allen Jr., the guy who invented the compound bow, is looking down and busting a gut at today's consumer-bowhunters. Allen (1909–1979) was a Missourian, a born tinkerer, and an outdoorsman. Frustrated by the ease with which whitetails sidestepped arrows from the fastest bows of the day, he began to experiment. And experiment. Using a borrowed physics book, he boned up on the leveraging principle of a block and tackle, then took a sawed-off recurve and added pulleys to both ends. It was crudeness itself: wooden eccentrics, a handle of pine boards, and oak flooring for the limb cores; the whole contraption held together with T-bolts, epoxy-impregnated fiberglass thread, and Elmer's glue. But the thing could throw an arrow. Imagine. The bow's design had remained essentially unchanged for forty thousand years. That's two thousand generations of humans before one came up with the idea of putting wheels on it. Allen's compound blew the doors off of everything else, forever changed archery, and gave rise to modern bowhunting. As well as the bowhunting industry.

Here's the thing. Allen didn't like to throw money around. According to a story told by his son, Wilbur was a counselor at a Boy Scout outing along Missouri's Osage River when word came that the white bass were biting. His fishing gear at home, he wasn't about to buy a whole new outfit. Instead, he picked up a 49-cent rod, a 39-cent eggbeater, and a small package of fishing line. He rigged the eggbeater up to a coffee can, attached it to the rod, and proceeded to limit out on bass. The few photos of him available show a tough old cuss. In one, he's sitting in the rear of a johnboat with a well-stocked tackle box, rods stowed and ready. He's wearing white socks and smoking a pipe. His expression says, *Get in the damn boat already.* And there's something in his eyes that makes him look—like virtually all country boys of his era—as if you'd need a posthole digger *and* a crowbar to get his wallet out to replace something before it wore out.

I feel him looking over my shoulder when I'm online browsing hot new bows. I picture a determined country boy failing again and again before rewriting history with wooden eccentrics and Elmer's glue. And then I go out back and shoot a few arrows with my old bow.

SCHOOL'S OUT

I hadn't initially wanted to chaperone the fifth-grade outdoor overnight, chiefly because I enjoy sleeping. Two things changed my mind. Although there were four moms signed up, the lone dad dropped out at the last minute, perhaps because he has a real job. Basically, I saw a chance to look like a hero and jumped on it. The other thing was that Emma—eleven and delighted with my participation—teeters on the very brink of adolescence. Within six months, this same child will sooner join a convent than publicly acknowledge any relationship with me.

I felt something amiss when, arriving late at the site, I found the woods silent. Same with the pond. Only the occasional lazy rise of a bluegill dimpled the surface. Canoes lay stacked on the shore. There wasn't a drop of water on them. I checked.

When I finally found Emma's class, they were being hustled off a creek, where they had briefly been allowed to collect aquatic specimens. They spent the next hour hunched over their paperwork—classifying, measuring, drawing, and describing. Then it was off to a lecture on the three types of rocks. It was as if the goal of getting out into the country was to replicate a normal, indoor school day as closely as possible. When I asked one of the site's instructors when there might be time for a child to paddle a canoe or fish, the answer was "Maybe tomorrow. If we get through everything else in time."

He said something about the after-dinner schedule, but an army of irate neurotransmitters had hijacked my brain and I could no longer process speech. Fearful of what might escape from my mouth, I pivoted and left. The intensity of my anger surprised me. As I walked, still shaking, my thoughts coalesced: For adults to take young, city-bound children out into the natural world and then refuse to allow them to engage that world in ways other than those that demonstrably boost their scores on computer-graded multiple-choice tests is an act of such negligence that it rises almost to a kind of violence.

Then I was driving and realized I'd reverted to what has become my default setting when children and water combine: I was looking for the nearest bamboo. Finding a stand, I cut eight lengths of it and secured them to the roof. Back at the pond, I began measuring line and tying on hooks. Whether these kids would get to fish was uncertain. But it damn sure wasn't going to be for a lack of poles.

The next morning, one of the moms performed a small miracle. Stephanie Uz—mom, U.S. Naval Academy graduate, and oceanographer—approached the same teacher, asked the same question, and got the same response. Unlike me, Ms. Uz kept her poise and pressed the case. The instructor attempted a flanking action, noting that parents always had the option of returning with their children another time for recreational experiences. Ms. Uz countered that many parents were immigrants who spoke little English. Others had no transportation. Others were single parents with multiple jobs and children. Still others had never fished or been in a boat themselves. How likely was it that such people could exercise this "option"?

Shortly afterward, the children were given free time until lunch, for boating, fishing, or just playing. I ran and fetched my poles just ahead of a tide of kids. "Every angler needs to get a worm!" I said, pointing at the nearby compost pile. Two minutes later they returned with worms: in bare hands, cups, and—in one boy's case—all four pants pockets. I began threading worms onto hooks. Shouts, screams, and laughs began to ring out as fish were hoisted into the air. I was too busy baiting, untangling, and unhooking to note any particular child. I didn't need to. I could feel and hear the change in the air. I do remember the indignant looks of children approaching with stripped hooks, incensed that at least one fish in these waters was a *thief.* I didn't see Emma. I was too busy being a father to children whose names I didn't know: fist-bumping successful anglers, rotating in those who hadn't had a turn, and complimenting the patience of those who hadn't caught anything.

Something was constricting my thigh. My lost child was touching base. She pressed her face into my side. "Daddy," she breathed, then ran away. And then it was time for lunch.

Ms. Uz, by your actions, you may have lowered the scores of numerous fifth graders on the standardized tests by which the commonwealth of Virginia assesses its children. On behalf of the parents of those children, I find it necessary to say: God bless you.

MY LATE SEASON

I should be sitting twenty-eight feet up and just downwind of a deer trail, not in some doctor's office with so many diplomas on the walls that I'm half expecting him to speak Latin if he ever does show up. But my back has been giving me trouble lately. I can barely bend over far enough to pull my shorts on each morning. If this gets any worse, I'll be getting dressed with one of those aluminum pole grippers that old people use to whack their grandkids.

Eventually he breezes in, MRI film in hand, and says I've got "disk degeneration consistent with that of a normal fifty- to seventy-year-old man." My first impulse is to pop the little dude in the nose. I'm fifty-six, 6 feet, 172 pounds. I can crank out fifteen pull-ups, bench most of my weight, and run an eight-minute mile (although that really tightens up my back the next morning). I'm insulted to even be included with seventy-year-olds. But saying so won't do much good, so I don't.

The spinal disks, the doctor explains, are like jelly donuts. (I'm not sure why he's using such a simplistic analogy, but I'm guessing it's my plaid shirt.) The donuts' outer layer encloses the jelly, which distributes the pressure when the spine is compressed. He gives me a you-with-me-so-far? look and I'm tempted to ask if he'd mind using cream-filled donuts instead, since those are my favorite. But I already dislike this man too much to joke with him.

Besides, all I really want is the damn cure.

But we're not done with the donuts. They can dry up with age. They can also get squished and change shape. The jelly can bulge or even get pushed all the way through the donut wall. This is known as a herniated disk, which is a condition I happen to have. The good news is that it isn't causing particular pain or I would have mentioned it by now. The bad news is that it's complicated by what looks like chronic inflammation. And some arthritis.

I am stunned. There must be some mistake. Over the years, I've become quite vain about staying fit, about still doing things many guys my age can't, even as the odometer keeps turning. This is supposed to happen to guys who eat at the drive-through window and whose feet never leave the pavement, not to a guy who climbs trees and can lift and throw a sixteen-foot canoe onto a roof rack. Herniated disk? Arthritis? I know zip about arthritis and don't want to. With my luck, it'll turn out to be like strudel.

I just sit there, suddenly terribly aware of my spine, the taken-for-granted tent pole from which the fabric of my body hangs. This magical chain of bones suddenly feels brittle and very, very vulnerable. I stare at my shoes. My eyes are blinking steadily, once per second. I'm vaguely aware of having just crossed into Indian country, to a place where all previous assumptions mean nothing. A faint feeling of terror uncoils in my stomach. I am afraid of the day I can't use a climbing stand, hike up a mountain, or pull my weight in a group of men. I knew that day was coming, I just thought it was further off.

The doctor wants me to do as little as possible for eight weeks to let the inflammation subside. Then we'd "reassess." He's telling me this on a late October day with a cold front moving in. A day on which I still intend to catch the evening hunt. "Not gonna happen, Doc," I say softly. "You have a plan B?"

He shrugs. "Do the least damage you can," he says. Take anti-inflammatories. Try to minimize wear and tear on the spine. Don't run. Do the core-strengthening exercises he'll give me instead of lifting weights. Eat good food instead of junk. Pay attention to what my spine says. If it says something hurts, stop doing it.

"I'm getting old, my spine's compromised, and there aren't any easy answers," I say. "Do I have that right?" He nods and says to call him if my condition changes or I want to discuss this further.

Fifty minutes later, harnessed, bow in hand, I tighten my stomach muscles as I bend to pick up my climber and shift it carefully onto my back. Something I've always counted on has been taken from me. But to focus on the loss is to double its power. Suddenly, my memory spits out whole lines of poetry I'd forgotten I even knew. They're about Ulysses, old and at home after all his adventures, yet unable to rest. In the final lines of Tennyson's poem, the old warrior contemplates taking his crew to sea once more:

> Tho' much is taken, much abides; and tho'
> We are not now that strength which in old days
> Moved earth and heaven; that which we are, we are;
> One equal temper of heroic hearts,
> Made weak by time and fate, but strong in will
> To strive, to seek, to find, and not to yield.

I hitch up my load, feeling the slight breeze on my face. Though much is taken, much abides. There are two hours of legal light left, and I'm heading into the woods.

MAKING THE CUT

As a frugal outdoorsman, my watchword has always been "If it looks stupid but it works, it's not stupid." I have cited this when using a sock as a coffee filter. I have quoted it when using a Frisbee as a serving dish, a dog bowl, and a bait bucket.

Once, in a waterfowl blind, someone noticed a funny smell. I said that it was my feet. No, the fellow said, that flowery smell. My feet, I repeated. I had put antiperspirant on them—a fairly widely known trick—to keep them from sweating, because if your feet don't sweat, the sweat can't freeze. And if the only deodorant handy when packing for a trip is Yves Rocher Jardins du Monde Provençal Lavandin roll-on for women, well, that's what you bring. So if it smells stupid but it works, it's not stupid.

Murphy's Laws of Combat quotes the maxim, but its origin remains unknown. My favorite example came from a story in the *Washington Post*. Back in 1996, senior military and civilian officials were being shown a new thermal-imaging system at the Marine sniper school in Quantico, Virginia. The scopelike device, which could detect the human body at great distances, was considered unbeatable. As student snipers attempted to approach the machine and their binocular-wielding instructors, the scope would occasionally beep, unmasking another sniper.

At a certain moment, a Marine gunnery sergeant nearby cleared his throat. All eyes swung to the shaved head and heavily tattooed arms of this upstart. The man was there to be seen, not heard. This was a breach in command. With exaggerated courtesy, attending officials invited the sergeant to speak. With all due respect, said the gunny, he could beat that machine. Sergeant Neil Morris was cordially invited to back up his claim. Off he trotted.

"For the next hour or so the officials scanned the woods and brush," read the *Post* account, "the device beeping each time it detected a student sniper in the meadow. Their confidence in the gizmo grew. But suddenly, a mound of dirt and weeds only 15 yards away rose up, with a rifle and an old brush-covered umbrella. From a rictus in a green and black face, Morris said simply: 'You're dead.'" A lone soldier using a $1.25 flea-market umbrella and some common sense had defeated a multimillion-dollar system designed by the defense industry's best minds. Morris became a legendary sniper, serving five tours of duty and amassing twenty-four years' experience in sniping and special operations. When he retired in 2001, he was the senior scout sniper in the Marines.

On a cold windy day last winter, after driving seventy miles to hunt and forgetting my hat, I thought of Morris. Knowing I wouldn't last ten minutes on stand without a hat, I reviewed the materials at hand for a field-expedient head covering. Road maps can be folded into a hat but not a warm one. An insulated coffee mug retains heat but is reluctant to assume a skull-conforming shape. Then, on the floor of the backseat I found a plush-toy golden retriever puppy. It was dirty and matted and smelled of old juice box, but its torso was about as long as my head. That it would look stupider than anything I'd done in a lifetime of stupid things was a given. But would it work? The hangtag specified stuffing of both polyester fiberfill and polypropylene pellets.

Fiberfill is an excellent insulation. Polypropylene pellets, potentially less so.

My first step was to amputate all four legs and seal the openings with the Gorilla tape I keep wrapped around my flashlight handle. Having used up the tape, I left the head on. Then I slit the seam up the dog's stomach. The fiberfill looked great. The polypro pellets—very tiny, very hard—were packed in small mesh bags sewn to the sides of the dog like sacs of synthetic fish roe. These I removed, along with a scrap of paper bearing a UPC code. Then—this was more unnerving than I care to admit—a red satin heart fell out. Why would anyone put a heart in a plush toy? It's not as if anyone but a psycho would cut one up. Finally, making very sure that I was alone, I slid the puppy onto my head. The sensation of warmth was instantaneous.

I hunted the entire afternoon in relative comfort. I never drew my bow, but a doe and two offspring—perhaps drawn by the juice-box scent—did stop to sniff the air as they passed fifty yards downwind. As I drove home, I briefly considered writing Sergeant Morris a note thanking him for his example and describing my own efforts under difficult circumstances. In the end I decided to hold off. There are limits as to what a hero should have to bear for his country.

CASTING A SPELL

For the past six months I've been seeing a woman who is way out of my league, and it's going so well I'm starting to wonder what she's hiding from me. Recently Michelle and I decided to flee the toxic fog that envelops D.C.—generated by countless class presidents who left Bugscuffle for the nation's capital, only to find that simple backstabbing takes you further in this town than a PhD in political science—for a weekend in West Virginia. We hoped to catch some cleaner air and maybe a few trout.

My mood improved by the minute as I scoped out the purposeful, trouty-looking river paralleling the road. When we finally arrived at Smoke Hole Caverns & Log Cabins Resort, I thought we'd hit the Lotto. There, right in front of our little cabin, lay a pond full of soft-finned torpedoes. One trout was so big I wasn't sure we could have fit it in the car's trunk. We watched a woman throw fish pellets from a waterside vending machine. The water roiled like a washing machine set to its "stubborn stain/squashed rodent" cycle. Inside the cabin, we found warnings posted that any guest caught fishing for the robo-trout would be "ejected immediately without a refund." In other words, no fishing before 10 P.M.

In the meantime, we bought licenses, rigged spinning rods, and went to scope out the river. There we met an older man, obviously local, carrying a six-fish limit back to his truck. He was dressed in chest waders, with an old aluminum creel over one shoulder and a landing net snugged against his back. I noted his tackle: a six-foot spinning rod with a couple of split shot riding eight inches above a gold salmon-egg hook. He said the fish were hitting bait—salmon eggs, worms, or corn drifted along the bottom—as well as small Mepps and Blue Fox spinners in the faster water.

A guy going out of his way to help obvious tourists like us wasn't enough to reverse my view of humanity, but it did give me pause. Then he directed us to the very hole he'd been fishing. "Little pool fifty yards below the bridge there," he said as he got into his truck. "Fulla trout." He put it in gear. "If you can't catch 'em there, you can't catch 'em anywhere." As he pulled away he gave me the faintest wink.

My heart sank. I knew it was too good to be true. I suddenly felt like the last lobster in the tank at a Cantonese restaurant on Saturday night.

"What's wrong?" Michelle asked.

"We just got jinxed," I said.

"What do you mean? He said it's a good place." She looked puzzled.

"It's code," I explained. "You ever ask a stranger for directions and when he says, 'You can't miss it,' you know that he really means you'll never find it? It's like that."

"You mean it's voodoo?" she said. "Come on, think positive. Let's give it a shot."

We did. We gave that and every other place we could find a shot. We tried salmon eggs, corn, and Gulp! Dough Trout Nuggets. We tried three sizes of spinners, in white and squirrel, with silver blades and gold blades. The next day we came back, fished those spots again, and fished a few new ones. There was one moment when I did have a trout on a Mepps for a few magical seconds. But the fish ran for heavy current and threw the hook almost before I knew it was on. Michelle reported a solid tap on her corn bait, but having never really fished before, she couldn't be sure. She did show uncommon aptitude for coaxing her line free of snags, both above and below the water. But neither of us landed a single trout.

In the end, despite ample opportunity, we didn't even fish the stocked pond. "C'mon, let's try it," I urged late on our second night. "It's not like we're going to keep the fish."

"No," she said. "If it turns out we can't even catch one in there, I don't know that I could stand it. Let's just come back and fish the river another time. And not talk to anybody."

"Oh, all right," I said, as if giving in. But what I really thought was how sensible this suggestion was. And rather than sour her on fishing, our failure seemed to have hardened her resolve. What's more, the contemplation of a return trip implied that she hadn't yet soured on me. I was suddenly struck yet again by the strangeness of the world's unfolding. It was only by our blanking on the fish that I realized what a keeper girlfriend I had on the line. I gave her a kiss and said, "How did a guy like me end up with a babe like you?"

"Damned if I know," she murmured. It was too dark to see, but it sounded like she was smiling.

CAULK THIS WAY

Think of the best hunter you know, and I'll bet a pack of Rage Titanium two-blade expandables that he started on small game. Squirrels taught him stealth. Rabbits schooled him in patience. When it comes to hunting, I've always defied conventional wisdom and blazed my own trail. It's no different with small game. These days, I'm hunting ants.

With the chamber open and empty, I step soundlessly out the back door. The weapon in my hands won't ever make a "Top 50 Classic Caulk Guns" list. It's strictly old-school: a cradle-type gun with a ratchet rod. Pitted with age, nicked from use, it predates models with a contoured trigger and spout-cutter hole in the handle. But this old gun will still lay a bead with the best of them, and it's got something no dripless, smooth-rod gun ever will—a story. My father used it for fifty years. I pick it up and I'm eight years old again on a hot summer Saturday morning. From the depths of the house, my father's voice rings out. "Betsy, I'm already late for my golf game. The damn bathtub looks just fine!" I smile and chamber the old man's favorite load, a 10.1-fluid-ounce tube of Dap Acrylic Latex Caulk Plus Silicone, Crystal Clear, guaranteed for thirty-five years. I lance the seal with a box nail and cut the nozzle at a blunt 30 degrees—I'm not decorating a cake here—and squeeze the trigger. The ratchet croaks forward. Two more croaks and I feel a slight pressure. The next squeeze will push sealant for real. Beware the man with one caulk gun.

As for the ants, they just showed up one day, as mysterious in their wanderings and numberless as caribou. Tackling a mountain of dishes,

254

I had just caught sight of the kitchen counter when I surprised the colony in mid-orgy around some leftovers. The main event was a slice of pizza, its mozzarella translucent with age. The ants registered my presence as if they were one multitudinous, humming organism, but they panicked and fled singly, every insect for itself. An agitated ant can sprint eight hundred body lengths in a single minute. Unfortunately for them, I'm really big and had time to get off six or seven shots of the cleaner I had in hand. I don't know what's in Formula 409, but I will say this: Besides tackling the toughest kitchen messes while delivering a streak-free shine, the stuff is pure hell on ants.

I strategized. I consulted. One friend actually recommended better housekeeping. "Simple," he said. "No food for ants, no ants." He is now an ex-friend. Another said the county extension agent, given a specimen ant, would identify it and recommend a species-specific remedy within three weeks. Nonstarter No. 2. It was a neighbor lady who put me straight: "Find the entry holes. Seal them." Bingo.

I was soon spending hours on hands and knees inspecting the crumbling sixty-year-old mortar between bricks for openings and found dozens. One looked like a live satellite feed of O'Hare Airport on Labor Day. At others, activity came in waves, as if ant cruise ships took turns docking here for the endless free buffet inside my house. I went through two tubes of caulk the first day.

I learned to soften my gaze and use peripheral vision, which revealed more ants faster than central vision. I thought nothing of hugging the dirt and following one ant as it trod a groove of mortar around two sides of the house and disappeared into a dime-size fissure, which I promptly sealed. The feeling was euphoric and addictive, so I disciplined myself to hunt only mornings and evenings. (Twice—I admit it—I went out with a headlamp and caulked until first light.)

When things suddenly went quiet, I knew better than to claim victory. They'd just gotten smarter. At last I found a highway on the brick side of the house's lightning-rod cable. When I sealed that hole, the entire two-way column broke rank and ran like retirees who'd just had their Medicare yanked.

And then it was over. The hordes were gone. I still hunt, still hug the ground to eyeball every vent and downspout, still soften my gaze to try to register movement.

Occasionally I'll find a lone scout, yards from his nearest kin, prospecting, hoping for a miracle portal.

Ants have their specialized functions and this is his. But I've gotten to where I can read their gaits, and I can tell his heart isn't in it. Some evenings, I return without even having primed my gun.

Hunters who've bagged a particular animal after months or years sometimes report feelings of listlessness afterward. The challenge, not the trophy, is what they love. It's the same with the ants and me. Strange as it sounds, I miss them. Yes, we were adversaries. But we also brought out the best in each other. Even now, I sometimes "forget" a slice of pizza on the counter for a couple of days, seeking that hunting high you only get chasing the smallest game.

RASH WORDS

It's election season, when unemployed megalomaniacs go on TV pledging to restore civility to politics while noting that an opponent is "a flag-burning cross-dresser who bites the heads off baby cockatiels." Meanwhile, no one is talking about the real threat: the killer poison ivy we are creating with global warming.

Global warming—which scientists have definitively traced to the carbon dioxide in sodas—is on the rise. By 2050, according to *National Geographic*, CO_2 levels will have increased by 200 parts per million, potentially threatening "one-fourth of the world's plant and vertebrate animal species with extinction." I blame the Chinese and the iPhone. This is because the Chinese people assembling them work twelve hours a day, six days a week. It's hot and thirsty work. And when they start popping open cans, it's over. The resulting environmental changes will be both good and bad. If you own a beachfront home, for example, you need to caulk it and register it with the Coast Guard. On the other hand, the prospect of hunting walrus in the Texas panhandle is kind of intriguing. (You have to figure that a hunt for a two-ton critter with thirty-inch tusks close to home will be by lottery. Write if you know where I can preregister.)

There will be some losers in the plant community. We know this from an experiment in North Carolina in which plots were subjected to 2050-level CO_2. Many plants, such as pine trees, started strong but then faded. But the study singled out one plant that took off running and never looked back. It recorded sustained growth rates 75 to 150 percent above normal. That plant was *Toxicodendron radicans*, or poison ivy. The Godzilla poison ivy wasn't just more "muscular" (one scientist's description). It also produced urushiol—the "poison" in poison ivy—at levels 153 percent higher than in the control plants. "That was a bit of a surprise," one scientist remarked.

"A bit of a surprise"? Pearl Harbor was a bit of a surprise. Urushiol two and a half times stronger than it is now could spell the end of outdoor human life as we know it. We need stronger urushiol like we need asbestos T-shirts. The stuff is so potent that it takes one-billionth of a gram to induce a serious rash. A quarter of an ounce could give poison ivy to every person on earth. Forget nuclear terrorism. If Iran gets hold of some weaponized urushiol, we'll all itch to death.

I've always been susceptible to the current stuff. Back at Camp Yonahnoka, contact was virtually unavoidable. And a boy's hands are in frequent contact with the other parts of his body. This is especially true when peeing, which is both a biological necessity and a competitive activity among boys. I usually developed an epic rash the first week of camp. This meant I got sent to the infirmary, where a woman my mother's age with freezing-cold hands examined the relevant area, which was then bandaged in Caladryl-soaked gauze that had to be changed thrice daily. My bunkmates, models of discretion, greeted my return with joy. "Hey! Aren't you Richard Rash?" one yelled. "Mind if I call you 'Dick'?" His mirth was such that he lost his balance and fell to the ground. This turned out to be the joke of the summer. The experience led me to cease urination entirely from the age of twelve to fifteen.

If you're one of those smug people who are "immune" to poison ivy, scratch on this: Just because you've never had it doesn't mean you never will. Get exposed enough times, the experts say, and nine out of ten people will succumb. For those of us who are already susceptible, it is possible to go from bad to worse. Last year, just as my girlfriend, Michelle, and I were headed to the airport, a localized case—the only kind I'd ever had—went systemic. I had it everywhere, even behind my ears. We stopped at an urgent-care place on the way to the airport. A physician took one look, ordered up syringes of prednisone and Benadryl, and stopped speaking to me entirely. "You said you're flying right after this—he the pilot?" Michelle said we were flying commercially. "Good. This may make him loopy," she said. "Don't let him drive, and keep an eye on him." As I was rolling up my sleeve, the doctor said, "Uh-uh. These are the other kind." I sighed. There was no give in her voice. I undid my belt and assumed the position. Michelle whipped out her iPhone to capture the moment. It felt like someone was shooting chilled Gorilla Glue into my butt.

Michelle later reported that I'd been so out of it by the time we got to airport security that they'd nearly sent me through on the conveyor belt. The next thing I remember, we were in Louisiana.

I used to think single-issue voters were morons. Maybe poison ivy turns you into one. So be it. All I know is this: The guy who's toughest on poison ivy gets my vote in November.

UNHOLY MACKEREL

Michelle, my girlfriend, and I spent spring break in Cedar Key, on Florida's Gulf Coast, where we hoped to forget that some bass lures now cost $150 and to rekindle the kids' interest in hopelessly primitive hook-and-bobber fishing.

Emma, twelve, had shown promise as an angler until she discovered the *Twilight* book series and her interest shifted to teenage vampires in love. Fishing-wise, I figured Jack, Michelle's nine-year-old, as the linchpin. I had helped Jack catch his first fish, but in the year since he had fished exclusively on a Nintendo Wii. To him, this was a no-brainer. Real fishing involved endless waiting, no guarantee of success, and whatever weather came along. Digital fishing offered nonstop action and fifty species of trophy fish at a constant 70 degrees. What concerned me was that Jack spoke of his Wii catches—the 310-pound Warsaw grouper, the 463-pound giant sea bass, etc.—as if they were real.

If Jack got the fever again, however, Emma would follow along. And if Emma went, so would Cole, five. (Cole, who had yet to show an interest in fishing, was a mystery. Highly intelligent, immune to self-doubt, he recognizes no external authority. He will end up a Navy SEAL, the president of GM, or a fugitive in Paraguay.)

On our second day, I hired a wonderful guide, Bill Roberts. He took us out a couple of miles to fish the flats for sea trout. After holding a rod for four minutes—or nine Wii years—Jack gave up and went forward to sulk. Michelle gave me a shrug, signaling that she was open for suggestions. I tried to give Jack my next hookup to reel in, but he wasn't biting. Having paid a guide, found fish, and even hooked fish,

I felt that the best way to improve Jack's attitude would be to grind him up and use him as chum. But you can't say this to a boy's mother, so I just smiled and shrugged back.

Cole played with a Gulp! shrimp for a while. Then he wanted to throw the anchor overboard. This was counterproductive to fishing, but Bill humored him. Meanwhile, Emma had gone to stand on the bow, spreading her arms dramatically and acting out the famous scene from *Titanic*. The best fishing hours lay ahead of us, but the kids were done.

On our last morning, we fished from a seawall in Cedar Key. I was throwing squid on an ounce of lead with Emma's pink Shakespeare Ladies' Spincast Combo—she had lost interest again and was daring Cole to eat ants—when I snagged what I thought was a chunk of oysters. I pumped and reeled, hoping to save the rig. When a sea turtle's head appeared fifteen yards out, I freaked. If a child were to see me harming a sea turtle—accidentally or not—I'd be labeled an evil man who deserved to have his blood sucked out by vampires. Fortunately, the turtle threw the hook. Five minutes later, Michelle handed me her rod, which had a small but muscular stingray on the other end. When I finally slid it ashore, a local man appeared, stood on the tail behind the barb, and twisted the hook free. "C'mon," I said to Michelle. "Let's go before one of us hooks a baby harp seal."

We drove to Jacksonville that night for a 7 A.M. flight the next day. We had found a great hotel deal on the airport's grounds. This was because it was under renovation. We were its only guests. While this meant no lifeguard at the pool, it also meant nobody to tell me I couldn't fish the lagoon behind it. With the sun setting, Michelle watched the kids at the pool while I picked up the pink Shakespeare, now carrying a three-inch white twister tail. At the water's edge, I cast and a fourteen-inch largemouth nailed the lure almost as it hit the water. It was pretty sporty fishing on that little rig. As I lifted the bass in the fading light, I realized how I'd missed being able to stick my thumb in a fish's mouth with the expectation of getting most of it back.

"Can I hold it?" came a small voice from behind me. I turned to find Cole, in his bathing suit, rapt at the sight of the fish. He must have been watching the whole time. His eyes were ablaze. The fishing gods had just blown fire into his soul. "Can I?" he repeated. As usual, I had totally misread the situation. It was Cole, the dark horse, who had broken from the pack in the final stretch and confirmed my hope for the future.

"Yes," I said, dropping the pole, my thumb still in the fish's mouth as I presented it to him. "You can absolutely hold this fish."

SON OF A GUN

My grandfather and namesake died when I was sixteen, still too young to be curious about old men. I do remember that as early as age nine, going over to my grandparents' apartment for brunch after church was the best part of Sunday. After ushering in the rest of the family, he would take me aside, lower his voice conspiratorially, and say, "My little .22's waiting in the closet for you." And off I would scamper to get the single-shot, bolt-action rifle, dry-firing it endlessly, mostly prone on the big Oriental rug in the living room.

It was a Ranger M34. I've since found out that it was likely made by Marlin for Sears, Roebuck. I studied that rifle. Its lines. It was unlike anything in my nine years of experience. It bespoke intention and consequence. It mattered. It was all purpose, simplicity, and restraint. There was nothing nonessential to that gun. Except for the slight fluting at the end of the forestock. And then I saw that even that curve was functional, preventing a sweaty hand from sliding forward off the stock.

I loved shooting that gun—the solid lock of the bolt, how the bead settled into the notch like the moon setting between two hills, the crisp click of the trigger. It was a bond I had with my grandfather. He had gotten the gun for my father and uncle John when they were boys and the family lived in the Canal Zone. With this gun and when he was scarcely older than me, Granddad said, my father had killed a fer-de-lance that he encountered in his tree house. And he told me that the gun would be mine one day.

By the time the .22 came into my possession, I was living in the city. I kept it at a friend's farm, where it became the official groundhog gun for about thirty years.

"I know it's nothing fancy," my buddy told me. "But that little .22's the most accurate gun down there." I wasn't surprised. I'd sensed its accuracy long before I ever sent a live round down the barrel. What surprised me was how much those words meant to me. As though they confirmed something about the three generations of Heavey men who knew that firearm.

I didn't realize Granddad had any other guns until Uncle John died. I was at the house near Annapolis while his wife was going through his papers. Lying on the piano stool were a Winchester Model 94 .30/30 and a Colt .380 hammerless stamped U.S. PROPERTY. When I asked Aunt Joan her intentions for the guns, she said, "I'm going to throw them in the Severn River. I don't like guns."

I didn't say anything but my mind was doing wind sprints. The Severn River, I knew, didn't care one way or another about those guns. Whereas I wanted them badly. I needed them. "Tell you what," I said casually. "I'm headed back that way. I'll throw them in the river for you."

The .30/30 handled wonderfully and would put a bullet inside an inch at a hundred yards. I knew that millions of deer had fallen to such lever-action guns and had tried hunting with it. But the top-ejection means it won't take a scope, and the iron sights go dark half an hour before the end of legal light. After watching a few deer disappear into darkness when I shouldered the rifle to shoot, I went back to a scoped .270. The smart move would have been to sell it. I didn't.

At first I'd thought the Colt was Uncle John's sidearm from the air force. But some digging revealed that such pistols were issued only to brigadiers and above during World War II. That meant it was Granddad's. All I knew about his war record was that it was a tough act to follow. My father chose the Naval Academy instead. Granddad had headed the Army Corps of Engineers 2nd Engineers Special Brigade, 400 officers and 7,000 men engaged in the evolving science of amphibious warfare in the Pacific. The 2nd ESB made eighty-two combat landings and engaged in the longest stretch of continuous combat operations of any unit in the military during the war. I came across a photo of Granddad from the time. He'd never been a big man, five foot seven might have been a stretch. But you don't notice that in the photo. You saw a man who was all sinew and willpower, even standing at attention in some sandy wasteland. The caption read: *Leyte, Philippines. 12 March 1945. Gen. Heavey with Aide, Lt. Williams, at ceremony to present Presidential Citation to Co. A, 542 EBSR. Coconut trees in background cut by artillery fire on day of landing.*

Collectors pay thousands for these military pistols. Granddad's is staying oiled and cased in my gun safe. I check on it every so often. I heft it in my hand and somehow feel connected to my co-conspirator at Sunday brunch so long ago, the old man who would lower his voice and tell me that his little .22 was waiting for me in the closet.

THE OLD WARRIOR

I was recently ambushed by a quotation that sang in my ear all night like a whippoorwill. "A warrior must learn to make every act count," it went, "since he is only going to be in this world a short while, too short to witness all the marvels in it." I didn't like these words. They made me anxious and unable to sleep. That's how I knew they were true.

I was still hearing them on a rainy afternoon in southeast Baltimore.

I hadn't wanted to visit A-1 Taxidermy. My girlfriend made me. "Joe Thomas is the last taxidermist in the city," Michelle had said. She'd photographed him once for a news story. "Old-school. I just think you should see it." She and the boys had errands nearby. They'd meet me there later and we'd go duckpin bowling. At my knock an old guy in a camo shirt and ball cap padded over. Inside was a little shop that had itself been taxidermied, stuffed with fiberglass and old-style skin mounts. Thomas was eighty-four, with watery eyes made bigger by his glasses. He sat down and started talking. His words didn't always follow a straight line.

He'd opened the shop in 1954 and although his pension from forty-two years working in Baltimore's steel mills was more than he needed, he still keeps the place open to stay busy. At thirteen he'd started working every day after school and all day Saturday, had been working ever since. He gave his paychecks to his mother, even after he got drafted in 1945. The army sent him to Newfoundland, where he saw a beautiful mount of a snowy owl and got the yen to learn taxidermy. His wife, Lucille, who died in 2000, minded the shop during his shifts at the mill. He seemed a harmless old coot, but I was sneaking looks at my watch.

266

The Old Warrior

Over the years, he'd seen it all walk through the door: uncountable deer and fish, a stillborn lama, a mouse walking a cat on a leash. Then there was the millionaire with two owls and a hawk who offered ten thousand dollars for mounts. Thomas told him that required a federal permit. The guy said only the two of them would know. Ten grand, he repeated. Finally, Thomas relented, but on one condition. "I said, 'I want the natural resources guy here when you pick 'em up.' And the fella says, 'Why? What's he gonna do?' And I said, 'He's gonna arrest you!' He got all red in the face and flew out of here." He shakes his head, amused. Rich guys. Some of them can't quite wrap their heads around the idea that not everything is for sale.

Michelle's two boys bust in, dripping wet. The younger finds a coonskin cap and a skunk tail, puts the cap on his head, the tail down his pants, and starts jumping around, announcing, "Look! I'm a crazy skunk!" The older runs his hands over the meticulously mounted animals, ignoring DO NOT TOUCH signs. Thomas doesn't even bat an eye at these transgressions. If anything, he seems amused. Michelle starts to rein the boys in, but he stops her. "They're fine," he says. They talk a while, then he tells the boys. "Got something for you." From his pocket he produces a handful of coins and counts five silver dollars into each boy's hand.

I'm stunned. Although I recognize this gesture, I'd almost forgotten that certain men of my grandfather's era would give kids money for no particular reason. (Try picturing Bill Gates handing children pieces of silver. You can't.) Joe Thomas knows that we enter and leave this world with nothing. And that he is therefore free to be generous in the interim. But there's something else going on here besides a transfer of money. Maybe one way a boy learns generosity is by receiving it.

I'm still taking this in when he tells Michelle he has already pre-paid his own funeral, picked out the casket, even got in it and had the salesman snap his photo. "I shut my eyes like I was dead, you know, but with one hand holding out my handkerchief. It's for the kids to cry on. We joke about it all the time." Those big, watery eyes turn, take me in, see my confusion. "To make it easier for them when I go," he explains softly. "So it won't be so hard on them." His words shoot through me like an arrow and my throat gets tight. I've been sitting here arrogant, judgmental, and utterly blind. This windy, shuffling old geezer is in fact a warrior—impeccable, selfless, and unflinching. This is a man who knows his time on earth is short and decided long ago to make every action count.

We say our goodbyes. Hours later, at the bowling alley, each boy will press two silver coins into my hand. "Here," they'll say. "You should get some, too."

Acknowledgments

So many people helped me commit this book that I can't pretend to implicate all of them.

Jean McKenna, who edits my column for *Field & Stream*, deserves special thanks. She has put up with me—with my difficulty in meeting deadlines, my incessant changes to copy after those deadlines, my general contrariness, etc.—for well over a decade.

My soon-to-be wife, Michelle Gienow, spent countless hours reading the manuscript and calling my attention to all sorts of errors so obvious that I couldn't possibly be expected to have found them myself. She provided advice, support, and encouragement.

I'm indebted to all the editors I work with at *Field & Stream*, who—while they pretty much know that I usually have no idea what a given trip was about until well after I'm back—continue to send me anyway. Thank you, Anthony Licata, Mike Toth, Jean McKenna (mentioned here again to make up for the fact that her name was misspelled in the acknowledgments for my last book), Dave Hurteau, Colin Kearns, Donna Ng, Kristyn Brady, Alex Robinson, Maribel Martin, and Nate Matthews. I promise to find those missing receipts.

I thank my great friend, Jack Unruh, an amazing illustrator, who did the cover of this book, as for my first collection of *Field & Stream* stuff and for *It's Only Slow Food Until You Try to Eat It*. He has to draw eleven caricatures of me annually and somehow makes it look like he actually enjoys it.

269

I thank Slaton White, the editor who first allowed me onto the pages of *Field & Stream*. I thank Sid Evans, the magazine's editor from 2002 to 2007.

And a special thanks to the people at Grove who have devoted many hours into the planning and realization of this book. I thank Morgan Entrekin, Jamison Stoltz, and Allison Malecha, who tracked down things so obscure that I don't even remember writing them.